EVERY SINGLE TIME

Republicans and the Illusion of Conservative Thought

Gene Enree

CONTENTS

PREFACE

I would like to start by saying 20% of the net proceeds from this book will be donated to the Wounded Warrior Project. Wounded Warrior Project is dedicated to helping our returning service men and women, integrate back into society smoothly and helping them to cope with possible injuries!

The project helps in making their homes handicap accessible as an example. Or it will help with rehabilitation and counseling! Wounded Warrior Project will give needed assistance anyway they can!

So I thank you on behalf of our Wounded Warriors for purchasing the book. My only hope is to help as many vets as I can! They deserve our assistance and we are very grateful for their service and for the important work they have done!

This book is a compilation of one man's more than 65 years of life's experience observing Republican's and Democrat's in politics. I guarantee you that you will learn many interesting facts and read impartial government statistics about the two parties. You will learn things you never knew and probably never thought that much about!

We will clearly learn who is giving the nation jobs and strong economies! This book is kind of a voter's guide for you.

We will see where one party has repeatedly given the nation expanding economies while the other party has not. One party has created strong business environments while the other lags far behind.

Many of you may not know this but Teddy Roosevelt was not a conservative President. He was in fact a very progressive President! He instituted new government programs, gave us reforms and policies designed to better society.

Come learn the policies that work in society and those which give us strong economies! You may even discover a few things about yourself. You may find out if you are frozen in your beliefs or if you open to thinking differently. You will learn a new political language Republicans commonly use and what our individual responsibilities to the nation really are!

We will be reviewing the political accomplishments of both parties! Call that part a little history lesson. But mostly we will be looking at the more modern post WWII time period. We will learn what the Parties records have been, so we can better judge what their future actions are likely to bring!

I believe once we have the facts, we may change our attitudes toward them. I realize changing some ones beliefs about politics is a tall order. I am also sure you do love your country and you would never support a party if they bring weak economies!

You will learn about healthcare, auto insurance and what we almost had. Learn who really gives us surpluses and who brings us deficit spending.

Learn some simple solutions for how we might solve the dropout problems in our public schools so as to create a better society. You may discover how it is we who are the weak link in our political system! We really are the ones not creating that great society.

We are responsible for our nation's problems, but we also can solve them. This book will be a learning experience for you! This book definitely is for political junkies. The book is guaranteed to get your attention! You will learn many things which most people do not generally think about!

Enjoy.
Gene Enree

ACKNOWLEDGMENTS

For me it has been a God send that the federal government has kept good job creation statistics for over 95 plus years. One of the important parts of this book has come to us from those federal statistics!

It should go without saying that when we have strong job creation we also have had good economies. When job creation has been poor we have seen contracting and sluggish economic times. Our government has provided this vital and impartial information which I thank them for!

In addition to the federal government I wish to thank the Republican Party itself for providing such a rich cast of colorful personalities. What more could a writer ask for than to have colorful personalities!

With Republicans we have people such as Joseph McCarthy, Herbert Hoover, Richard Nixon, George W. Bush and even the great President Ronald Reagan himself to work with! Today we have people such as Donald Trump, Ted Cruz and Mark Rubio. Honestly how can any party provide a more interesting group of individuals than the current stars of the Republican Party?

We have had the Sarah Palins, Michelle Bachmann's, and Rand Paul's, of the world! Thank you, Republican's thank you thank you so very much!

These people have a very rich history to examine! In some ways the book has been easy to write. There has been no shortage of material. One only needed to organize their thoughts and use honest American values to identify short comings.

I also wish to acknowledge help from David Wogan and his team for their help in bringing to the public this work. They have accomplished much with my very limited budget!

And most of all I would like to thank the public for supporting the Wounded Warrior Project. Your purchase of the book is appreciated by those men and women who deserve our help!

Thank You

THE OVERVIEW OF POLITICS

I am sure you understand politics is a large subject with many nuances. It is easy to misunderstand and we must put effort into learning about the subject.

I want you to think about politics as though you were completely new to the subject. As if you had no knowledge of what each party stands for and what their policies are. It is with that clean mind set you need to rethink your party loyalty. We need to learn what each parties approach to solving the nation's problems is.

Now if you were to find out, party A actually creates jobs 4 times faster on average than party B does on average, I am sure that would be a factor in swaying your opinion and party loyalty. If you were to find out party A believes you will increase commerce by cutting the consumers tax rates you will digest that?

We have a couple choices here to make. One approach is we can cut the middle classes tax rates which gives them more purchasing power and keeps businesses busy, active, needing employees and also add to bottom line profits. Or you could do what party B wishes and keep those businesses profitable by cutting their taxes directly, but that does not add to commerce!

I think if party A actually brings society values which are both religiously and socially correct you will remember that. Where party B believes making those kind of changes only ends up costing corporation's money and profits so they tend not do that. Who are you going to gravitate to?

If Party A has balanced the budget 2 ½ more often than party B you will note that. Since surpluses are constructive to the economy. If party A has brought the economy back repeatedly from recession and party B constantly puts the economy into recession, any reasonable person would not want for that to happen to your citizens and the country!

If you suddenly realize one party does a lot of underhanded or dishonest things where the other party does not you probably will gravitate to the more honorable party! You do that because you yourself are an honest, good person and you believe in proper values.

If one party has a long history of improving society through structured government and the other party only wants less government involvement in our lives, you will see and weigh that. These are all things we as voters must learn.

So we have a lot to consider about politics. We must develop our knowledge as to what we get with the 2 major parties. We must learn what the real result of supporting a party brings to us! We should learn that a healthier and happier life does not necessarily come from greater wealth!

By nature it follows that when you want smaller government, with fewer regulations, less involvement and lower taxation you will have less commerce in the economy because government will not have money to spend or contract for services.

When you remove government spending from the economy you can't help but bring contraction upon the economy. You are removing money from the system. Fewer government contracts will reduce profits and increase unemployment.

But when the government does have the money they will contract for services and invest in infrastructure as an example. When that money is spent it will quickly returns to government in the form of new taxes being paid by the contractors through profits and employee taxes. Government spending is not long lost money at all. It is only gone for a relatively short period of time.

A healthy and strong economy comes to us with commerce created by government spending and as more sectors of the economy becoming active. Government is an integral part of the economy!

I remind you with a strong economy it makes it possible to have the programs needed for the nation. A strong defense; social programs; workable infrastructure in the form of roads, schools, police and other government agencies are all important to a healthy economy.

Now I would like to say that when it comes to politics, people often have strong feelings about the party they choose to be loyal to. They usually become stubbornly locked into their perception of how politics works.

I believe having strong feelings are one thing but don't you think those feelings should be reinforced with proof or facts in some way? For example if you believe Republicans are good for the economy that should show itself in the economic statistics!

I say if you think Republicans give us better economies, that's fine but show me some proof! Show me the strong economies Republicans bring us. You need much more than a conservative commentator talking negatively about the opposition. You need some real proof!

So I must ask, are your loyalties based on actual facts or have you simply fallen victim to your love for one party over the other? I totally understand the attraction to conservative thinking. I have always been somewhat conservative myself. I believe it is the responsible way to live and to act.

Seems to me one thing to find out is this. Is there a way to actually see when we have a strong economy and then to see who is creating that economy? So can a strong economy be measured? There are plenty of voices on both sides of this issue, and those voices will claim their Party creates the stronger economies!

Well I believe the following measurable things do indicate a good economy. When businesses are enjoying lots of commerce that clearly indicates a good economy! Since their business is good and they are busy their staffs are overwhelmed, and thus that creates the need for new jobs. More transactions lead to higher profits and since they are more profitable they are paying more in tax!

So job creation is a very important indicator. Another good measure is if the business has stock, the stock will appreciate as investors witness the better times and the growth. Another indicator is with a growing economy government assistance programs are not needed as much. Unemployment claims fall. More employees and more commerce create revenues to the government!

All of those are measurable things. So I do believe growth in the economy can easily be seen, and when we witness a strong economy it is very measurable at every level!

Fewer people needing food stamps, new unemployment claims, lunch programs and falling crime indicate a healthier economy.

There is more money in government to fund our military and social programs. A strong economy is seen in many ways!

I think we all realize it is human nature that once a person decides they are for a party it is very difficult if not impossible to change that thinking. Political loyalty is a wickedly powerful subject matter. People become locked into their beliefs and often will not change! There is little I can do about those voters.

I believe the only way to really change some ones thinking is with facts and evidence about what their party brings to the economy. Perhaps factual evidence will alter their thinking. We should force voters to look at their party in the proper light! I will be doing a lot of that in this book.

In the course of reading this book you will discover, growing economies do not come to us with the Republicans. In fact what we actually usually get with Republicans are contracting economies at best or collapsing economies at worst!

With Republican and their conservative policies we never see lasting job creation, because when you remove government spending, you are removing a big part of the economy! With Republicans we never see long term evidence which indicates growth.

Now I think it is safe to say Republicans really believe Corporations are over taxed. That is why they always want to cut their taxes. While Democrats believe it is the middleclass who is over taxed. So I have no choice except to leave it up to you to decide which way to think about this issue!

I hope at least we can agree commerce and job creation are key indicators of a strong economy. Both parties say they want to see job creation.

So basically that leaves us with a situation where we can cut taxes for a corporation which is good for them of course. Or we can create a strong economy which is also good for corporations and it is good for workers too! Both parties talk about the importance of job creation.

So I say consumption becomes an important consideration. Doesn't it make sense that if you want to create consumption the easiest way to do that is by lowering the tax burden of your consumers? You want to leave more money in the consumer's pocket to give you that additional commerce!

You will learn why the conservative approach is not the best path to a larger economy. We need to be clear about what Republican economics brings.

We know Republicans believe in an economic policy known as Supply Side Economics. President Ronald Reagan made that famous. Democrats believe in a policy known as Keynesian Economics, or as I prefer to call it, Consumer Focused Economics!

We need to understand how the party's economic policies are different from one another? They both look at similar things like the availability of merchandise, consumer demand, corporate taxation, profits, money supply, interest rates, etc. But both economic strategies have very different approaches!

With Supply Side Economics, the stated goal is to increase the supply of products to the marketplace. You do that by cutting taxes for the producers, distributors and the retailers. That should lower the cost of those products. When products are less expensive that ought to increase consumption by making them more affordable!

With this Republican policy, the theory is you help retailers to sell more of their products by lowering their tax burden which lowers the cost of production. If you can lower the cost of the merchandise enough, the theory is more people will be able to purchase that product!

However there is a limit to the amount you can cut government expenses for businesses. But you can also work the exact same problem from the other side of the economic equation. Instead of trying to lower the cost of merchandise you can increase the demand for products by increasing the spendable income of those who are the consumers!

Democrats believe you can increase demand for products by increasing consumption. Simply allowing workers to keep more of their income will increase consumption. With slightly larger pay checks consumers will be able to budget for more things!

I also believe you can increase demand without creating inflation if you use a balanced and yes conservative approach. I believe this is what Democrats believe in. Democrats believe in a conservative consumer focused approach by creating stronger demand!

We will be talking about all of this more in a moment. It sounds like Democrats use the same policies as Republicans, but they really are totally different from one another. Democrats know that increasing the wellbeing of the middleclass will increase consumption and create jobs in retailing and manufacturing.

Republicans think they can bypass the middleclass and give their aid directly to the corporations in the form of lower corporate taxes. The Republican model will keep the corporations profitable but does not add anything at all to consumption which has a large effect on retailing and manufacturing jobs. You will have less of that with the Republican economy!

JOB CREATION AND
RESPONSIBLE VOTING

Let's face it, life is tough, and sometimes we have to put great effort into just living our lives and figuring things out. Maturity does not happen without effort. Simply the act of living will require decision-making and thought on our part. I would hope we never want to be un-educated or make lots of bad decisions!

Voting is a right which comes to us at age 18. Would it not be a shame for you to waste or misuse your vote, throughout the course of your life?

In writing this book, I doubt I will change many strong Republican-minded people. Confirmed Republicans know what they know. They just know Republicans are better. I know, and do understand this thought process. However at the same time I am pretty sure most people would never support a party that has a bad effect on the economy and our nation. We all should love America first!

Trying to give people knowledge is my goal for this book. With more knowledge we be a better judge of politics and politicians. With knowledge we will become better voters.

For example here is a basic fact for you to digest. When looking at all politicians since the end of WWII, from Harry Truman through George W. Bush, Democrat administrations have created jobs more than twice as fast as Republican administrations. We should have agreed job creation is vitally important to a strong economy! I will get to the job creation statistics which will prove that to you very soon.

But think about this, if you remove the one Republican who did create a few jobs which was Ronald Reagan during his second term, the average Democrat is actually 4 times stronger at job creation than are Republicans. So from that statement, you will see Democrats are in fact the true job creators by a very wide margin.

So one may conclude Democrats are the ones giving us the strong economies!

Anyone can say anything but job creation is an important part of good economic times. Remember job creation can be checked in the statistics surrounding the economy and we will be looking at that!

If you had no doubt that Democrats create jobs faster than Republicans surely you would support Democrats, right? Not because you like or love Democrats but because they are giving you the strong economy!

Just like some of you support Republicans today, you probably do that because you believe they are creating jobs and giving us strong economies. You are of the mindset that Republicans have policies which are good for the nation!

I think we agree when commerce is good, profits are going to be better. Both businesses and new employees will be contributing more in taxes. Government is being better funded and from that we can conclude in general, taxes should not need to be raised because the economy is strengthening. We are in a good situation!

But how can we understand politics correctly if we only listen to people like Newt Gingrich. He is a well-known former Republican congressman and personality who is telling you things like "If you want a food stamp society elect Democrats"! In My Opinion Newt is telling you some very false things when he implies Democrats give the nation weak economies! We will get into all of that soon.

I realize if you are a Republican, you probably dislike Democrats. OK that is understandable and Newt is providing you the re-enforcement you need for your beliefs. But you are not thinking the right way. I say if you are lazy about the facts or to close minded you probably will be embracing a lot of incorrect things! It is easy to do.

Since all politicians, Republican and Democrat tell you they want to see job creation I believe job creation information is vital to understanding the economy! Job creation statistics are one of our holy grails of statistics.

Government needed a way to monitor the economy so they began tracking job creation back in 1920. Government needed a measure of what was happening in the economy. Accurate job creation statistics are vital to both the economy, economists as well for voters in general!

In today's world we usually hear from Republicans how President Obama is not using correct policies. I think those statements are really off base since President Obama has been creating jobs at a very good rate for some 60 or 70 months now. First he had to undo the damage his predecessor did to the economy!

If you have been paying attention to the news just recently President Obama is on track to creating 3 million jobs this year. That is a good number. Everyone must admit he is far surpassing what George W. Bush actually did for the nation!

We know during growing employment times, staffs are being overwhelmed. More commerce is being conducted and with that we generally do see shrinking deficit spending as more revenues are being collected. Not from increased taxes but from increased commerce. As the economy expands burdens on government services can be lifted.

Strong job creation statistics are vital to a healthy economy. President Clinton had strong job creation, he created around 22 or 23 million jobs and we ran surpluses for four years. All of that is important and is clear evidence of the importance of a strong economy!

So if you accept these facts about the economy it follows that you need to learn about who is doing the better job of creating jobs, right? Naturally we want to know which party is better at that. By rights, I would think that should control whom you support with you vote!

Well as I said it just so happens that the federal government has been tracking job creation statistics since 1920. The federal government is as impartial as you can get. The agency has employees from both parties working in it. They make sure they are giving us honest information. They understand the importance of job creation to the nation!

For my book I use the federal government's statistics because I believe they are honest and accurate. I will give you the links to where you can check the information for yourself on the Internet. Have a pen and paper handy. This is one area where our government has done a very good job.

Now this is a tricky thing, because Republicans claim they want the economy to be good. But why is it that the effect of Republican policies always results in the contraction of our economy? Republicans consistently give us contracting or collapsing economies. That is an important fact for you to understand! It is the difference between growth and contraction in our economy!

Job creation statistics are very important in many ways! They determine things like interest rates and lending standards. The statistics determine where income tax rates need to be. It all is information that fuels debates in Congress. Job creation statistics are very important statistics for the nation and for us to understand. When we get to them, please give them a proper look!

There have been nine Republican four-year Presidential terms since the end of World War II. Did you know Ronald Reagan by himself accounts for half of all Republican job creation in that time period? If you take President Reagan out of the picture, we are left with seven very weak, slow growth Republican Presidential terms. Why on earth would Americans ever want slow job creation?

I do not care how you get your education about politics. I do not care whether it comes through reading, or via a good variety of television, radio or through lively conversations with others. It's all good. The goal for you should be to have a well-rounded education. It is good to have knowledge and be aware of what is happening!

This book is sort of a test for you. If you do not like to read what is here, I would say you are flunking the open minded test. You may be a stubborn closed minded Republican!

I also recognize there does come a point when you can't teach a dog any new tricks. Some people get to the point where they just are not interested any more. They know what they know and they cannot be told anything different!

I want you to understand simple sounding catch phrases work with a lot of voters. Both Republicans and Democrats use them. All people can be taken in by catch phrases.

For example when a Republican says they are for less taxation that is a huge hook. It is a nice sounding catch phrase that individuals who do not think much, love to hear.

People will often vote for Republicans when they are pledging tax cuts! They do not need to think about anything else or who Republicans want to give tax cuts to. They just need to hear Republicans want to cut taxes and then they are good. Their mind is made up and they know who they will vote for!

But there is a lot to this subject of tax cuts. There are many different types of tax cuts. There are tax cuts for working people and there are tax cuts for the wealthy. There are corporate tax cuts! So do you think tax cuts for corporations are the best way to improve the economy?

I believe we must ask what type of tax cuts are Republicans talking about? Will those cuts contribute to a growing and vital economy? Will their Republican tax cuts lead to increased commerce?

DEMOCRATS GIVE US THE STRONG ECONOMY

Now I have to ask you to think about this for just a second. Wouldn't you think if Republicans had a better way of running the country, #1 voters would keep them in power? #2 their good governance would be seen in the statistics surrounding the strength of the economy. Republicans would stay in power and be re-elected because they are giving us good economies!

It usually stays that way until people realize the policies are bad and are not working. That is the only reason Republicans ever seem to get voted out of office. People tend to want to believe in conservative values.

We will see how Democrats always hand Republicans strong economies. Democrats leave the economy in good shape, but Republicans really don't!

Democrats get removed from office because Republicans successfully make voters believe Democrats are over taxing and over regulating. They will say with Democrats you have fewer freedoms. But you will see for yourself in the actual statistics, the truth is the opposite of that!

Republicans end up giving Democrats contracting slow economies at the end of their stays in the White House according to the statistics. Republicans tend to ride the better Democrat times down to the bottom.

Think about what I just said. This is where you must be honest with yourself. I will show you the statistics, which ought to confirm what I say.

How did President Clinton do, when he had an all-Democratic congress helping him during the first two years of his Presidency? President Clinton created seven million jobs in just 2 years. That is a huge number of jobs being created in a short period of time with a smaller population. No one has come close to that number!

So I have to ask you a simple question, did Democrats have good results or not in Clinton's first 2 years? Democrats had the entire economy, government and policy under their control. They caused the economy to expand. If you were being honest with yourself you would say yes they did a pretty good job!

We had record job creation and record profits at the corporations. The economy was both strong and good for everyone and government was being better funded. President Clinton's was using Consumer Oriented Economics, and it worked great!

There is absolutely no reason why Republicans could not do the same things if they wanted to. Democrats would never hinder Republicans from using correct policy. Republicans should just learn from what has worked and what we already have done in the past. Giving support to the middleclass will create a good economy for all!

Now it took four years but in addition to massive job creation President Clinton policies began running surpluses. The economy was allowed to thrive, with that Democrat economic policy in place!

I guarantee you, people like Newt Gingrich will try to claim credit for the good times created during the Clinton administration. But the real reason was the tax cuts given at the beginning of the Clinton years which spurred the economy forward. That is where the strong economy came from!

Now this is important to remember. Those Clinton tax cuts were only scheduled to last for five years. Then, congress would need to extend them. After year two Republicans controlled Congress. At year 5.5 of the Clinton Presidency Republicans had to make the decision. That was the time when Newt Gingrich was then the speaker of the House of Representatives!

Now Republicans and Newt Gingrich could have extended the tax cuts, but they chose not to do that. That should show you their acumen in economic matters. Because we had surpluses Republicans felt the government was being over funded. I guess somehow Republicans think running surpluses is incorrect policy, really? If we do not run surpluses how are we supposed to pay down the debt?

Republicans then weakened the economy further by cutting corporate taxes and raising them on the middleclass. This was an additional factor which killed commerce and led to the return of deficit spending and weaker consumption. In my opinion Republicans are not very wise when it comes to the economy. Republicans just seem to have a natural ability to do the wrong things!

You see this is the difficult thing for the country, for people and especially for Republicans to get. When governmental policies support the middleclass, the economy will boom. Giving tax breaks to the middleclass is good for all of us including the corporations. It causes the economy to explode and we know this is how the corporations and professionals make the big money!

Those are tremendously important reason to vote for more Democrats in our government. Democrats have shown us they constantly do the right things when it comes to the economy!

President Obama has stopped the collapse of the economy from George W. Bush. That was the first job which had to be done. Then we saw the economy rebound! What more could we want?

I simply say, do a little research just by reading this book and see how the economy improves under Democrats and their policies of supporting the middleclass. I will give you the links to check all the stuff for yourself when we get to the job creation statistics!

Now consider this, since F.D.R. was in office and not counting any of the F.D.R. recovery years at all or President Obamas first term, because he had to deal with the George W. Bush collapse. Democrats have created roughly 56.3 million jobs in their 28 years in the White House. Compare that to Republicans who have only created 34.2 million jobs in their 36 years in the White House with half of those Republican jobs created by one President Ronald Reagan. We are talking about the time period from the beginning of President Truman's Presidency though President George W. Bush.

To me this is clear evidence Democrats give us consistent good job creation and expanding economies. Republicans have the record of giving us contracting economies, which do not keep up with population growth *every single time* they gain power! Who or why would anyone want a contracting economy?

When you look at a year-by-year comparison, in the post WWII era Democrats have created jobs more than twice as fast as

Republicans. That evidence is a clear indication that commerce has been much stronger under Democrats and profits better for corporations!

What I just told you is based on those federal job creation statistics. Are you going to discount the federal government statistics? Are you going to try to claim it is not accurate information?

Anyone can find pro Republican blogs out there that will say the things you want to read. But why would the government be wrong! By what motivation would they provide incorrect statistical information?

With the Democrats we are talking about job creation which is faster than population growth, verses job creation slower than population growth with Republicans. That is the difference between a good economy, verses weak and sluggish economies. For the economy to be good job creation must be faster than population growth!

However people such as Newt Gingrich will try and tell you Democrats only bring us food stamp societies. He is so wrong about that. He is and filling your head with a lot of misinformation and nonsense. But because it plays with the press those who wish to believe negative things about Democrats will just take it as reinforcement of their beliefs!

Do not forget government spending grew like crazy under Presidents Reagan, George H. W. Bush and then again big time crazy under George. W. Bush. We had big deficits then! Those presidents would not tax the corporations or lighten taxation of the consumer to try and support the system. Thus we ended up with a lot of deficit spending!

Republicans love to spend money, even though they talk against that. This talk is the illusion conservative Republicans want you to believe. Republicans want you to think they are responsible but they really do major deficit spending because they have not given us a vibrant economy!

Republicans will start taxing the one part of the economy they should go lightly on. Republicans fundamentally are creating the weak economy they claim they do not want to have. That is a Republican illusion!

Republicans today have not embraced Teddy Roosevelt's values. Republicans are doing exactly what Teddy Roosevelt was trying to limit. Today the Tea Party wants to be quote n quote, super responsible. Do you call blocking progress, weakening the economy and not raising the debt ceiling responsible?

Did you notice how the then Senate majority leader Mitch McConnell was not supporting the Tea Party policies of shutting the government down to get what they want. In the old days Republican desires for no government at all seemed more important than the legitimate needs of the people?

Republicans and Tea Partier's never wish to collect revenues from corporations. Where then do you think Republicans will collect the needed revenues? The answer is from you and me. I remind you every dollar that comes out of middle class pockets has got to harm consumption!

You must realize for the economies sake, we should spend government money during weak economic times. Not the strong times, just the weak times. Even though, we do hate to be doing that.

But Republicans know it will be easier to win the White House back if the economy remains weak when a Democrat occupies the White House. Basically Republicans are playing politics with the economy instead of doing what is right for you, and me! But we all know they do that!

Aren't those all meaningful reasons to dislike the Republican Party? I believe it is Republican behavior which is harming progress and a better economy. We just need to use correct economic policy to have commerce being conducted again. Not taxing the middle-class will create the consumption we all want!

I have often heard Republican candidates and individuals say we should adopt a flat tax! Everyone would get taxed equally and therefore it would be fair to all. They will say it could be a new low tax rate such as 15% which is much better than the current high 39% max tax rate. On the surface this sounds fair and better.

But here is the problem. If I say to you I want a flat tax too, but my tax rate will be 75%, since everyone is taxed equally my tax will be fair too. Just because I want a high flat tax we should ask, will that rate be good for the economy. The answer is of course it is not good because you are literally taxing the life out of all people. Clearly you will ruin the economy. People will not have disposable income. Their lives will not be very good. Because of that fact, in this example a flat tax is not a good tax!

But it would be fair. All people will be taxed equally. I must ask, is it wise to do something which is fair if it harms the people and the economy? Would you honestly do something like that?

I have heard a 15% flat tax kicked around that would fund the government. But let's look at this idea. Someone I know is a teacher and she earned $72,000 dollars and paid $12,000 in tax. But that was not all income tax. She also paid Social Security, FICA and un-employment taxes from of her earnings. That is about a 16% tax load. So to get to where you are paying a 15% income tax, you probably would have to earn around $90,000 to $100,000 per year or more. I am guessing on that.

So basically with a flat tax of 15% everyone who earns less than $90,000 will be paying more in income tax, than those who earn more than $90,000. They will pay less in tax. The net result is you are taxing those who are less capable more, and those who have plenty of cash are taxed less. This is great for the wealthy and the well-off but hard on average people. Does this sound like correct policy to you? But Republicans want that.

This is typical Republican logic. Tax those at the bottom of society more and make it better for those who already are doing fine. People at the bottom are struggling and working hard just to make a go of it. Suddenly people earning $20,000 per year will have to pay $3,000 in income tax plus all of the other taxes too, instead of just a few hundred?

The flat tax harms those at the bottom and helps those who are living in the greatest country on earth. It is a country which offers them so much and provides so much opportunity. America is a country you should feel fortunate just to live in. Your good life comes to you because we have an organized government and that must be paid for and should be willingly supported.

If you wish to live in a country with great roads, have police and fire protection, good schools, and have the strongest military in the world you should support your government. If you are a high income person you do live much better than low income individuals. The system works correctly as it is structured. We all have a wonderful country.

The flat tax idea is a bad idea. With a flat tax you are holding the bottom of society down. That is not the American way. I want no part of that! The graduated income tax has worked well for the nation and it is truly the fair tax policy.

LEARNING A NEW LANGUAGE
"REPUBLICAN SPEAK"!

N ow there is something else I want to make you aware of. Did you know Republicans have their own language. It is a special speak which most voters do not understand, or even think that much about. I call their language "Republican Speak". It is understood by Republican insiders but not widely understood by most voters!

Republicans know they must make their policies sound good to the middleclass. They must make things like cutting taxes for the corporations sound reasonable and correct. So how do Republicans make corporate tax cutting sound reasonable?

Well Republicans use what I call double speak. That is to say they use different meanings than what you think. They will call for a tax cut, but will not tell you whom it really is for!

For example if they wish to give a big tax cut to the wealthy or the corporations they will include a very tiny cut for the middle-class. Then when campaigning for the package they will primarily talk about the tax cut the little guy receives. Basically they want you to believe they are helping the little guy!

Republicans will get together in their caucus and are told how to address a given subject. They are told exactly what to say and how it must be said. I believe the average middleclass person would never support corporate tax relief if they knew that was basically what they were doing when supporting the Republican tax plan!

Let me explain how I figured this language out. My wife and I like working crossword puzzles. Of course crosswords use lots of double meanings. Working them has taught me what frame of mind to be in when listening to what Republicans have said. I learned Republicans will use vague language to describe something like a tax cut!

Because of the crosswords I know I must question are Republicans talking about middleclass tax cuts or something else. You should assume they almost always they are talking about corporate cuts.

For example in a crossword puzzle the clue might be stone. We are all thinking rocks, gravel, to harm someone or to get high, etc. But for the puzzle the correct answer is peach pit. Republicans use these uncommon meanings as their normal way of speaking. It is your job to learn "Republican Speak".

I have learned if Republicans do not specifically call for a middleclass tax cut, which is intended to help no one other than the middleclass, 90% of the cut will be going to the wealthy. Republicans will hide who the real beneficiaries are with their "Republican Speak"!

It takes a while to catch on to it. Occasionally Republicans think they are speaking only before loyal Republicans as was the case when Mitt Romney told a crowd he thought the majority of Democrat voters were basically takers from the system and this explains why they vote for Democrats. According to Romney Republicans do not believe average Americans are good constructive people. Personally I take offense to that!

This is another of the Republican illusions. The illusion being Republicans will be cutting your taxes, and preserve the economy for you in a meaningful way. The illusion is they are looking out for all of us!

With Republicans and their typical tax plan it is just a bait and switch operation! They can point to how they gave the middleclass a tax cut. Even though everyone knows the lion's share of the cut is going to the wealthy or the corporations instead of the middleclass!

Please learn to understand "Republican Speak"! Republican's use this artful speak, to pass things they really want but with the needed middleclass support!

RECOVERING OUR ECONOMY!

Have you heard Republicans say President Obama has botched the recovery? Last month Feb of 2016 240,000 new jobs were created. Is that a botched recovery?

To put it bluntly that is just blatantly screwy talk. I think he is doing pretty a good job given he has had no support at all from Republicans. Where has he botched the recovery? In my opinion the economy has been coming back fairly well!

He has created about 14 million jobs or so since the bottom has been reached! Where George W. Bush created only about 350,000 jobs total after his 8 years in the White House! How can you possibly think Democrats are not good for the economy? Where has he botched the recovery?

President Bush was losing 700,000 jobs per month at the handover of power. President Bush was very, very close to being a negative sum job creator!

To really fix an economy the right way, it makes sense that we need a co-operative government. The two parties need to work together in the right direction. With Republicans we have not had co-operation!

Whether you like President Clinton or not, you have to admit the Clinton Presidential years were great years for the economy. In fact they were the best years we have ever seen. They were also very good years for businesses, and they were great years for the government too. They were good times for everyone!

Everyone was making money, the wealthy, businesses and corporations as well as working people. Employment grew by between 21 and 23.5 million jobs with President Clinton. You cannot look past that and think that somehow he did not do a great job. Everyone wants job creation like that!

This was a perfect example of what can be achieved when you have good policies. The best things for America happen when we constructively work together using proper economic policy. Republicans will not work with the Democrats!

Would you trade the great Clinton years for the lethargic and slow growth years we had under George W. Bush? Is there any comparison? Are you one of those stubborn Republicans who cannot accept that a Republican killed the economy? At some point you have to be honest with what has happened!

I actually know people who have lost their business because of the sluggish economy George W. Bush gave us. Yet they stubbornly believe it is somehow because of Democrats, or high taxes. Anything but the lack of commerce. It is anything but because of the bad economic policies, Republicans brought us!

By the end of George W. Bush's first four year term, he did not create any jobs at all. That was after taking over the strongest economy in the history of the world! How can that even be possible?

In President Bush's two terms his job growth rate started out at a 0.05 percent new job creation in his first term! That essentially was no job creation. Then that was followed by only a 0.23 percent new job creation each year in his second term! Can any reasonable Republican defend a record like that?

The economy was weak because there was no consumption. There was no consumption because the middleclass did not have disposable income. Why was that? The middleclass were taxed higher by the Republicans!

President Bush had an all-Republican congress helping him with his policies. There was no effective Democrat opposition. Republicans had everything they wanted and could have hoped for in that government. Yet they crashed the economy! Why would that be? I thought you people believed Republicans know what they are doing.

Isn't killing the entire American economy a big enough deal to make you leave the Republican Party? If you cannot leave them after they have done something like that, you are just being blind to reality! There is nothing that will make you mad with Republicans.

Republicans will say cutting spending is going to bring the economy back. But when you cut spending essentially you are cutting jobs in the economy and you are contracting the economy. You will be making unemployment and the recession worse. Republicans will try to portray that as responsible policy, really?

I ask you to please learn Republican Speak and stop being played for a fool. Wouldn't it be a shame for you to waist your vote all through your life. Start critically thinking about what Republicans are saying and doing. Democrats are bringing us good economies even though Republicans will claim the economy is a total mess and Democrat policies are wrong!

LEAVING YOUR PARTY
ON PRINCIPLE, PLUS
<u>LOVE AND HATE!</u>

I feel now would be a good time to talk about how I came to leave the Republican Party. Changing party loyalty is never an easy thing for anyone to do! It was not easy for me.

In my youth, even though I was never overly loyal to either of the two parties somehow I felt Republicans were generally more in tune with my beliefs. I felt closer to them.

However with time I began to see and feel honesty and integrity are important qualities a person wants to see from their political party. For me those were issues in determining my party loyalty!

It took me around 20 years of my adult life to sort my feelings out concerning politics. In the end I had to leave the Republican Party for several different reasons. The primary reason I left back then is not the same reason I cannot support Republicans today!

Some 25 years ago I came to the realization that Republicans did not have the level of integrity that was in line with my personal standards. I realized Republicans will to easily disobey or break our laws when they feel like it or disagree with the law or government policy!

It was all too easy for them. I will be sighting numerous cases of that for you. But it all added up to a situation where they were not a party for me.

Now I don't wish to sound to righteous, or morally perfect. But I believe a political party must conduct itself with certain minimal standards. First among these is the party should always have honesty as a core part of their values and behavior. This goes to issues of trust between the party and the voter.

In addition to trustworthiness, wisdom is a factor in choosing who you will support. A person wants to believe their party is moving the nation in the right direction and making good choices. So whether you agree with me or not on many of these issues, I would think you would want to see wise behavior from your chosen party!

Now I believe that people usually do gain wisdom as they age. It is a normal progression in life. I believe people are going to be wiser at age 40 than they were at age 20. They will be wiser at 65 than they were at age 40, and so on. As we age we do grow and end up seeing things differently. Unless something like dementia takes over we will be wiser as we age. We have seen more of life and we are more experienced.

We need to be aware of the extent to which Republicans will go to garner votes. This subject truly is where the old saying comes from "that all is fair in love, war, and politics."

Some 30 years ago I began to have serious reservations about the Republican Party. I was seeing a pattern of dishonesty in their behavior that was not acceptable. I was not immediately rejecting them, but as I considered all of Republican actions in government, I soon realized I must look at the whole picture!

I began to realize their values were not totally in line with my values. I was not seeing a lot of honesty or integrity in their action, or the positions they took and the policies they promoted!

Since I do expect honorable behavior from myself, I did not feel it is too much to ask that Republicans share my basic values. In addition like anyone else, I kind of expect their policies to work properly!

So when I finally left the Republican Party, the economy was not on my mind at all. It was their behavior! Today the economy is the primary reason why I can no longer lend my support to Republicans.

Let me take you through my progression as a voter and see how it compares to you. The first Presidential election where it was legal for me to vote was during the second term re-election of President Richard M. Nixon. At that young age, he seemed right to me. He was getting us out of the Vietnam War. He opened the door to China. On the surface he was doing things in what seemed like sensible, reasonable and conservative ways. I liked all of that!

In addition I had my whole life ahead of me. I had all of the dreams and desires that any young man would have. I wanted a girl, a career, a home and a normal chance to live life! I did not want to be one of the last young men to die in Vietnam!

When I turned 18 it was right at the beginning of the new draft lottery. I thought to myself, I was willing to do my part if I was drafted. But I also did not want to join the military for more than two years of service. I felt I would take my chances and try to get into something safe like the motor pool, or supply or maybe the artillery. I would use my smarts to not be a grunt front line soldier if possible!

Fortunately for me my draft number was just high enough that the draft did miss me. But it was pretty close!

If you are old enough you may remember during the Nixon Presidency, the Watergate Affair broke just before the re-election in 1972. As I said I was young and not yet very wise. I did vote for President Nixon in spite of the coming news, and he did win! Today I regret that vote.

But because of my youth I did not appreciate what Watergate really meant. I had heard about the break in but that was about it. Within a couple years or so President Nixon had to resign his Presidency and he did resign it in disgrace!

Looking back in hindsight I do feel, his resignation was the correct thing that needed to happen. But I also thought to myself that probably was a one-time event. He was a man with flawed qualities and he got caught!

The Watergate Affair taught me a little lesson. I started to realize I needed to be more aware of what was going on in politics. I had to be more careful with my vote. I began to think supporting President Nixon might have been a mistake. But like I say I was still young, idealistic and conservative. I still felt I would have to judge people more on their individual merits rather than on their party affiliation!

In the next election Gerald Ford was our acting President. I supported him against Governor Jimmy Carter. I did not know that much about Governor Carter. Of course, I was on the wrong side there. Gerald Ford lost to Governor Jimmy Carter.

But after observing President Carter I came to like him very much. For me he seemed to have a pretty high level of honesty and integrity. He seemed like a genuine good man. Politically to me he was a fresh change. I felt I could trust him as my President. I liked his honesty!

I believe President Carter was dealing with many difficult issues. Yes he did have high inflation during his Presidency. But I also felt the inflation was given to him from the Republicans!

Consider this President Nixon actually had to put price controls on our economy because of high inflation? Inflation under President Ford had reached as high as 9.7%. That was also high inflation. So I felt President Carter was not really responsible for the high inflation. He just had to deal with what he inherited. He was trying to control the overheating economy which had been left to him!

The melt down of the Three Mile Island reactor happened during his Presidency. Of course the Iran hostage crises happened. But President Carter also won the Nobel Peace Prize in 2002 for the Camp David Peace Accords between Egypt and Israel. This has reaffirmed my beliefs in his Presidency.

He also emphasized human rights in international politics. He was responsible for the new Panama Canal Treaty. President Carter did have very high job creation numbers and that for me was a very big positive!

So while inflation reached a higher level under President Carter (around 11%). The economy was already going haywire from Presidents Nixon and Ford!

By the end of his Presidency I liked very much what I had seen in him. There was real honesty there. I supported him for re-election against Governor Ronald Reagan. So far in my political picks, I was not doing very well.

Once Governor Reagan was elected I soon realized President Reagan was a very good speaker, perhaps one of the best ever. He made me feel good about America!

I believe he did worry the Soviets a great deal with SDI, The Space Defense Initiative. President Reagan then spent the Soviets into bankruptcy pursuing it. This had great value in getting the world to a safer place. The breaking of the Soviet Union's military power and economy was extremely important to our country. It massively reduced the threat of a nuclear war for our nation and for the world!

In general I thought President Reagan was a good President. He had won me over. I liked his speeches, but then that darned Iran/

Contra Affair happened. Who in their right mind would sell 2,000 surface-to-air missiles to the Iranians? Especially at a time when they openly hated America? Where was his integrity or his wisdom on that issue?

I always wondered if that might have been part of a secret deal with the Iranians to keep our hostages a little longer until after the election. But I guess we will never know that for sure. Those missiles were designed to shoot down jet airplanes. We could be talking about commercial jets and civilians lives here!

This was a real eye opener for me. As you know, I believe Presidents should always be honest and operate with the highest integrity. Additionally President Reagan intentionally went behind congresses back, against their direction to help the Contras and sell the missiles!

The Reagan administration knew they were breaking the law. He was specifically told not to give aid to the Contras, but his administration did it anyway.

That shows me great disrespect for the American people. President Reagan did take responsibility for that action and apologized to the people!

I think that action was a turning point for me. I had to re-think if I could ever give my support to a Republican ever again. First I had to deal with President Nixon's actions and then this. Seemed like when I vote for them I always get dishonest behavior coming back at me in return for my vote!

I thought how could I support Republicans when they so openly break our nation's laws on a regular basis? Plus they showed me that they have no common sense when they sell surface to air missiles to the Iranians!

I came to believe President Reagan and President Nixon together had little respect for the nation, our laws and citizens! I thought how will that dishonest behavior affect the morals of our people?

If you are thinking it is OK for a political party to disobey our laws and it is no big deal, then that is exactly what I am talking about. Morally you have begun to think it is OK to disobey our nation's laws!

I remembered that President Nixon basically used dishonest tactics to try and win an election. He wanted private information from the Democratic National Party Headquarters. He clearly was behind a crime there! President Nixon was actually responsible for trying to bug Democrats campaign offices. I hate to say it but President Nixon was behaving as a common crook!

In my mind, President Nixon did things that were akin to being a traitor to the country. As an American President you are supposed to be above dishonest behavior. I believe we as voters expect that!

Our President is tasked to protect our election process. We in America are supposed to enjoy free, fair and "HONEST" elections 100% of the time. In my mind there can be no compromise on an issue like this. It goes to the integrity of the American system of government! It goes to my integrity as a voter!

If you think what he did was not that bad, how would you Republicans like it if President Obama was responsible for doing a crime like that? What if he tried to steal Republican campaign tactics? Or what if he ordered the bugging of Romney's campaign headquarters?

Would that still be OK for you? Of course that would not be OK. That would rightly be a gross impeachable offense! What if he tried to cheat his way to re-election by stuffing ballot boxes? All of this is very dishonest behavior and we would not accept it!

President Nixon avoided paying income taxes that were owed, so he cheated there. For me I realized these were becoming huge issues. President Nixon expanded the Vietnam War into Cambodia. His Vice President Spiro Agnew had to resign his office over extortion, tax fraud bribery and conspiracy charges. Looking back, I now feel that entire administration was nothing more than a large group of crooks.

Then President Reagan was not that honorable either. He had the whole Iran Contra Affair. Then, you have to consider what happened to our economy under George W. Bush and Herbert Hoover. How can you feel good about Republicans after those realities?

This is what happened in America. Ronald Reagan fired 13,000 air traffic controllers! How safe were our sky's then?

Jeez, Republicans have actually given us Joe McCarthy, Ted Cruz, Derrell Issa, Rick Santorum, Richard Nixon, Herbert Hoover, George H. W. Bush, George W. Bush, and Ronald Reagan. These people have either ruined the economy or people's lives! In the big picture Republicans are not improving America!

Today Republicans would like to give us people like Ted Cruz, Mark Rubio and Donald Trump. Are you guys kidding? It had become clear to me that Party is not in line with my values! They were becoming regressive over the top conservatives!

Before beginning work on this book I had no clue. But now I think to myself, how could I ever support Republicans? They have such a long record of bringing us inappropriate people. I felt I could no longer be loyal to that party. They always conduct themselves way below what I would expect for America. Recent history has totally reaffirmed my beliefs. I am nobody special but even I am above that behavior!

Then I began thinking back through all of the various Presidents. I started considering their records. Looking at President Dwight Eisenhower, I realized he was not that great of a President either. In the end even he did not live up to my personal standards!

I do realize President Eisenhower is generally beloved and he was a war hero and all that. But stop and think. He did lose the race into space against the Soviets, both in 1957 with the first satellite, and then again in 1961 with the first astronaut! He used our CIA to overthrow a democratically elected government in Iran. That blew our chances to establish the first stable democracy in Iran and in the middle-east!

Eisenhower put the Shaw of Iran back into power there. The Shaw was hated by his own people and we caused it! President Eisenhower's action ended up giving us the hated Iranian government we see today. Pretty much everyone thinks Iran is trying to develop nuclear weapons!

Cuba went communist during Eisenhower's watch. He did invade several Central American countries in the name of protecting American corporations. He allowed North Korea to remain a Communist nation at the end of the Korean War and look what they are doing today! Plus he is the one who began the policy and training of rebels in the Bay of Pigs invasion on the Island of Cuba! Eisenhower did much to create problems for America!

I am not sure he could have done much about some of those things. But many bad things happened under his watch and some of those issues could have been handled differently. Plus he did give us a badly contracting economy as witnessed by the job creation statistics! We will be looking at job creation soon.

After the Watergate break-in and the Iran/Contra Affair, Republicans had totally lost me. Looking at the big picture, when you consider people like Joseph McCarthy, Herbert Hoover and George W. Bush, I realized I could not stomach them any longer. Those people have no morals, they are not good for the nation and their economic policies do not work!

It was very easy for me to become a Democrat. President George W. Bush just reaffirmed my beliefs about how bad Republicans really are. He used in-appropriate Republican economic policies, which ruined the entire economy of the United States of America.

His Republican policies very nearly gave us a modern Depression. Do you people appreciate how bad a modern depression would have been for America? With a depression you are talking tens of years of terrible economies!

Do you realize President George W. Bush took over the strongest economy in the history of the world from President Clinton, and then gave us a near depression economy in its place? He could not even keep a little of the good times going. How can anyone be loyal to Republicans after something like that? Open your eyes and be honest!

Even though Democrats built a few safe guards into our system, they very nearly were not enough to save the collapse of the entire economy. That should show you beyond any doubt, that some regulation is a good thing. I believe we actually need more regulation not less. Democrats were being wise by bringing regulation in. Republicans always want less of that!

George W. Bush gave us the Iraq war. That cost us 4,300 American lives. Many families have suffered unbelievable loss from that war!

This all led me to think, there has got to be something hugely wrong with the way Republicans think and govern. Their philosophy is flawed! So I wondered if there was some way to warn people about the Republican Party. That is why I decided I had to write this book!

I realized Republicans never take care of our economy. With Republican policies, we only get short-term profits at the corporations. The middleclass was left to deal with financial hardship and economic collapse. The middleclass will be left holding the bag again!

Republican policies will work in the short term, but not in the long run. Time keeps marching along and we cannot live our lives not knowing what the future holds. We cannot plan a future without stability!

Ladies and gentlemen, in short Republicans are lacking in so many areas. Financial wisdom, personal honor, and integrity were all lacking. Republicans are ruthless people who are thinking about short term gains only. They believe if they have enough money for today, they will be able to survive tomorrow somehow. I cannot support Republican values!

Republicans will give you a collapsed economy, and not think twice. Republicans know how to make a buck as the economy is collapsing. That is the bottom line of what Republicans bring to us. I do not believe we want to go in that direction!

Republicans do destroy our economy *"every single time"* they come to government. I am here to tell you this is another of the illusions Republicans want for you to believe. They want you to believe they are good for the economy, but they really aren't!

After I examined our job creation statistics, and saw what President George W. Bush did, I was extremely frustrated with Republicans. Something had to be done.

I formulated my thinking on the importance of job creation in the economy. None of us knows these things in the beginning! Typically we are not given job creation statistics in the course of our education.

It is up to us to seek this information out. We must learn it. We must see and read the statistics with open eyes. We need to learn how job creation is not happening at all with Republicans. If they are not creating jobs, why on earth would you vote for them, that makes no sense!

If I tell you Republicans are not creating jobs, you will just assume I am an anti-Republican author when I say that! But what I just said is backed up in the job creation statistics. So if you are going to be an intelligent voter, you must pay attention to employment. I will be giving you the federal statistics, plus the links to check my information for yourself. For starters please Google the following.

"Job Creation by US Presidential"

Find the Wikipedia article. Then read and study what is there. Like I said, I will be giving that information to you in more detail very soon.

By studying the information, I soon realized *"every single time"* Democrats come to power in the White House, we do see expanding economies. Job creation is up, as seen in the statistics. Deficits are shrinking and commerce is up! Everything is good!

So that means there is more business activity. We have more employees who are paying taxes. Businesses are turning greater profits and paying more in tax because of the increased commerce. Government is receiving greater revenues too. Everything is the way we want it!

When you align yourself with Republicans, all they want to do is to promote things such as increased gun ownership. They do that because they need the gun lover's votes. So if you want more weapons in society, support Republicans.

Republicans want to make it more difficult for poorer and older voters to be able to vote. What is with that? Republicans are trying to require people to have picture I.D.s. to vote. Again what is with that?

For an older person or someone who is disabled or is a poor person that maybe just enough hassle to cause some of those voters to not even get registered. Republicans view those people as voting for Democrats thus they make picture ID a requirement to create that hassle!

Seems to me, picture ID has never been a constitutional requirement to vote. So Republican voting policies would seem to go against the constitution!

Republicans are so paranoid about how we should always follow the constitution yet here they are requiring something in voting which is not required by the constitution! So when it is inconvenient for Republican's to follow the constitution they won't!

John McCain wants us to get tough with Russia and other nations like Iran and North Korea. How are we going to get tough with them if we do not have a strong military! How are we going to have a strong military when we have weak economies!

So if you are in a hurry to see your sons involved in serious wars, without proper equipment I say it is more likely to happen with Republicans. They certainly do not create strong economies!

They don't use carefully thought out policy before making decisions. They tend to jump off the deep end. Can you imagine if Trump were our President?

It is my opinion government should not bring Religion into society. We must keep an absolute separation of church and state in place. If one religion is promoted by the government, how can we claim to be any different from say the Taliban?

I think most of us understand we should keep those two parts of our lives separate. Religion is a PERSONAL part of our lives.

I want you to live your life correctly and according to your beliefs and values. I have no desire for you to live your life according to my beliefs. You can be a Christian, a Muslim, a Hindu, Baptist, a Jew or anything else. I just do not care. It is your life, not mine. All I ask is that you live your life in peace and do not harm others!

Most of us share basic universal human values. Everyone knows it is wrong to kill except in the case of self-preservation. It is wrong to steal that which does not belong to you! Those are simple human values we all share!

Republicans would like for you to think Democrats overtax, and Republicans don't. Republicans would have people think Democrats overregulate. Republicans would have you think they stand up for more freedoms than Democrats. People might think Republicans will not deficit spend, or create to-much government. All of that is false and a part of the illusion they create! Those things are all they have done!

Republicans try to tell you President Obama has not accomplished much. I personally believe he has been one of the more productive presidents we have ever had. How can they think that? How hard was it to bring in the Affordable Care Act?

Republicans oppose the raising of the minimum wage even in the smallest amount. Even though most Americans believe it needs to be raised, and know that will help the economy. Republicans in the name of corporate profits are not supporting minimum wage increases. Republicans will not support equal pay for women doing equal work, as in the Lilly Ledbetter case.

I feel Republicans should just get out of the way and let the Democrats see what they can do with the economy. Let the Democrats work the problems. If they screw it up the people will hold them accountable at election time!

Naturally we do not wish to have excessive government spending. I understand that and nobody likes doing it. However when the economy is ill you need to support the economy to minimize the damage. Not spending money during the slow times will only weaken the economy further!

For me those are reasons to no longer support Republicans. But there are many other reasons for me to not support them! Job creation is anywhere from twice as fast, to as much as six times faster with Democrats than it is with Republicans depending on the time period you are looking at!

That just happens to be the record the country has compiled over the past 95 years. I am only looking at job creation statistics compiled by the government from President Harding through the President George W. Bush Presidency!

Creating jobs is something Democrats do. I believe you can count on them to create a good economy. However, stubborn Republicans will still vote for those Republicans politicians because they are not closely looking at their party!

Do you realize Republican Senator Olympia Snowe of Maine has left Congress because she is tired of Republicans and Democrats not working together? She was/is a Republican. Republicans are virtually unwilling to give ground to Democrats on any issue.

I bet Republicans will not co-operate on the successor to Judge Scalia. From Republicans we never see compromise, they never co-operate and offer no alternative plans. Being obstructionists is not a constructive part of being in government!

I honestly believe if we want to make America a better nation, we do need Democrats in the majority in all of government. Because Republicans are not ones for making changes or progress!

Do you remember Mitt Romney when he started Romney Care in Massachusetts? Which basically was the only workable model for healthcare plan in America including the mandate, (or tax). Why, was the Romney plan OK for Massachusetts, but Republicans would not support a national version of it?

I never understood that opposition from Republicans, except they never wish for anything good to happen under Democrats! They do not seem to care about Americans!

Well Republicans will always oppose Democrats regardless how correct the issue is. Republicans will also protect the corporations over protecting the people. I sometimes believe Republicans oppose Democrats just to be in opposition. Republicans must be on the other side of Democrats on most issues!

Do you remember how Mitt Romney was first a pro-choice guy on reproductive issues? But then just to satisfy the conservatives in his party he started siding with the religious right. He sided with the ultraconservatives basically to look acceptable to them!

Mitt Romney has claimed Barack Obama is a failed President. Would you honestly say President George W. Bush was a successful President? President Obama has not driven our economy off of a cliff!

Under President Bush Chrysler and General Motors were heading straight for the bankruptcy courts. Romney would have let Chrysler and General Motors go through bankruptcy. He has been no friend to American auto workers.

What does that tell you about him personally? Do you guys think about this stuff at all? How can Republicans claim President Obama is not an effective President? All Democrat Presidents including Truman, Kennedy, Johnson, Carter, Clinton and now even President Obama have given us growing economies with a lot of job creation!

Compare that to Presidents Hoover, Eisenhower, Nixon/Ford, Reagan/George H. W. Bush and George W. Bush who have all collapsed our economy. As I said this always happens!

It might be a different matter if Republicans would let President Obama do what he wanted with the economy, and then the economy fell apart. However, when Republicans interfere with his efforts from the start, aren't they essentially trying to sabotaging him? Then Republicans will claim he has failed while they are the ones who have worked to restrict his policies!

Now I am not telling you how you should be thinking about politics. But, I guess I am telling you how you should be thinking about economics. I just want you to use your head before you vote.

In the cold harsh honest light of day, can you honestly say Republicans are working for a stronger economy? Especially when the net result of Republican policies is they cause the economy to contract! Why would you support polices like that?

Do Republicans merely work to increase corporate profits? Do they believe the middleclass is not important to the economy? Or do they just work to hold Democrats back?

Look at the type of people the Republican Party puts forth. You have people like Newt Gingrich and Donald Trump. How many wives have those guys had? How moral are they? Have they been good men?

Then on the other side, we could have had Rick Santorum, Pat Robertson, Mike Huckabee, Mitt Romney, or even Rick Perry. Do you guys really want those strong religious minded people to be making decisions about anything? Would you like to have people like that appointing Supreme Court Justices?

Recently five conservative justices on the Supreme Court ruled against women in preserving that a privately held for profit corporation can deny women contraceptive medicines in their medical insurance! This is something which is a part of the Affordable Care Act. Hobby Lobby now has a financial advantage over their competitors. It is unfair and allows them to force their values to an extent upon their employees.

Remember Presidents appoint Supreme Court justices. If you want Hobby Lobby to support their female employees we need to make sure justices support our nation's values!

What about Sarah Palin and Michele Bachmann? Do you think those gals are Presidential material? These women are attractive but not politically in tune with most of the people I know. In short I think they are female nut jobs!

Do you remember how Michele Bachmann told a story about how a woman came up to her and said how her daughter became retarded after receiving the HPV vaccination shot? I believe that was later proven to be an untruth, there was no such woman ever found. So Michael Bachmann had inappropriate values for someone being considered for the Presidency!

Then Sarah Palin could not even name a magazine she likes to read! I think probably because she never reads magazines. Now I realize she is from a town that may not have lots of up to date publications in Wasilla Alaska but at least just give an answer!

Now I am sure your personal experiences are different from mine. But hopefully we have come to realize taking care of consumers is critical to strong consumption and that is vital to a healthy economy. Those were some of the reasons I do not believe in the Republican Party today. They do not live up to my values as an American!

CONSIDERING THE
IMPORTANCE OF STATISTICS

N ow if you were going to read one chapter, this would be the chapter to read. In this chapter you will find impartial job creation statistics. These are statistics which have been compiled by the Federal Government. The Federal Government employs both Republicans and Democrats and you can be sure it is good, honest information!

The government and the employees in the Department of Commerce will not permit favoritism being given to either Party. You may check the accuracy of my charts for yourself. I will provide you the links.

There are only two charts in this chapter, the government chart presented the way the government provides the statistics. Then we have my chart presented the way I think the information should be given. My chart it will contain the exact same statistics which the government uses but arranged in a different way. That is the only thing I have done differently.

Our country would not be able to guide itself correctly without honest economic information. So Congress tasked the federal government with keeping track of job creation statistics. The gathering of statistics started back in 1920. The government knew that job creation was very important information as it mimics the state of the economy!

For example if we did not see job creation that would be an indication the economy was in some sort of distress or contraction. That would shed light on the state of our economy. Changes to economic policy would be identified and new policy enacted to stimulate the economy as needed!

Both parties talk about the importance of job creation. In fact Republicans always complain about how Democrats do not create jobs. But you will see for yourself what the statistics are showing. Democrats are way stronger at job creation than are the Republicans!

Now job creation tells you the following things. First it obviously tells us how many people are actually finding work. Second, if jobs are being created at a good rate for example that is an indication that commerce must be good also!

Third, increased commerce indicates companies will have greater earnings. Fourth, the increased commerce causes staff to become overwhelmed which then creates a need for additional hiring. Businesses and corporations must hire employees just to meet the increased sales and supply issues!

Fifth, business and corporations become more profitable, which is good for stockholders and good for earnings. Sixth, you are reducing the need for government services such as food stamps and un-employment etc. Seventh, government revenues rise due to the increased commerce and the new income tax generation from employees and from business activity itself.

Eighth, retailers and manufactures must increase manufacturing to replace sold merchandise. Ninth, government does not need to raise taxes on anyone because government is seeing improving revenues. Tenth, the nation may be able to start running surpluses and the national debt begins shrinking!

So when you are seeing jobs being created in the statistics, we are seeing a better business environment for businesses and for people. People are finding work and that is always good; they are supporting themselves. Government is better funded. Those things go hand in hand and, it is what we want to see!

Job creation statistics do closely correlate with the economy. The government set the statistics up to be straight forward with no frills or giving any favoritism. The government then makes that information available to economists, news organizations and to the public!

Both parties should be commended for having kept the system honest by not interfering with the gathering of, and/or the presentation of that information. In this respect I have to give the government and the politician's high marks for delivering an honest product and good information!

Really in this chapter there are only two charts for you to read and consider. This is where you really see how the two parties are doing in that most important area of giving us strong economies. If either party has good economic policies, it will show up in the job creation statistics. That makes total sense since job creation only happens as our economy grows!

Polls do consistently indicate the health of the economy is more important than any other statistic to American voters. It seems like with every election the economy is more important than foreign policy, immigration issues, border security, birth control, gay marriage or even the Affordable Care Act. They all take a distant second place to job creation!

We know voters will replace a party which brings us bad economies. The federal job creation statistics I sight are what they are. I did not make them up. Nobody has skewed them.

I certainly will not twist the information for this book. Because I know every Republican out there is going to be checking me on it. I will even give you the links to the government information so you can check it all for yourself.

I have created two charts. The first chart will be the federal job creation records presented the way the federal government collects and presents that information to you. But then I do the second chart differently. In the second chart I use the exact same statistics but I divide the two parties into two side-by-side columns!

I put all of the Presidents in chronological order within their party. The Republicans are on the left side. Then I put the Democrats next to them on the right side. Again, everything is in chronological order and they are the exact same statistics!

So then I ask you to just compare the two parties side by side. The way I put my chart together is the way I feel the information should be presented to the public. It directly compares the parties. The public can see how well each party has done!

But first we need to understand what the charts are saying to us. Let's say a President's takes over from another President who averaged a 2.6% new job creation rate! If the second President happens to have a slow and even decline in job creation to 0% new job creation at the end of his or her 4 year term, they would still average about 1.3% new job creation over their entire term!

It is that way because in the early part of their term job creation was high, and at the end it was 0 so that president will average 1.3% new job creation over the 4 years even though they left us no new job creation!

Does that make sense? We will actually see Presidents who have worse job creation numbers at the end of their terms than what the statistics are showing because their job creation rates were declining!

You will see many Republican Presidents are actually leaving us very poor job creation, while Democratic Presidents typically leave us stronger economies than what their averages show, because their numbers are rising!

Democrats are strengthening the economy. The actual job creation rate at the end of their term is usually higher because the figure given is an average number for the entire term!

When Republicans come to power in the White House we end up with contracting economies. Why is that? Well that can only be because Republicans use different economic policies. Those new Republican policies happen to be policies which were not good for the economy, so the economy begins to contract!

Job creation went down, commerce went down and government revenues went down. Our economy actually went into contraction. It happens *every single time* with Republicans!

If George W. Bush really wanted to do something to better the country, I believe he should come out and say, I have seen in my own economy that Supply Side Theory just does not work. Please, do not use it!

We must now analyze the job creation statistics. The whole time period from Warren G. Harding through Herbert Hoover was an unsophisticated time within our economy. Banks and brokerage houses were unrestricted and had few rules. There was no sensible regulation going on.

Then we had the new deal years of F.D.R. followed by the outbreak of WWII giving us wildly skewed information in favor of Democrats. Again that is all inaccurate information!

Those statistics are so in favor of Democrats, and they came to us as a result of very weak times. I believe they provide no useful guidance for the picking of future presidents today! The time period from Harding through Roosevelt has a lot of inaccurate and useless information for the comparing of modern economies and picking of future Presidents!

Needless to say the Great Depression and WWII skews the statistics wildly in favor of the Democrats. Thus I just throw it all out!

So I started tracking the economy at what I felt was an honest neutral point. A point where the effects of the Great Depression, were no longer with us and a point at where a Democrat President was following a fellow Democrat President! So I started with President Truman. This is where some basic safe guards and regulation had been built into the system and where the economy was somewhat returning to normal!

Prior to Harry Truman and after George W. Bush we have some twisted inaccurate information. As I said President Obama's first term has been statistically bad because of the mess he inherited from George W. Bush. It was not his fault. He took over the economy just as it was falling completely apart! Our economy was driven off of a cliff by President W. Bush.

But I believe President Obama's second term will be fair game to consider. His entire first term was spent straightening out the mess he inherited from his Republican predecessor!

I considered Truman through Bush because during those years the economy was somewhat stable and normal. Even though President Truman had to deal with the difficult situation of converting the economy from a wartime economy over to a peacetime consumption economy! He still did OK.

I believe it would be unfair to President Obama to have him log job loses created by another President. Unless you wanted to let me subtract the job losses from the Republican totals? Then we would have to add the jobs President Obama actually created after the bottom was reached during his first term to his totals. Not doing so would be like saying, Republicans have ruined the economy, but you Democrats must take the losses. Thus I just throw the first term of President Obama out the window. It is simpler that way!

So once we understand what the statistics are saying to us, we can begin to judge which policies seem to be working better. I believe we will come to the proper realization that one party really is better for the economy than the other party. Everyone wants good economies after all!

The statistics are gathered and compiled each month. They are constantly updating the picture of the economy. The results are presented each month, each quarter, each year, and then again at the end of each Presidential four-year administration. We do have good records that show how the economy has done!

It all ends up being the actual Presidential job creation records used for this book. First we will be looking at the statistics the way the government provides the information to us. But then we will be looking at the same information the way I feel it should be presented: comparing the parties' records easily side by side to help you make an informed decision as to which party is better for the nation!

You may compare the accuracy of my charts for yourself. Again I will give you the links to that information and where to find it on the Internet. Keep in mind small percentage changes in the charts indicate big changes in the economy!

Now in researching for this information, I have found something out. There seems to be more Republican blogs out there on job creation than there are Democratic ones. I had to wonder why that was. I thought to myself, maybe Republicans feel they need to counter the obvious negative record for the Republicans that the actual federal job creation statistics seems to show?

Perhaps the Republican blogs are trying to do whatever they can to rehabilitate so to speak, their parties image in the public's eye. Take my word for it, you probably will find those same pro Republican blogs. I caution you to only consider the federal statistics. For any other site is going to give information which is skewed by their particular viewpoint.

You will need to go to the following web site. The federal Governments job creation statistics! Google

"Jobs Created by U. S. Presidents"

I am pretty sure Republicans know when they have more web sights on a subject they will get more views and the truthful sights will not be seen as much. I cannot say for sure if it is that simple, but who knows for sure. That is why I only consider the federal statistics.

Sometimes we will hear that the government is revising the information! With more time they obtain more complete information. So we have to give the statistics a little time to settle out. This is all normal.

Now let me make this very clear to you, I am not your government. I am just an author. I will use the same government statistics that are a part of the public record for this book. But then I will present the information to you in a way the government cannot. It will still be honest and fair information but presented where the public can make simple side by side comparisons. It is very easy to see the economy rise and fall!

I believe the Federal Government should provide job creation statistics as a service to the people. Just present the information properly and in the most informative way. Make it easy to compare the parties against each other. I believe the government should not present the information in a way where it is difficult to see what the parties are actually bringing.

Because this is my book and I can do whatever I want. I want you to clearly see Republicans do not create jobs. I do want you to see how the economy collapses with Republicans *every single time* they come to power. In effect, conservative Republicans policies consistently ruin the economy!

I feel it is kind of a duty for me as an American to properly present the information for your benefit. Just so you can see that there are differences between the parties. Perhaps you will change who you support!

We should not have to go to non-official web sites to get twisted information which says what you want to read. Instead the federal statistics should say exactly what you want to read. For Republicans the statistics should show the economy strengthens with Republicans!

If I repeat myself I apologize. Record keeping began back some 95 years ago in 1920.

Find the Wikipedia for your source of information. The same impartial government statistics I use in this book will come up for you. I believe the federal job creation statistics are a pretty accurate record. Those statistics mimic the economy very well. For me this is your holy grail of which party is the better party!

According to economists everywhere, if you want to heat up the economy, simply allow the middleclass to keep more of their money. Give them more disposable income. That one act will lead to an increase in consumption all across the economy.

My only desire is for you to read my work and ask yourself if it seems to make sense or not. So I say you should accept the government statistics. They do have value, and the government's statistics are correct. What information source can you trust more than federal government information?

As a Democrat, I believe the middleclass is the base of the economic system in America. Republicans do not share that basic belief. Republicans believe that corporations are the heart of the economy. So In My Opinion that is one major thing which Republicans get wrong.

It is up to each of us to find out the information contained in the records. That is what I have tried to do here. I believe this is where you may reluctantly learn to support Democrats.

First I will be giving you the statistical information in chronological order. This is how the federal government provides the statistics, with no regard to Republicans or Democrats, just one President after another. When it is given that way, it is very easy to see why the public does not pick up on the problems and how big they are!

However, when we break the information out into statistics by each party, you will definitely begin to see the huge difference between the two parties. Simply look left to right.

In the first chart you will see the actual number of jobs created per Presidential term. Usually Presidents have two full terms, but not all do. So when looking at the first chart, you will see that job creation information followed by what that equaled in terms of a percentage gain or loss in jobs, for that four-year Presidential term!

After we observe the federal chart, I will give you the exact same information in my chart. However I will put all of the Republican Presidents in their own column. I do the same with the Democrats. In this chart the difference between Republicans and Democrats will be much easier to see and compare!

When we compare the parties side by side it is eye opening, because you will notice consistently higher job creation by

Democrats. Understand small percentage changes in employment represent very large changes in the economy!

You will see Democrats are better at giving the nation strong economies than are the Republicans. Why on earth would we want to turn back to slow and lethargic economies?

I feel new job creation must be right around 2.5 percent per year in my opinion to keep up with population growth. Below that you will have a contracting economy, and above that an expanding and growing economy! Newt Gingrich please pay attention here this is the true reality for the American economy!

In the first chart you will see a percentage number given for the number of jobs created in percentage terms. Then separately you will see what that equaled in actual numbers!

Now the percentage information is given in a slightly different format, so it can become confusing. In short the percentage number gives you the average percent change of jobs over a four year period of time. It is the per year average over four years!

Example: If one percent new job creation is indicated, that means that President averaged, new job creation at the rate of one percent new jobs created each year, during his entire four-year term. Or a 4% total gain of new jobs after 4 years!

A 1.0 percent change is a well below average percentage change. Changes approaching 2.5% are meaningful differences, starting to become good. I am just trying to help you understand the charts.

The first Presidential term noted is actually two Republican Presidents. Calvin Coolidge succeeded Warren Harding midterm! Together they created a total of 4.5 million jobs in 4 years. President Harding was assassinated mid-term! Coolidge finished Harding's term in the White House!

That was not bad job creation at all. That was an average growth rate of 4.23% new jobs created each year, for a total job growth rate of about 17 percent new jobs created during the entire four-year Presidential term.

This by the way was the best job creation numbers booked by any of the Republicans! They took over from Democrat Woodrow Wilson whom we have no statistics for! So we do not know if he gave Harding a strong economy or not?

Keep in mind it was the beginning of the roaring 20's. It was a time when we had almost no regulation of our banks, or in the lending industry. We also had an overheating and wildly expanding stock market. There were few rules and restrictions. Things were pretty freewheeling in those days. That is exactly what Republicans want for today's economy!

As I said before the first chart is how the government provides the information. It is interesting to read, but it is hard to really notice any particular patterns in the statistics. Unfortunately this is how most people view the statistics.

I believe it is why most people miss the significant differences between the two parties. People really do not understand how much better for the economy Democrats have been. They also do not pick up on how bad for the economy the Republican philosophies have been!

Each year the population of America grows. That population growth has an effect on the percentage changes. It will take more jobs being created, to actually change or reach a given percentage of change!

I do feel it is important to look at both numbers but I myself put more value in the percentage changes. In my chart I do not have room for the actual number of jobs created anyway so I omit them!

So here we go…the job creation statistics we have all been waiting for. I will be dividing the information in to the pre Harry Truman era, and then from the Harry Truman era on.

Prior to Harry Truman the information is wildly in favor of Democrats, mostly because it was a less sophisticated financial time. Few protections were in place until F.D.R. added them!

First there was the Great Depression. Then we had all of the recovery years credited to the F.D.R. administration. That information in my opinion really is not accurate information to consider. So I do throw out the skewed information! I throw out everything surrounding the Great Depression!

If we did not separate those two time periods, we would have crazy information. As I said I also will not consider President Obama's first term. Because he had to absorb all the job losses created by President George W. Bush. And they were huge job losses as the economy imploded!

So let us start looking first in chronological order. Here are the impartial government statistics.

PRESIDENT			Total jobs added in four Years	% change per year
21-25	R	W. Harding/Cal Coolidge	4.50 Million	4.23%
25-29	R	Calvin Coolidge	2.60 Million	2.13%
29-33	R	Herbert Hoover	Lost −6.40 Million	-5.41%

Remember He lost an average 5.41% jobs each year, of his four year term, or had 22% total job losses over his four year term.

33-37	D	Franklin D. Roosevelt	5.50 Million	4.97%
37-41	D	Franklin D. Roosevelt	3.28 Million	2.53%
41-45	D	Franklin D. Roosevelt	7.42 Million	5.00%
45-49	D	Harry Truman	2.77 Million	1.61%
49-53	D	Harry Truman	5.47 Million	2.93%
53-57	R	Dwight Eisenhower	2.74 Million	1.34%
57-61	R	Dwight Eisenhower	0.79 Million	0.87%
61-65	D	J. F. Kennedy/Johnson	5.90 Million	2.64%
65-69	D	Lyndon B. Johnson	9.85 Million	3.91%
69-73	R	Richard Nixon	6.85 Million	2.38%
73-77	R	Nixon/Gerald Ford	3.94 Million	1.29%
77-81	D	Jimmy Carter	10.34 Million	3.06%
81-85	R	Ronald Reagan	5.32 Million	1.43%
85-89	R	Ronald Reagan	10.78 Million	2.69%
89-93	R	George H. W. Bush	2.67 Million	0.62%
93-97	D	Bill Clinton	11.58 Million	2.64%
97-01	D	Bill Clinton	11.31 Million	2.33%
01-05	R	George W. Bush	0.06 Million	0.01%
05-09	R	George W. Bush	1.23 Million	0.23%

I know that chart seems like just a bunch of numbers, right? It just is a chart, BORING. But that is how the government provides the information to you. However when you put the statistics together the way I do and compare them side by side, you will see quite an amazing pattern or difference!

I have not changed the statistics in any way other than to arrange them by party. When doing this we will see how well each party has done. In My Opinion a 2.5 percent job creation rate is a good target rate. Our individual working years run usually run between 40 to 45 years!

Now in my chart I will give the average yearly job creation in percentage terms only. I feel it is only important to keep in mind how fast the jobs are being added and how fast the economy is expanding!

Of the nine post WWII Republican administrations they have only had one term of job creation over 2.4 percent new jobs created. Of the seven Democratic administrations, five of those administrations are at 2.64 percent or better and three of them are at 2.93 percent or greater! The lone best Republican was President Reagan who had one term at 2.69% new job creation!

Term after term job creation is much higher with Democrats verses what Republicans give us. Don't forget Democrats are taking over weaker economies from Republicans and they manage to give us good numbers. While Republicans always take over strong economies from the Democrats, then they ruin the good economies and give us low job creation in its place!

In fact, Republicans use policies which leave the economy in contraction *every single time* they come to the White House. How far down would the economy go, if voters did not replace them with Democrats?

Fortunately the voters do see the decline and crash coming and they usually remove Republicans and their policies from office before we hit bottom. This is the way politics seems to be progressing.

O.K. so now we are going to look at the job creation charts the way I would like for this information to be provided to the public. With Republicans organized in one column, and Democrats organized in their own column. In this chart you can just look left to right and compare the two Parties side-by-side. I believe this is how the government should provide the statistics. Make it simple for voters to see the job each party is doing!

I would like to say the general time periods match up well too. It is not like we are comparing older Republican times to modern Democrat times. We have had a fairly consistent shifting of power back and forth during the times after World War II. OK so here we go let's comparing the statistics the right way!

Republicans	% Jobs Added Per Yr.	Democrats	% Jobs Added Per Yr.
Harding/Cool	+ 4.23%	Roosevelt	+ 4.97%
Coolidge	+ 2.13%	Roosevelt	+ 2.53%
Hoover	Lost -5.41%	Roosevelt	+ 5.00%
Eisenhower	+ 1.34%	Truman	+ 1.61%
Eisenhower	+ 0.87%	Truman	+ 2.93%
Nixon	+ 2.38%	Ken/Johns	+ 2.64%
Nixon/Ford	+ 1.29%	Johnson	+ 3.91%
Reagan	+ 1.43%	Carter	+ 3.06%
Reagan	+ 2.69%	Clinton	+ 2.64%
Bush Sr.	+ 0.62%	Clinton	+ 2.33%
Bush Jr.	+ 0.06%		
Bush Jr.	+ 0.23%		

Source — Google, "Job Creation by U.S. Presidents"

If you look at this chart closely do you see or notice various patterns? Look at the Republican list and skim over the job creation percentage numbers. Make yourself a mental note. Sometimes the numbers are in the same general area with Democrats slightly better. Other times Democrats are way better!

Then notice how Democrats consistently leave higher job creation for the Republicans. See how Republicans take the high job creation numbers and turn them into declining numbers! Except for the situation we had with Ronald Reagan, who did manage short term growth in job creation. But still that Republican economy collapsed. It was not a lasting model for George Bush Sr.!

Republican President George H. W. Bush had to endure the collapse President Reagan created. I will explain that situation a little more, later in the book.

Now look at the Democrat list and skim over the job creation numbers. Isn't it obvious Democrats are creating jobs at a faster rate, on average than are the Republicans? Democrats are creating jobs faster than population growth, which means workers are in demand. Workers have become a priority within the system and are being paid better. This means they can consume more of what America produces. It is good times in America with the Democrats!

President Truman had to deal with the complete changing of the economy from a wartime economy, producing war supplies to a consumption economy. Yet he grew the economy at rate of 1.61 percent job creation in his first term, up to 2.93 percent new jobs created each year of his presidency during his second term. So Truman gave us a growing economy after the amazing recovery we accomplished with 12 years of fellow Democrat President F.D.R.

The next President is Republican Dwight Eisenhower. Under him the statistics show the economy was declining, contracting and collapsing. His job creation rate first went down to 1.34 percent, in his first term followed by just .87 percent new job creation during his second term! This was the first of many Republican contracting economies during the post WWII era. I will point out Republicans always give us contracting economies!

Then with Presidents Kennedy and Johnson we returned to growing and expanding economies! Kennedy/Johnson gave us 2.64 percent new job creation for that first term. That was followed by the highest job creation rate we have ever had at 3.91 following WWII. That was percent of new jobs created in Johnson's lone second term. Again Democrats gave us very good growth according to the federal job creation statistics! Johnson was the best post WWII presidents at new job creation!

But, when President Nixon and Ford come in they brought back their declining Republican job creation. First it was an average of 2.38 percent new job creation as President Nixon was riding the Democrat economy down, followed by 1.29 percent job creation for the Nixon/Ford Presidencies.

Why on earth would you support a party which gives us declining job creation? Republicans in that situation have returned us to a weak economic environment. Business was not good!

In general, Republican job creation is not keeping up with population growth. Republicans are doing a poor job when it comes to maintaining the economy. You can forget about growing the economy, and commerce was not good either. People were going bankrupt and so on. Profits at the corporation were down also!

Then after Nixon/Ford we get to Democrat President Jimmy Carter. With President Carter we have a return to good growth in the economy. He created about 3.06 percent hew jobs created each year of his single term.

He and the Democrats gave the country a good growing economy. People were employed, paying taxes, corporations were doing well and we did not have huge deficits facing us either!

Then with President Reagan and George H. W. Bush they ultimately gave us a collapsing economy. President Reagan's job creation started out at 1.43 percent and actually went up to 2.69 percent in his second term! I will explain why that was later in the book. He got the short pop in the economy which comes when you start using Supply Side Economics in a somewhat healthy economy!

But then for fellow Republican George H. W. Bush his job creation went on down to just .62 percent new job creation by the end of his only term. That was because Republicans do not support consumption in the economy.

In one term George H. W. Bush caused the economy to crash. He did not drastically change economic policy. Showing us that Supply Side Economics does not working for the nation in the long run!

Now you need to understand what happened during the Reagan's Presidency. Democrats held congress and they knew that Supply Side Economics would not work, so naturally they opposed Reagan bringing it into government. This was a correct move!

But it was also a different time. It was not yet the time of total unending opposition politics like it is today. When Democrats saw that Reagan won re-election campaigning on less taxation and using Supply Side Economics, it was clear if they did not support President Reagan several felt they would be voted out of office!

So in Reagans second term Democrats did not block him from bringing that policy in. The policy came in and it was tried, Reagan did get the short term boost to the economy which always happens when you enact that policy into a somewhat moderate to good economy!

Both parties talk about how important it is, for jobs to be created. Everyone wants to see job creation. But so far isn't it Democrats who are the ones actually creating the jobs? Remember small changes in the job creation percentage rate are actually big changes for the economy!

President Clinton succeeded Presidents Reagan and Bush Sr. He gave the nation a record breaking expanding economy. I say record breaking because he did create the largest number of actual new jobs of any president in his first 2 years! 7 million jobs in 2 years was a lot of job creation!

He was also shrinking the massive deficits Presidents Reagan and Bush Sr. had left to him. After 4 years he actually began running nice surpluses. President Clinton had 2.64 percent new job creation followed by 2.33 percent new job creation in his second term. Yet that lowest percentage number for President Clinton was still a larger % gain of people finding work under him than seven out of nine Republicans!

Then we had the total disaster of George W. Bush. He gave us no job creation in his first term, and that was followed by just 0.23 percent job creation during his second term. We essentially were right back to no job creation and a very sick economy with him!

Term after term Republicans kill our economy. Any reasonable American would stop supporting Republicans if they knew this was going to happen!

We know President George W. Bush ran every aspect of the economy into the ground. The housing and auto industries were all collapsing. We had personal and commercial bankruptcies happening left and right. The manufacturing and retailing industries were all collapsing under his Republican Presidency! He did that with the help of his Republican House and Senate! Democrats did not mess him up, because they did not have any control!

So even when Republicans had the one thing they always wanted, which was complete control of government, they still gave us a very sick contracting economy. I thought all that Republicans ever wanted was to have complete control. Folks if you want growth you must elect progressive Democrats!

Looking at the chart more closely, all but one Democrat administration have been better at job creation than seven out of nine Republican administrations. One of the two Republican Presidents who did beat the worst Democrat administration was still worse than 5 other Democrat administrations. So you have a situation where the vast majority of Democrats are better for the economy than are Republicans!

President Nixon had a nearly 2.38 percent new job creation rate in his first term. His ending job creation was low, at just 1.29 percent. His average was better because he took over a very strong economy from President Carter. This all made Nixon's average looked better than it actually was!

The only two Democrat administration with a worse job creation record was the first term of Harry Truman who had absolutely no peace time economy to work with and President Clintons second term which was 2.33% verses Nixon's 2.38%! I am sure Nixon was simply riding the better Democrat economy on down!

So, basically we have a situation where five out of seven Democrat Presidents were better at job creation than, seven out nine Republican Presidents. How can anyone accept a situation like that? That is a huge fact which must not be overlooked. It was almost like every Democrat President was better at creating healthy economies than every Republican President!

President Reagan at 2.69 percent just barely beat two Democrats who were both at 2.64 percent new job creation. President Clinton had one term at 2.33 percent and then Harry Truman's first term at 1.61%.

We came very close to having a situation where five out of seven Democrat Presidents were better at job creation than all nine Republican Presidents. From all of this information I do not see or understand how people can think Democrats are not good for our economy! You must take negative Republican comments with a large grain of salt!

Clearly there is something flawed in Republican economic policies. If Republicans were more or less as effective as Democrats at job creation these statistics would show reasonable equality. Republicans would have their share of good job creation presidential terms.

Job creation is the holy grail of statistics. Republicans are not giving the nation job creation and growth! This means Republicans are not giving the nation a prosperous economic environment where all people and businesses alike can get ahead.

So basically the statistics are backing up what I have been saying to you. You should bite the preverbal bullet and realize Democrats are not only good for the economy but actually they are way better!

Seven out of nine Republicans fell below the worst Democrat President who himself was dealing with huge economic problems at the end of WWII. I thought you Republicans believed Republicans give us strong economies.

Simply ask yourself a very simple question, why would seven out of nine Republican administrations have worse job creation than all of those awful Democrats who never do anything right? I hope you are starting to see the light.

How often have we heard Republicans say the economy is bad under Democrats? Even today Republicans are talking down the Obama economy. I guess you people have completely forgotten the economy we had with George W. Bush!

I am not saying Republicans are bad, I am not saying they are evil. It just is that their conservative approach does not work when you apply it to economics. The economy never responds well to a weak middleclass which is what Republicans give you!

So seven Republicans and one Democrat administration did not have job creation which kept up with growth of the population. They fell way below the 2.5% job creation threshold. All of those guys gave us sluggish economies.

Truman had a good reason to not have good job creation numbers during his first term. At the end of the war there literally was no household manufacturing at all! His economy did not have a lot of consumption happening because there were no products being manufactured or available!

Referring to the charts Republicans have always received good economies from Democrats. But when a Democrat takes over from a Republican President, that Democrat President usually receives a sick to slow economy. So the Democrat must first repair the bad Republican economy to a normal level before they can then give us a good economy. That is like having to climb two mountains instead of just one!

Democrats have given us surpluses five times. Republicans have given us surpluses only two times, and they have had the White house for more years. You people want to think Republicans are better for the economy? Are you still going to believe that when you view these statistics?

What are you Republicans going to try and say to justify your beliefs? Democrats always exhaust the good economy so there was nothing left there for Republicans to build upon? If that is the case how come *every single time* Democrats take over from Republicans the economy reverses direction and becomes strong again? If Democrat policies were bad why would an economy ever improve?

Harry Truman started with a Democrat economy and gave us our first good economy since the end of WWII. You cannot credit his economy in any way to Republicans! President Truman's low job creation number was due to the ending of WWII, it was not due to some problem with Democrat policies!

At the end of WWII we had millions of service men and women returning home from war. These young men and women were marrying their sweet hearts, starting families and needing the merchandise for the living of life.

Jobs were not plentiful. War contracts were cancelled and many workers were without work. It was a double whammy for the economy. It took manufactures several years to tool up the production lines. It all involved time to get the economy moving again. It is no wonder Harry Truman's first term was weaker!

Now looking back at my chart, Republicans are on the left side of the chart and Democrats are on the right side of the chart. Simply comparing the parties left to right, nearly every Democrat has a notably higher job creation number than the Republicans, on the left hand side.

It looks pretty lopsided in my opinion. Let's talk about this for a second. Looking at the entire first chart back to the beginning Republicans have a grand total of only four terms where job creation was over 2%, while Democrats have had a total of nine terms with job creation over 2%!

Democrats have one term of job creation at 5 percent! Democrats had 3 terms with job creation over 3 percent! One of those was 4.93%. Democrats had 4 other terms with job creation over 2 percent.

Republican had only one term of job creation over 4 percent at the beginning of the roaring twenties. They only had 3 terms where job creation was over 2 percent. One of those again was at the beginning of the roaring twenties! And another one was after taking over a very strong economy from Lyndon Johnson where it would be nearly impossible to average a low number. I say to you most of the Republicans with good job creation is not from them creating jobs but from them riding Democrat economies down!

Now just looking at the modern era as I prefer to do, we already know Democrats create jobs 2.1 times faster than Republicans. Folks to me this is very strong evidence that Democrats are way better for the economy than are Republicans.

But I want you to consider this. If you remove the one good Republican President, President Reagan from the Republican totals, because he was not your average Republican. He was the only Republican in the modern era to have some job creation! If you remove him and now average the remaining Republicans, you will get to where the average Republican creates jobs four times slower than Democrats!

That is a huge difference. How do you justify your support of Republicans?

I believe you can remove any individual Democrat President from the totals you want and not have much effect on the Democrat averages. Pretty much all Democrat Presidents have been good at job creation!

I consider the beginning of the modern production and commerce era to be the post WWII time period. That is where I prefer to give the closest look at the economy!

Economic policies do change when Republicans and Democrats come to the government. A person does have to wonder why the parties are so different from one another. Seems like everyone ought to be able to agree on what good economic policies are!

Republicans simply do not get it. They will never recognize or learn from the good economic policies, which Democrats have repeatedly used! In fact they will claim Democrat policies are bad. Go figure?

However I say since average Democrat Presidents are 4 times better at job creation in the modern era than the average non Reagan Republican, what would you expect to see from Republicans in the future? Will we have a Reagan style Republican, or a George W. Bush style Republican!

Will we have more of the policies of cutting the taxes for the corporations while keeping them higher on the individuals? Are you thinking we are going to have stronger commerce when the middleclass has less spending money? Surely that does not make any sense, does it?

You know I am not using any of President Obama's first term since he was handed a total mess from President George W. Bush. We want to consider normal average statistics. Just like I have not talked much about the Great Depression years, or Herbert Hoover's record! We will not count President Obama's first term because of that huge broken economy he was handed!

I think you would agree it would be unfair to credit President Obama with all of those job losses. Those losses were not created by him, so he should not be held responsible for them! To my way of thinking the Obama administration is the only administration where major job losses did not fall on the party who actually caused the problems.

Here is another very important point. You will see the economies that Democrats receive from Republicans are always slower, collapsed economies. Not most of the time, but literally 100% of the time. Republicans on the other hand always receive good and strong economies in general from their Democratic predecessors. Newt you need to pay attention here and learn something!

Democrats are climbing all kinds of mountains when they take over from Republicans. If you think of yourself as a good American you need to rethink your support of Republicans. I tell you it really is not that bad when Democrats have the government and the economy under their control!

Certainly it is better than what Republicans do for the economy! But you Republican supporters only believe Democrats are bad! It is not that hard to change your party loyalty. Just get use to thinking in the correct way. Democrats are good for our country! I am not saying they are perfect, no party is. But they pretty clearly do a better job in general!

THE IMPORTANCE OF CONSUMPTION TO THE ECONOMY!

Consumption is the most powerful economic fuel any economy can use. Fortunately for the economy at the end of WWII, it was consumption that really fueled growth at that time. It was strong consumption that saved the Truman Presidency. Within a few short years consumer goods returned to the market place and our economy began to hum again!

Consumption is a good thing, and the lack of consumption was the problem we had at the end of WWII. The problem at that time was there was nothing being produced which the people actually needed.

Just like the lack of consumption is the problem we had at the end of the George W. Bush Presidency! But the problem for him was different. The people did not have the money to make the purchases to begin with. President Bush did not maintain the financial strength of his consumers in the middleclass!

Anytime you remove spending power from the middleclass you will slow the economy down. Since Republicans constantly do that, they are repeatedly responsible for giving the nation slower economies!

Less commerce equals smaller profits at the corporations, which leads to less work all around. There will be less manufacturing as products are not being bought up. Republicans are actually harming corporations with their conservative policies! Obviously they are harming working people too!

So if you think Republicans are better for the country why would the economy become stronger when Democrats bring more progressive policies to the economy? Is it really that simple? Conservative policies lead to contraction, while progressive policies bring increased commerce. Well that is how it looks to me!

No President has to be smart to ride a good economy down! All that a President must do is have bad economic policies. Anyone at all can ride a good economy down. It takes some skill just to maintain an economy let alone cause it to grow!

In mid-January of 2015 President Obama was threatening to veto another tax break extension the Republicans were trying to pass. This shows to me that Republicans are totally wrapped up in these beliefs that cutting taxes for the corporations and the wealthy is a better policy!

Having profitable corporations is good but should not be the primary goal of the economic system. I believe we should not support Republicans unless they totally revamp their economic beliefs.

It seems like if Supply Side Theory really worked, the economy should have gotten better when the master of Supply Side Economics was at the controls. The economy would have been at whatever level and then grown and stayed stronger. But in the end Reaganomics caused an economy to collapse!

I don't suppose you remember that President Bill Clinton had an all Democratic House and Senate for his first two years, what happened there? President Clinton and Democrats totally rejected Supply Side Economics that's what. They enacted Consumer Focused Economics. The focus was on taking care of your middleclass consumers!

President Clinton set the all-time record for job creation in absolute numbers. He created seven million jobs in his first two years and the corporations were seeing record profits.

So President Clinton rejected Supply Side Economics, and he gave tax cuts to working people. His tax cuts were scheduled to last for five years. He supported the middleclass with tax cuts and minimum wage increases. This was the opposite policy from what Republicans were trying!

President Clinton brought those tax cuts in with an all Democrat Congress! And please do not forget, he left George W. Bush the strongest economy in the history of the world!

The worst thing Republicans did toward the end of the Clinton Presidency was they would not renew the tax cuts that had been given to the middleclass. This was a very basic misunderstanding of how economics works by Republicans. That mistake by Republicans would have kept the economy expanding were it not done!

Please keep in mind changes in government policy always take time to happen. They never happen as fast as we would like. But President Clinton's tax cuts took us to the peak of the surpluses. As soon as those tax cuts were taken away by the Newt Gingrich congress the economy began to seriously contract!

During the final six years of President Clinton's Presidency, Republicans had total control in the House and were either ahead or tied with Democrats in the Senate. The period of little co-operation from Republicans had arrived. Yet Newt constantly tries to take credit for the surpluses and good economy President Clinton created! In my opinion Newt is really the one who ruined our economy!

At that time Republicans were working as hard as they could to undo his policies! Republicans vehemently opposed Consumer Focused Economics. However there was nothing they could do to make big changes until the tax cuts expired. It was about year six when Republicans did not renew the tax breaks for the middleclass! Newt Gingrich and the other Republicans took support away from the middleclass and the general economy!

In addition Republicans compounded the economies problems by giving more tax cuts to the corporations. That was not necessary since corporations were doing just fine with Consumer Focused Economics. That combination over time badly hurt revenues to the government, and did nothing to increase commerce. Republicans had reversed Clinton's policies!

Since Republican policies did not have an effect on the economy until tax filings for year 6 of the Clinton Presidency it was not long before the economy began to contract. Basically the economy was expanding and had upward momentum until Republicans undid the Clinton tax policies. The collapse began in year seven of President Clintons Presidency!

We all know by the end of year 6 the great and growing surpluses we had began to wane away! Surpluses in year six would probably have been even larger than they were, had the beginnings of incorrect policy not already been in place!

Clearly by year seven we were suffering the full effect of higher taxation of the middleclass! The middleclass simply was not maintained. We should have kept paying down the national debt. The entire economy would have been busier but Republicans just changed course.

After all that many of you still say Republican policies are good for the nation? For crying out loud we were already entering the future George W. Bush collapsed economy years? Geez folks figure this stuff out, it really is not that complicated. Quit being stubborn in your beliefs!

So now we get to the total disaster of the George W. Bush Presidency. As I have repeatedly said, this man did destroy our economy. You Republicans probably just hate to hear that, but that is the reality; it is the truth! He and his Republican policies destroyed the America economy and nearly took down the world economy!

In the end with the single action of higher taxation of the middleclass, Republicans cut the legs out from under the strong economy. Do you people get this?

Have you forgotten in President Bush's second term he was losing 500,000 to 700,000 jobs per month at the end! Folks George Bush could not create any jobs at all. For years Republicans and George Bush claimed they had the correct conservative Republican policies but look at what we got!

George Bush had a total Republican government helping him all of the way. Democrats did not foul up his economic scheme! This is just another great illusion Republicans feed to you! They tell you their policies are better, but we know now what the truth is! Are you going to forget that?

It really bothers me that people would support a party that has such a long history of bringing harm to the nation. To me this demonstrates how powerful political loyalty becomes to average voters. People just stop thinking and lock themselves into incorrect beliefs!

How much damage do you need to see before you become upset with this? This man's party has destroyed the economy in America for now the fifth consecutive time. Going clear back to 1920 every time Republicans are in control of the economy it ends up as a very bad economy. That is why they do not stay in power!

Do not tell me Republicans are better for the economy. There is no comparison, and literally all of the growth this nation has experienced has come to you from Democrats. You can't argue Republicans create jobs when the federal job creation statistics show the opposite!

I remind you those statistics are not Democrat statistics! That information is compiled by both Republicans and Democrats working hard at producing honest information for economists, news agencies and the public to use.

It is honest information. How can you possibly support Republicans when our government is not adequately funded? How are we supposed to have a strong nation and a strong military when the economy is slow, sluggish and failing?

Do you professionals believe your lives will be better when your taxes are slightly lower, but the whole economy is struggling? Will a slow economy with massive unemployment, under-funded government, a weaker military, worse roads, schools and infrastructure bring you more happiness when everything around you is collapsing? Are you only thinking about your immediate wellbeing? How can you think that when America has given you so much!

All I am saying is Republicans should adopt some version, any version, of Consumer Focused Economics. Take care of the consumer. Republicans should make Consumer Focused Economics their own policy. Wouldn't it be great if we always had proper policies and a strong and healthy economy?

The wellbeing of the nation is way more important than the success of any one party! You could claim the statistics happen to be bad for Republicans once in a while, but not "every single time." You can't say it has just been bad luck! Republican policies are bad and they bring contraction to the economy!

Remember when it comes to job creation statistics, our government must remain impartial. Our government will not make a party look good or bad. They are not permitted to make a big production out of these statistics. They pretty much deliver the news in a plain Jane way. They will not provide the information to you in the informative way I have.

If the statistics were presented properly our population could make simple side by side comparisons. People would make better choices. I say if we are going to stay a healthy democracy, then we should present the statistics in a way where the population can see what each party is doing for the good of the nation! Do not bury the information in hard to understand charts.

Why politicians do not site job creation statistics is a mystery to me. The only thing I can think of is, there must be a rule or something that says you cannot campaign on job creation statistics. However, I am not bound by any of those rules if there are any. I am simply an author.

I took the total number of jobs created by each party. Then I divided by the number of years that each Party was in the White House. I then divided the higher Democratic number by the lower Republican number to come up with the ratio between the two parties. That has revealed a flat out drubbing of Republicans in my opinion. But this is not a sport. It is seriously important stuff.

Since WWII Democrats have created jobs at an average rate of 2,010,000 jobs each year they are in the White House. Republicans on the other hand have created an average of around 925,000 jobs each year when they are in the White House!

Today job creation is happening. Deficits are shrinking. The price of oil is plunging. More consumption is happening. We are steadily seeing the economy return to good times. I know it is not a complete recovery yet, but we are moving in the right direction. Just give it more time!

Ann Coulter you need to open your eyes. President Obama has been the great savior of our economy this time! This is in spite of the fact he is not getting any co-operation at all from your Republicans friends! You should be ashamed of yourself and the Republican Party for your opposition voice. You are holding America back!

We could cut corporate taxes rates to zero but what good would that do if you still do not have healthy consumers? You still will not sell things or make any money. With Supply Side Economics you will only get the sluggish results we have seen in the statistics. Republican policies do not increase commerce!

You should take this chapter to your heart. For goodness sake, common sense says you should never vote for Republicans given their policies and the results!

Much as you hate the idea of voting for Democrats you do not vote for them because they are Democrats, or because you love them. You vote for them because they use the correct policies for the economy.

You Republicans should quietly step aside and let the Democrats fix the economy. Let Democrats put us back on a growth path, and do so without opposition. If Democrats get it wrong they will be voted out of office soon enough. You do not need to do anything!

We are all Americans first! We should support a strong economy which benefits all. It is not important to support one party or the other. It is only important to support the policies which work in the economy. Until Republicans adopt Consumer Focused Economic policies you really must not support them with your vote!

THE GREAT DECEPTION

I think we should take an even closer look at the statistics. There really are many things here to be learned when we dig into it a little bit.

Consider this, the slowest 20-year period of job creation for Republicans was both terms under President Eisenhower then we have George H. W. Bush who is followed by both terms of his son President George W. Bush! In those 20 years of Republican Presidents they created only 7,443,000 jobs. Please keep that in mind.

Now again since the end of WWII and not counting any of the F.D.R. recovery years! The fewest number of jobs created during a 20-year period of time by Democrats was over 34,335,000 jobs!

That would be both terms of President Truman, followed by Kennedy/Johnson. Then President Johnson alone, followed by President Jimmy Carter. Now these are long term comparison of job creation. It pretty much gives you a stable long term picture of both parties ability to create jobs for the nation and strong economies for the middleclass!

7,443,000 verses 34, 335,000 is a huge difference. This simple statistic clearly shows Democrats do not give the nation "**BAD**" periods of job creation, while Republicans do. These are long term averages!

So in the slowest periods Democrats have created 4.4 times more jobs than the Republicans have created in their slowest period of job creation. Now how can any of you claim or believe Republicans are better for our country?

Here is the actual job creation numbers for our U.S. Presidents after WWII.

REPUBLICANS		DEMOCRATS	
Eisenhower	2,743,000	Truman	2,772,000
Eisenhower	745,000	Truman	5,470,000
Nixon	6,852,000	Kennedy/Johnson	5,900,000
Nixon/Ford	3,947,000	Johnson	9,855,000
Reagan	5,316,000	Carter	10,338,000
Reagan	10,781,000	Clinton	11,576,000
Bush Sr.	2,672,000	Clinton	11,315,000
Bush Jr.	56,000		
Bush Jr.	345,000		

Now let's compare the best economic periods for both parties. The best 20-year period of job creation under Democrat President's was 48,984,000 jobs created! That was Presidents Kennedy/Johnson, Johnson alone, President Carter, and then both terms of President Clinton. Those Democratic Presidents created 48,984,000 jobs in their 20 years!

Those Democratic Presidents created 48,984,000 jobs in 20 years and that was more than of all Republican President combined since the end of WWII! I am talking about all 36 years of Republican Presidents!

Republicans only created 34,387,000 jobs, total in 36 years. Nearly 50% more jobs were created by Democrats in their best 20 years with a lot less time! And Republicans had nearly twice as much time in the government.

Are you still thinking Democrat Presidents are somehow bad for our economy? Anyway you try to arrange the statistics Democrats always do a much better job!

Now I realize I am not counting any of Barack Obama's first term. As I feel he had to absorb the job loses he inherited from his predecessor! Just like we are not considering the Great Depression! We do not wish to consider skewed information.

Mind you I have not picked the worst Republican President's here. All of the Republican Presidents since the end of WWII collectively have done a terrible job of creating jobs when you compare them directly to the Democrats. Please remember both parties have stated the importance that job creation has in the economy! So that should be important to you too.

Again that should tell you there really is something horribly wrong with the way Republicans are trying to handling the economy? For some unexplainable reason many of you still support those Republicans just because they are Republicans.

How wonderful that is, they are Republicans. For you there is no other reason needed. They are Republican and there for they are doing the right things and are better! Have you ever considered your thinking might be flawed?

I will say to you I believe Ann Coulter, makes an idiot of herself when she talks about how wonderful President Reagan was! She will claim he was the great savior of our American economy?

But President Johnson created only 900,000 fewer jobs, nearly 20 years before President Reagan had his best term. Even President Carter created 10.3 million jobs 8 years before Reagan's best term! That is only 450,000 fewer jobs than Reagan's best term.

But that was more new job creation in percentage terms than all Presidents other than President Johnson! Of course Clinton who came after Reagan exceeded his numbers in actual terms even though for 6 years he was receiving no co-operation from Republicans on middleclass tax cuts!

I have to ask what kind of an American are you? I am not saying Reagan was not a good job creator, he was. But he was nothing extra special. He basically was as good as your basic Democrats were for one term. He was the only Republican who gave the nation some jobs. But his model did not last it was not lasting job creation and growth!

For some of you there is no evidence which will change your thinking. Some of you actually have the nerve to make negative remarks about Democrats and they are the ones who are creating the strong economies. With your stupidity you are pretty much demonstrating your wisdom level to the rest of us!

I want you to digest this fact. The best 20 years of Democrat Presidents created 47% more jobs than all 36 years of Republican President's combined. Be honest with yourself, it is only through stubbornness or personal greed that you continue to believe Republicans are better for the nation!

The best Democrats on average created 2,449,000 jobs every year for 20 years. That is a great average for Democrats!

The worst 20 years of Republican Presidents did not come close to equaling either President Jimmy Carter's lone term or Johnson's lone term. I can't believe some of you talk badly about them.

Clinton created more than 11 million jobs in each of his two terms! Obama is now creating job at a very good clip too. I am sure he will be over 10, 11 million jobs for his second term!

Four out of seven Democrat Presidents individually have created more jobs in their personal 4 year terms, than the worst five Republican Presidents combined in the post WWII era. Doesn't all of this say to you Democrats in general do not give us bad economies? In fact Democrats give us good economies!

Jimmy Carter had the third best four-year period of job creation in absolute numbers, and it was the second best in terms of a percentage gain. I do not care what you say, but in terms of job creation President Carter was good for the nation. In my opinion he deserves to be regarded better than he is by the Republicans!

President Lyndon Johnson managed to create 9,855,000 jobs during his lone 4-year term in office. President Johnson also did balance the budget one year, and both of the houses were Democratic. All of those accomplishments were done while expanding the Vietnam War.

President Johnson also started the expensive great society push. Bad as Johnson may have seemed to us at the time, he did the best job of creating new jobs in America. He created good revenues for government, as witnessed by the balanced budget. How can anyone say Democrats are not good for the economy?

Johnson started the Welfare system. In spite of that we had a strong and growing economy which in my mind far outweighs the welfare problems. And guess what, after all that money was spent on welfare, we are still here as a nation. Our country is still whole. Our wealthy are prospering more than ever. The economy has continued to function. That awful welfare system has not ruined the economy at all!

I tell you those Republicans have this economy stuff all wrong. The problems come from Republicans because they know how to play politics. Republicans will ignore the reality of the good Democrats have accomplished. Then sometimes they will even label what Democrats have done as bad. Republicans are totally nuts when they think Democrats are messing up the economy. That is just reality!

I have been trying to push the idea that having a dynamic and vital growing economy with lots of commerce being conducted is our Holy Grail of economics. But all Republicans have to do to win elections is tell people Democrats overtax, restrict your freedoms, or over regulate. Voters are not properly considering what the true facts of our economy really are!

Don't you think it is better to have a job and pay some tax's verses having no work at all and living with low taxes? What good does that kind of a situation do for you?

I myself have never felt the heavy hand of government. For me there are no big problems here. All of the problems sighted by Republicans, I believe have been created in Republican minds. There are no real issues with our government! Our government is just organized, and that is not a bad thing at all.

Our society will not be good if we do not fund government. Our government provides a workable structure for our system. Fair laws, honest business practices, needed regulation and correct oversight give us a healthy successful system.

Sometimes I wonder if the new Republican strategy is to ruin as much of the economy as they can. They do this to create a situation where our government can no longer afford to fund any social programs! Republicans believe once programs end, taxes can go down.

Well a few will live well but many will suffer. Is it worth it to do that when you can still have good times when Democrats are giving you a healthy economy?

Sure corporations will be spared the few bucks it costs to keep the system functioning. But business will not be good because of bad commerce. We will have growing wide spread poverty and rampant social problems with that model.

We know Republicans will deflect criticism by saying they really want to save those program's but, because of the weak economy we can no longer afford to fund them. They will just say we do not have the money. "It is the economy stupid."

Geez, are you guy's going to fall for that simple line, over and over again? Republicans will then claim they are just being **"responsible"**.

We have to understand what the *new goals and strategy of the Republican Party really are*. First ruin the economy, by cutting taxes for the corporations or the "job creators," reduce regulation and tax the middleclass heavier. I guarantee you with that policy you will kill the economy!

With that model corporations will still be able to squeeze out small profits even though the economy and business environment is very sick. But why would anyone want corporations to be profitable while millions of people are struggling to survive?

Wouldn't businesses rather have a strong, healthy and vital economy! How is that a workable economic model? Stop and think why would anyone support that?

Mind you, I do understand no one likes paying for welfare. I get that. But there are times when women with children are in a tough situation and they really do need some help.

Gee whiz, America really can afford to have some compassion for others built into the system. It should make us feel good to be a generous country. Today everyone understands we will try to stop abuse when it is found!

Remember what Teddy Roosevelt told you about the big trusts. He said "they are ruthless entities in the economy." And "the corporations are solely focused on profits".

Republicans in some respect are way ahead of us Democrats. I believe Republicans are looking past the collapse of the American economy to the future of the world economy!

My view is Republicans really are not concerned that much if America fails. Republicans know the corporations will still be capable of making money and surviving in other countries even after America has gone down. Under Republican policies the corporations and the wealthy will survive. Corporation will set up business in whatever economy is doing well!

Republicans will cause the downfall of America if we let these policies in. It's not that they are trying to kill America it is just their ruthless survival of the fittest mentality that Republicans live by. Corporations will survive in Europe, Japan, Russia, China, India, Brazil or where ever if they must. It does not have to be America!

None of us will have Social Security, Medicare, Unemployment and other programs, because America will be a broken country. Our economy will be non-existent, our military will be weak, but the corporations will be doing just fine wherever the economy remains strong!

Republicans will then try to convince you, this is the formula that must be used to preserve the economy. According to Republicans, it is how the middleclass will live better. I simply say to you do not buy it.

Republicans are not talking about middleclass Americans when they say these things. They are talking about the future middleclass population of the world economy. They are talking about the people who can function within that new ruthless world economy! This is your Republican speak again.

Currently our middleclass does not have enough disposable cash. The corporations are not benefiting as much as they could from the weakened middleclass masses. In general the middleclass needs to be wiser about this whole subject. You need to think this out! What are you really getting with Republicans and their policies? Collapse and contraction is what!

To me Barack Obama has been a very good President. He is working to strengthen America. America is not lost at all. He is trying to build up the middleclass. Our economy is getting stronger! The stock market is near an all-time high!

So for you the issue to figure out is which party is correct? The only important tool I have to convince you are the job creation statistics and my logic. To me job creation is pretty clear evidence!

Your vote should go to those candidates who want to make the economy as strong as possible. The middleclass will evenly spend their money throughout the economy. Allowing the middleclass to keep more of their earnings is a very cost effective way to keep the economy strong and it benefits all!

Many years ago Republican President Teddy Roosevelt warned us about the large trusts. I am paraphrasing here a bit, he advised us "we must drive the special interest groups out of politics." and "the citizens of America must effectively control those mighty forces, forces which they themselves have called into being."

That is to say, it has been the middleclass that has made those segments of society powerful. It has been a healthy middleclass which has created the wealth of the corporations simply by their existence. The middleclass created the opportunity for the corporations to thrive. Now the middleclass needs to keep some control over what they have created.

Corporations should be thankful for the middleclass. Corporations should demand from Republicans that they keep the middleclass strong!

I believe Teddy Roosevelt's advice to us was wise then, and is still true today. How smart is it to allow corporations to basically buy elections with all of their money? Do we have a better country when corporations are pouring millions of dollars into elections?

As I recently told you the Koch brothers announced they will be spending 900 million dollars on Republican candidates and causes this election cycle. Do we really want to allow one family to spend that kind of money on our elections, is that fair to the rest of America?

We need to protect our Democracy and our economy. We do not need to protect the corporations.

Please remember, I am on the side of the corporations. I want them to do well and make tons of money. But I also want that to happen through a strong and fair economy. I want for corporations to earn their profits and not just get windfall tax breaks.

Teddy Roosevelt also said, "There can be no effective control of the trusts, while their political activities remain intact." He knew how it works, when powerful corporations are involved in politics. We should not allow that to be!

I know for a fact, business people would prefer healthy economic times with slightly higher taxes, to sluggish economic times with lower taxation. Unless of course you are a Mitt Romney type.

He is actually someone who has been in the business of profiting off of the liquidation of good companies!

Clearly a balance is needed. Voters need to become wiser. Mitt Romney is no fool. But he is also nothing more than a good businessman taking advantage of the system this great country provides!

We need to be very clear about whom we are helping and who we elect. If people would just let Democrats structure the economy properly and stop focusing on their personal taxes, everything will work out fine!

PRESIDENT CLINTON

Ann Coulter has said she thinks Ronald Reagan was the great savior of the American economy. Let's look at that. I believe the true savior of the American economy was President Clinton! He was so much better in so many areas!

First he added around 23 million jobs and began running surpluses. He also completely reversed the direction the economy was going under George Bush Sr. until Newt Gingrich and the Republican controlled congress reversed his policies and brought back a weak economy and deficit spending!

How can Ann Coulter think President Reagan was good for the economy when he tripled our national debt and never balanced the budget even one time? How can she label him as the great savior of our economy when he gave us massive deficit spending and created jobs slower than three Democrat Presidents!

The only positive thing you can say about his Presidency is he had the highest job creation of all Republican Presidents. But he was only fourth on the list in terms of job creation rates. All of the other Republican presidents lag far behind him so he is the only bright spot among Republicans to sight! Who else among Republicans can Ms. Coulter sight?

Are you going to fall for Ann Coulters baseless claims over job creation statistics? You have to be smart enough to reject what they are trying to get you to believe. Ms. Coulter and FOX News are just flat out feeding you such a line!

President Clinton may have been disliked for aspects of his Personal life, but if nothing else he did a very good job with the economy. To me creating jobs is far more important than some in appropriate affair.

He kept the economy and system strong to properly maintain the things which are important in our society! Because of what Mr.

Clinton gave the economy we were able to make sure government programs would continue!

Consider this, the only Republican President to ever give us a balanced budget was Dwight Eisenhower! He accomplished that twice, in 1956 and 1957. I commend him for that, it is not easy to achieve!

However during the modern era, starting with Harry Truman, Democrats have balanced the budget five times! Like it or not Democrats have balanced the budget much more often than Republicans. President Clinton actually balanced the budget 4 times! But you hate him?

Another Democrat you Republicans hated was Lyndon Johnson. He too was able to balance the budget one time. He did that while the Vietnam War was heating up, and after 3 or four years of Democrats in the White House and in Congress.

Democrats were in control of government in the Johnson years. Then Democrats were in control when President Clinton brought in his middleclass tax cuts!

President Clinton did not get his tax cuts on day one of his Presidency. His tax cuts began after Congress and the President enacted changes. Once started they were scheduled to last for five years and it does take a while to turn the economy!

It was not until year five of his Presidency when we began to see surpluses. Those tax cuts lasted until about year five and a half of his Presidency. Or you could say well into the 6th year by the time you get to tax filing season!

The surplus in year 6 might have been even greater than they were had the tax rates not been changed. Republicans killed the strong economy with their changes!

Because all of the years through year six saw lower middleclass taxation the economy ran growing surpluses. The negative effects of allowing the middleclass to pay more in taxes was not being felt in a big way until year seven of his Presidency. By year seven the surpluses were clearly disappearing!

It was year seven of the Clinton Presidency when the full effects of the higher taxes on the middleclass were being felt in consumption. Our surpluses at that time began to wane in a big way!

When Newt Gingrich along with the other Republicans did not extend the tax cuts for the middleclass we knew that was going to harm those who are doing the consumption. It must, because you are taking money away from the consumer!

Higher taxes on the middleclass, coupled to lower consumption plus lower taxation of the corporations, all led to fewer revenues flowing through to government and a less strong economy! This explained the return of deficit spending.

Republicans will tell you it is because of Newt Gingrich and proper Republican policies that the economy ran surpluses. Wrong; as soon as Republican changes came into play the economy reversed direction!

President Clinton's surpluses grew from 122 billion in year five, up to roughly 230 billion dollars in year six of his Presidency. Those were very good numbers. We were paying down our debt!

At the end of the Clinton Presidency he warned Republicans to be responsible and keep the surpluses going. President Clinton warned Republicans of giving big tax cuts to corporations and he warned them of taxing consumers to much. He gave Republicans all of the correct advice!

Republicans naturally did not listen. Republicans will never listen to a Democrat even though President Clinton was right about maintaining a strong economy!

George W. Bush and the Republicans were back in total control of our government. Republicans policies continued to weaken the economy. They began running larger and larger deficits!

Here are some good sources of information on the subject. Check them out for yourself.

• En.wikipedia.org/wiki/United_States_federal_budget

and

• Articles.cnn.com/2000-09-27/politics/clinton.
  surpluse_1_budget-surplus-national-debt

Republicans harp about balanced budgets and responsibility in government all of the time. Yet they have not given us a balanced budget since the 50's. Republicans have not even moved the economy toward those balanced budgets. Republican economies are always moving us toward greater deficits!

So this is another illusion Republicans are using on you. They will say what sounds like logical things. They will tell you they know how to run the economy. But we only see collapse with them!

If I were in the Democrat leadership, I would point to the economic problems Republicans bring us. The record does not lie!

Whether you like President Bill Clinton or not, you must admit he created more jobs during his Presidency that any other administration in our history. His job creation numbers alone equaled close to two thirds of all of the jobs created by all of the Republican Presidents, all of them including Ronald Reagan combined since the end of WWII! Do not even think about saying Democrats are bad!

For Republicans, Keynesian Economics is basically a dirty word. I do not understand their thinking at all. They just refuse to acknowledge what has been successful in the economy!

Had President Clinton's economic policies been carried forward our grandchildren would have been very proud of us today. The economy was exploding, our deficits were shrinking. Government was enjoying nice surpluses. Why did we ever turn away from that? President Clinton had the right approach!

If you kept the tax cuts in place for the middleclass that would have maintained consumption. Over time with a strong economy you could start giving measured tax cuts to the corporations. Yes you want to maintain the surpluses but keep the surpluses controlled. It is a balancing act!

Today with Republicans coming back to power, they are trying to bring us back to full blown Supply Side Economics. Do we really have to repeat the same mistakes of the past for the sixth time? Be wise and do not return Republicans to office as long as they believe in Supply Side Economics. They will harm us all with those policies!

When it comes to economics President Clinton was an amazing President. He did the right things and we all prospered as a result. He had us heading in the right direction. He truly is the one who saved the economy!

I know you Republicans hate to read these things but that happens to be the truth. President Clinton was the real thing. He is the one who saved the economy!

Ann Coulter I believe you are a very unwise and uneducated commentator. You are sharp spoken, thoughtless and frankly sometimes rude commentator! In My Opinion you are one of America's great idiots! How the heck did you ever get hired by FOX?

SO ARE TAX RATES
<u>IMPORTANT?</u>

Another question we have is how does America's tax rates compare to other nations? There is much concern on the part of Republicans for our tax rates. They think our government collects too much in taxes. So I say let's make a rough comparison of how our nation is being taxed compared with other nations!

This will be a short chapter. Based on comparisons to other nations I feel we are somewhere around the middle of the road. Some nations will pay a little more in taxes, while others will pay a little less. It is hard to compare directly because we do not have the value added tax in this country, where most other nations do and it is an important part of their tax structure. Plus our individual states have different tax policies from state to state. But we do have basic numbers which we can look at!

My goal with this book is to try to turn peoples' thinking away from concerns about how high their taxes are, to focus on how much better their lives will actually be once we have higher revenue generation do to increased commerce in our economy. Businesses will be doing better along with the working class. We all want commerce and we appreciate having jobs!

The only important issue for me about taxes is this. At what rate do we wish to pay down the national debt and can we keep good levels of commerce happening? I am sure we would all agree it is unfair to lay a lot of our debt upon our children!

Therefore I believe surpluses in the budget do become somewhat important. If possible, we would like to see the national debt shrinking to a more sensible level. I believe we should have surpluses each year until our debt is much smaller. In my opinion, running surpluses should be the norm for a long time!

Now I just got these figures off of the Internet. I did not do a lot of research for this chapter. According to a chart I looked at these numbers are the maximum tax rates you might expect to pay in those various countries. These would be the tax rates for the highest earners. Use this chapter for general information!

Now in our country tax rates do vary from state to state. And it is hard to put an exact number on any of these other countries. So these statistics are very general. They are statistic for conversation and are probably not completely accurate. But here you go some tax rates for you to look at.

COUNTRY	MAX. TAX LOAD FOR INDIVIDUALS	VALUE ADDED TAX	CORPORATE TAX
Denmark	51.7%	25%	corp. flat tax 25%
Finland	51.0%	24%	corp. flat tax 20%
France	75.0%	20%	corp. flat tax 33.33%
Germany	47.0%	19%	Average 29.8%
Iceland	46.0%	25.5%	corp. flat tax 20%
Italy	43.0%	22%	corp. flat tax 31.4%
Japan	50.0%	8%	corp. flat tax 38%
S. Korea	41.8%	10%	10 - 22%
Sweden	57.0%	25%	corp. flat tax 22%
United States	55.9%	0%	0 to 38% corporate tax

Looking at these figures I do not see where Americans pays high taxes! The United State income tax figure takes the national max income tax rate, (around 39%) plus the average of state and local taxes nationwide to get an average tax load of about 55.9% for individuals. But we do not have the value added tax to pay in America. So the tax rate is higher but we have no value added tax!

When you figure in the value added tax we probably are a little below the average for industrialized nations. In other nations I believe the value added tax is added on all new purchases!

In other words if you buy a new car or new furniture you pay the value added tax when you make the purchase. The value added tax varies from nation to nation. I remind you this chart is very basic in nature. Plus I am not a tax expert at all!

I feel our federal corporate tax rates are high compared to the rest of the world. But to get into the highest rate your corporation would have to net at least 18 million dollars. Plus our tax system does allow for many massive tax right offs. Write offs of all kinds. Write offs the corporations do use!

For example corporations will write off all of their capital expenses. They will depreciate their equipment, machinery and buildings. They will write off their R&D, their advertising and their tooling up expenses for production! Often we hear corporations writing off hundreds of millions of dollars in expenses against their profits and really not pay taxes at all.

All taxes are complicated, especially America's taxes. But I say to you do not feel sorry for the corporations they usually are doing fine!

Where my niece lives is in Edmonton Canada, corporations there pay a 25% as a corporate tax. But in all other Provinces of Canada corporations pay 40%. In the United States rates runs from 0 to 38% depending how profitable you are and how many write offs you have.

I hesitate to give these tax rates because I am not familiar with the tax system in any of those other countries. I barely have knowledge of how it works in America!

In the chart I looked at, those countries which have variable taxes seem to give a range. Those countries which do not give a range I assume have flat tax rates. But like I say I could be totally wrong. The point I'm making is this, in general terms we are all about the same. No one country is very high or very low compared to America!

And as I have told you many times, taxation is not the key to profits! Low taxes do not have that much to do with profits. Having lots of commerce makes good profits possible. I consider tax burdens small potatoes compared to the profits which will come to us all, with strong commerce.

Can anyone disagree that commerce is the name of the game here? We all would like to see good levels of commerce being conducted. Commerce is the key and that is the important goal!

IT IS TIME TO
SWALLOW YOUR PRIDE

I believe it is time for Republican voters to swallow their pride, bite the bullet and learn how to give maximum aid to the economy. If Republicans truly loved America, they would stop doing what I believe they already know does not work. They would quit thinking about the corporations and taxes and start thinking about the middleclass, commerce, their consumption and concern for proper wages being paid!

If Republicans would do that they could begin to attract voters for the right reasons. Republicans could truly become a strong economic and political force in America. There is nothing stopping them except for their stubborn pride.

I sure do not want to cut taxes for the job creators and then just hope it leads to job creation. We already know that tax cuts given to consumers will put more money in middleclass pockets. We also know the middleclass will spend most of their money! That consumption will fuel your economy. You will have growth when the middleclass has more cash to spend.

When you give tax cuts to the middleclass, that money is not lost at all. That money is actively being spent in businesses. Those businesses pay taxes. The businesses have employees who will be working more and paying taxes too! The merchandise when sold must be replaced, so you keep manufacturing strong. Looking at the big picture, tax cuts for the middleclass are not as big of a hit to the government as you might think. We all want greater consumption!

IMPORTANT PRESIDENTIAL ACCOMPLISHMENTS!

I n this chapter we are going to be looking at the individual Presidential records. I believe it is important to understand which party brings about a better system for the people and for the whole nation. We really need to look at Presidential accomplishments!

We also need to understand if a given president had a congress helping or opposing their work. Did the president bring the new policy in, or did it come in because of the opposition party in congress and so on. We need to understand who to give credit too. This is one way to rate the parties.

This is important when we are choosing which party to be loyal too. We want to know which party or candidate is doing the most good for the whole country! We should not have preconceived notions.

So we will be looking at all important Presidential accomplishments. I am also going to be looking at the congressional records. Sometimes congress brings laws and policies too government too!

I am going to grade the presidents and the congresses as fairly as I can. I will present the information and let you make up your own mind. I will put a simple value on their various actions. It will all become clear in just a minute as we go through the chapter!

Remember we are trying to determine which party is better for the nation. That is the purpose of this chapter! We will be totaling up the records at the end of the chapter. I hope this book will guide you through the political jungle.

I will list each President, along with the well-known accomplishments that each President has been credited with. You may remember most of their accomplishments. But I might be refreshing your memory too!

I like to think the Teddy Roosevelt era kind of marks the beginning of more modern times. In my view it separates modern America from the expansion era and Wild West times.

I will break the statistics into the post F.D.R. period and the period from Teddy Roosevelt through F.D.R. I do this to help us understand if the party is currently helping. It will all become clear in a moment!

As the divide between the wealthy, the middleclass and the poor widens we need to keep track of who is helping the whole country. Who is maintaining the entire system!

We want for businesses and corporations to rise to the top because they are good and fair companies. We want for our companies to be successful while taking care of their employees and their customers. We do not want companies to rise to the top because they are ruthless or heartless.

I am going to start with Teddy Roosevelt. Most people of the time and even today considered Teddy Roosevelt to have been a good President. I would agree with that. Back then it was a different time, with different values. But I believe over-all, he was a good President given that particular time period.

I will be listing the things that historians have considered notable achievements of each Presidential Administration. We will determine if their actions have lifted the quality of life for the nation. Have their actions strengthened the economy, the people and the country?

OK, so let's start by looking at President Teddy Roosevelt, Republican.

1901-1908 THEODORE ROOSEVELT, REPUBLICAN
26TH PRESIDENT

President Roosevelt had a Republican House and Senate for his entire Presidency!

1. President Roosevelt will always be credited with the building of the Panama Canal. I believe the Panama Canal would never have been constructed without an assertive Teddy Roosevelt!

   The Panama Canal was a major accomplishment, which took a strong patriotic personality to push it through. It did much for our businesses, for shipping and in making America a strong economic nation. It linked the Atlantic and the Pacific Oceans for the United States and the world.

2. He also took measures to break up the large trusts. Trusts were the equivalent of major corporations today. He had a reputation of being a trustbuster.

   Even though he broke up several trusts, the people who were at the head of those trusts made even more money after the trusts were broken into smaller companies. Again he tried to keep the powerful interests in check so that they did not abuse the American system. He did in the end give our country what turned out to be a better economic system!

3. He was the first American President to set aside public lands for what in the future would become our National Parks and Forests. It was another good accomplishment. This action preserved some of the most pristine and precious lands in the nation for all Americans to one day enjoy!

4. He started what became known as the Food and Drug Administration. At the time he started it, it was known as the Meat Packing Act. It went a long way toward the delivery safe food to the people.

So I rate Republican President Teddy Roosevelt and his all Republican congress with four positive accomplishments which were beneficial to all Americans. Analysts have said Teddy Roosevelt in general was a good President for the country. I would agree with that. Teddy Roosevelt did not try to destroy the trusts. He merely tried to keep them in check and broke them up into smaller companies!

Remember we will be totaling up the scoring at the end of this chapter. We will see how each party has done.

1909-1912 WILLIAM HOWARD TAFT, REPUBLICAN 27TH PRESIDENT

President Taft had both Houses of Congress Republican during his entire four years in office.

1. June 16th, 1909 President Taft began collection of the Federal Income Tax. This in my opinion was a good thing.

2. April 8th, 1912 President Taft formed the Children's Bureau. This over time became what we know today as C. P. S. Child Protective Services.

   The Children's Bureau was tasked with reporting on birth rates, and infant mortality rates. They reported on juvenile courts, orphanages and the general welfare of children in America. This was an organization that really has its roots back in 1903 again with the Teddy Roosevelt Administration. No question, it was a needed organization that gave us good results.

I rate President Taft with two positive achievements for our country. Believe it or not, collecting an income tax in my mind has not been all bad for our nation or our system. Where would government be today without revenues? How would government have been able to build roads, schools and hospitals without a little stable financial source of income?

The Children's Bureau was extremely important to society. That was an important part of reaching a basic level of sophistication in America. This was another part of giving the nation some proper structure to society. I give President Taft and his Republican congress two points for bettering the nation.

1913-1920 WOODROW WILSON, DEMOCRAT
28TH PRESIDENT

President Wilson had both Houses of Congress Democratic for his first four years. Then he lost the House for his fifth and sixth years. He then had Democratic Houses again for his seventh and eight years!

1. December 23, 1913. He started the Federal Reserve System. This brought a little civilized banking and standardized rules to the money system of the nation. This was the beginning of a more sophisticated money system.

2. In 1914. He started the Federal Trade Commission with the power to issue Cease and Desist Orders to powerful corporations.

3. In 1914 WWI breaks out. Eventually President Wilson enters World War I on the side of the Allies after the Lusitania was sunk. He will not get points for that.

4. May 8th, 1914. He passes the Smith-Lever Act. This was an act where the Federal government pledged to match state and local funds for the education of farmers. It was critically acclaimed for being a progressive method for the funding of those programs. It became the model for improving society.

5. July 17th, he signs the Federal Farm Labor Act.

6. August 25th, 1916. He establishes the National Park Service Act. This established the first national parks system in the country. Though President Teddy Roosevelt did set aside lands for the public, President Roosevelt and the Republican congress at the time did not fund them as our parks. Finally the federal government had begun the funding of the National Park System. This was a good development for the country.

   President Teddy Roosevelt and the Republicans did not fund our future parks, their roads, lodges, rangers and ranger stations, etc. The land was there, but nothing else until President Woodrow Wilson and Democrats funded them.

7. September 3rd, 1916 President Wilson signed the Adamson Act creating the eight-hour workday, and the 40-hour workweek for railroad workers. He also signed child labor laws into effect.

   This established protection for children so that they could not work during their childhood! The Adamson Act brought us the 8 hour work day and 40 hour work week! This became the standard work conditions for all Americans.

8. February 14th, 1919 President Wilson establishes the League of Nations in an attempt to create a better world. This was an early version of what in later times became known as the United Nations.

   Though it was a noble effort, the League of Nations was destined to fail do to European countries demanding excessive reparations from Germany after WWI. This in the end was a contributing factor leading to the outbreak of WWII.

9. May 19th, 1919 President Wilson adopts the 19th Amendment giving women the right to vote. How important was that? What person in their right mind would say it is not right and correct to give women the vote?

We have many women today in Congressional and in Senatorial positions and perhaps one day soon a Presidential position. It goes without saying that women do have a voice which deserves to be heard. If you are a sane man, you will support the idea that women are 100% equal to men!

By my count six major Acts came in with total Democrat control of both Houses. Two came in with a split in government. So I give seven points to the Democrats and one point to the Republicans. Since the two accomplishments are equally credited to both parties. Both parties in this case had to work together.

There were no points given for entering WWI on the side of the Allies. In the future I will not mention those accomplishments where I do not award points.

1921-1923 WARREN G. HARDING, REPUBLICAN
29TH PRESIDENT

President Harding had both Houses of Congress Republican. President Harding had two years in office, before he was assassinated.

1. November 23rd, 1921 He establishes the Maternity Leave Act. This was an important Act for the nation, for women and for families!
2. June 5th, 1922, He establishes rules limiting what striking coal miners could do against employers and watching out for the best interests of the nation. He created basic rules for striking. He also was protecting the coal supply.
3. January 2nd, 1923, The Teapot Dome Scandal erupts.
4. April 9th, 1923, The Supreme Court Rules that the minimum wage laws for Women and Children is unconstitutional. That went against fair play for women and children in my book. But that was a conservative Supreme Court, not elected officials!

I am going to give Republicans two points for President Harding's Presidency, not knowing exactly what the problem with coal miners was all about. However if I remember correctly it was an effort to try and keep coal moving during winter months. It prevented unions from holding the nation hostage to the unions during those cold winter months!

That would be very important to everyday Americans at that time. Since coal was used in homes as well as in industry. It set down basic rules that critical industries cannot be crippled by strikers during vulnerable periods such as winter months. Of course the Maternity Leave Act definitely deserves a point.

I did not subtract anything for the Tea Pot Dome scandal. Nor was the Supreme Court ruling on the minimum wage for women a matter of control by either party.

1923-1928 CALVIN COOLIDGE, REPUBLICAN
30TH PRESIDENT

Calvin Coolidge had both Houses of Congress Republican for all 6 of his years in office.

1. March 18th, 1924 President Coolidge establishes a 2 billion dollar annuity fund, payable to WWI vets in 20 years-time.
2. February 26th, 1926 Calvin Coolidge cuts the Federal Income Tax rates. This leads to further weakness in government revenues. This may have been a contributing factor in the coming Great Depression which hits in November of 1929.

I will give Republicans 1 point for the one beneficial thing that was done for the average Americans during the Coolidge years, the two billion dollar annuity fund payable to WWI Veterans.

1929-1932 HERBERT HOOVER, REPUBLICAN
31ST PRESIDENT

Herbert Hoover had Republican control of the Senate for all four years of his Presidency and the House was Republican for the first two years. Remember the Great Depression raged for three years and a couple months of the Hoover Presidency.

1. Herbert Hoover began construction on Hoover Dam. It became one of our nation's important construction projects during the Great Depression.

2. March 28th, 1929 The U. S. State Department helps Standard Oil in obtaining oil drilling rights in Bahrain.
3. November 29th, 1929.   The stock market collapses and the Great Depression begins.

Unemployment during the height of the Depression went to 31 % or 32%. Basically almost 1/3 of Americans were out of work. Life was hard and jobs were scarce! That was an absolutely staggering level of unemployment when compared to the current unemployment levels and our present economy.

Needless to say, during the Great Depression countless businesses of all types failed. Commerce was very weak and business was bad.

That problem was basically left to Democrat President Franklin D. Roosevelt, and the Democrat Congress and Senate to try and rebuild the American economy from its broken state. Quite understandably the country totally turned away from Republicans at that point due to the magnitude of the problem!

Let me refresh your memory for a moment about the Great Depression. The Depression began in November of 1929. That was after all most nine years of Republicans having control of government!

President Hoover had fully three years and two months left in his Presidency when the Depression began! Hoover and the Republicans took no action to stop the Depression! Any reasonable person would say Republicans own the depression.

Just like Republicans today, President Hoover did not want to spend any money to pull the nation out of what would be called the Great Depression. Of course it was a less sophisticated time with few protections for the economy. I do understand that!

President Hoover and the Republicans believed in letting natural economic forces fix our problems. There was no real regulation of banking during those years. To say the least our system collapsed!

It did take a few more years before the economic situation became known as the Great Depression. In that economy, people had no discretionary income. Many businesses suffered or went under.

The White House, Congress and the Senate were all Republican at the onset. The public rightfully turned to Democrats to try and fix the mess we were in. Bad as the Depression was, I give Herbert Hoover 1 point for initiating work on the construction of Hoover Dam. That project continued during the Great Depression. It helped thousands of men to survive and it helped them to support themselves, and their families.

1933-1945 FRANKLIN ROOSEVELT, DEMOCRAT
32ND PRESIDENT

President Roosevelt had a totally Democratic House and Senate for all of his years in office. He was facing monumental financial problems when he took over the Presidency.

1. March 9th, 1933 F.D.R. establishes the Emergency Banking Act of 1933. This act closed financially unfit banks. He bolsters the remaining banks in an attempt to preserve the banking system in the U. S. His goal was to create confidence on the part of the people in using the banks again! This was a very important factor in saving America and our financial system as we know it.

2. March 21st, 1933 F.D.R. establishes the Civilian Conservation Corps, putting tens of thousands of unemployed young men to work in our national parks and across America. They were building roads, bridges and buildings. The new deal was essentially all deficit spending. I am not sure how many women got work out of the CCC.

3. May 12th, 1933 F.D.R. starts the Federal Emergency Relief Act as well as the AAA, Aid to Agriculture Act. This was important in saving thousands of farmers and their farms.

4. May 18th, 1933 He passes the TVA, Tennessee Valley Authority, for the building of dozens of dams to control flooding and to generate power throughout the Ohio valley. It also made a lot of work for the middleclass.

5. June 16th, 1933 He passes the NIRA, National Indian Rights Act.

6. F.D.R. also starts the PWA, Public Works Act.

7. F.D.R. starts the NRA, National Recovery Act.

8. F.D.R. is credited with the Federal Banking Act.

9. F.D.R. established the Federal Bank Deposit Insurance Act, of 1933.   This is known to us today as the FDIC insurance corporation, keeping banks and savings safe!

10. August 5th, 1933 F.D.R. establishes the NLRB, National Labor Relations Board. This allowed unions to have collective bargaining powers. This ultimately led to an acceptable middleclass life style for many Americans. A large part of our constructive and prosperous lives is due to this law.

   Republicans today are working to take that away from Americans. In Wisconsin, Governor Scott Walker has actually taken collective bargaining away from state workers. This weakens workers along with the general incomes of the citizens. Governor Walker also wishes to privatize our schools so they are no longer public schools. Which means individuals will need to come up with money to educate their kids, are you kidding me!

11. November 8th, 1933 F.D.R. starts the CWA, Civil Works Administration. Again this was putting thousands of workers to work building America and making the country better. F.D.R. literally was trying to spend our way out of the Great Depression. Spending during weak economic times goes against Republican thinking even today!

12. Jan 30 -- 31st, 1934, F.D.R. passes the National Gold Reserve Act of 1934.

13. February 2nd, 1934 F.D.R. establishes the National Import-Export Bank. This was an important factor on foreign trade issues and in providing a way for establishing loans to foreign entities purchasing American products.

14. April 28th, 1934, F.D.R. establishes the Home Owners Loan Act. This was an action that saved millions of ordinary homes in the country from bank foreclosures. This was an important element contributing to holding the nation together.

15. June 6th, 1934, F.D.R. starts the SEC, Securities and Exchange Commission.

16. June 19th, 1934, F.D.R. starts the FCC, the Federal Communications Commission. Remember radio was a new industry!

17. June 28th, 1934. In an attempt to stop farm foreclosures F.D.R. starts the Federal Farm Bankruptcy Act. Saving still more farms from foreclosure.

18. January 4th, 1935 F.D.R. begins the Social Security Administration. Social security provides a basic retirement income to millions upon millions of Americans. How wonderful it is that our parents and grandparents could benefit from this program. Of course one day, we ourselves will benefit from Social Security too.

19. May 6th, 1935 F.D.R. creates the WPA, Works Progress Administration.

20. May 11th, 1935 F.D.R. begins the Rural Electrification of America.

21. July 5th, 1935 He creates the National Labor Relations Act and collective bargaining board.

22. August 14th, 1935 F.D.R. signs the Social Security System into law, including bargaining for labor and unemployment insurance.

23. March 29th, 1937 United States Supreme Court upholds the minimum wage laws for women.

24. June 25th, 1941, F.D.R. establishes the FEPC, Fair Employment Practices Committee. Protecting people from discrimination due to race, creed, or color. This was the first of the civil rights laws in the nation.

25. June 22nd 1944, F.D.R. establishes the G. I. Bill of Rights. The G.I. Bill of rights allowed countless veterans to purchase homes, or get college educations!

26. In 1940 he begins the Lend/Lease Act to aid England.

I am going to give President Franklin Roosevelt and the Democrats in congress a rating of 20.   He clearly did a great deal of good for the nation. He did all of the right things to save the nation after the Great Depression hit. The rating could have been much higher but I did combine many of his smaller accomplishments to give him what I feel is a fair overall number!

1945-1952 HARRY S. TRUMAN, DEMOCRAT
33RD PRESIDENT

Harry S. Truman had both houses Democratic for his first two years. Then both houses went Republican in years three and four. Then both houses go back to the Democrats again for years five through eight of his presidency.

1. Feb. 20, 1946, Truman signs the Unemployment Act into law.
2. March 21, 1946, He creates the Federal Employee Loyalty Act.
3. June 20, 1947, President Truman vetoes the Taft Hartley Act.
4. Feb. 2, 1948, President Truman asks congress to secure the Civil Rights of Minorities.
5. April 2, 1948, He passes the Marshal Plan, aiding in the reconstruction of European Nations.
6. July 26, 1948, President Truman signs legislation desegregating of the Armed Forces.
7. July 15, 1949, President Truman signs the National Housing Act.
8. Oct. 26, 1949, He raises the minimum wage from .40 cents to .75 cents per hour.
9. Aug. 28, 1950, Truman amends Social Security.

Harry Truman was also a strong supporter of the United Nations, and of NATO. He supported the formation of the Jewish State in Palestine. He was a strong supporter of the Marshal Plan in Europe. He opposed the Communist's to keep them out of South Korea.

I give President Truman high marks for being a good President. I give him six points and I give one point to Republicans for their part in the 1947 - 1948 legislation.

1953-1960 DWIGHT EISENHOWER, REPUBLICAN
34TH PRESIDENT

President Eisenhower had a Republican Congress and Senate for the first two years of his Presidency. In the last six years both houses were under Democratic control.

1. August 19th, 1953. President Eisenhower has our American CIA organize the overthrow of the democratically elected Iranian President. He brings back the Royal family, the Pahlavi's to the throne of Iran. He was what we know today as the Shaw of Iran!

   After the overthrow of the Shaw, we then had to deal with an Islamic fundamentalist regime, who generally hated all things American. We currently must worry about their growing nuclear capabilities. It was during the Eisenhower Administration where we lost our chance for a real Democracy to exist in Iran and perhaps in the Middle East!

2. June 18th, 1954. Our CIA sponsors a coup in Guatemala.

3. August 1st, 1956. Eisenhower signs the Social Security Act for Women. Saying they could retire at age 62. As well as allowing the disabled to begin drawing benefits at age 50.

4. September 9th, 1957. Eisenhower signs his first Civil Rights Act into law.

5. May 6th, 1960. He signs another improved Civil Rights Act into law.

6. In 1960 we lost Cuba to the Communists.

7. We also lost the race into space in 1957.

8. President Eisenhower establishes the Federal Highway System for America.

9. In 1956 and 1957 Eisenhower delivers balanced budgets to the nation.

I am Giving President Eisenhower a rating of three and the Democrats credit for three things, since Democrats did control both Houses of Congress when all of laws and notable acts actually passed into law! Eisenhower balanced the budget twice, co-operating with Democrats!

1961-1963 JOHN F. KENNEDY, DEMOCRAT
35TH PRESIDENT

President Kennedy had a Democratic House and Senate for his entire Presidency.

1. March 1st, 1961. President Kennedy establishes the Peace Corp, which creates wonderful experiences for thousands of Americans helping out millions of people in countries all across the world. I would say the Peace Corp gave America a good reputation in the world community.

2. May 25th, 1961. He announces America's intention to build a spacecraft to fly men to the surface of the moon, and return them safely back to earth. This started the space race with the Russians and created many new high tech industries including the computer industries.

3. President Kennedy correctly guided the nation through the Cuban Missile Crisis.

I give President Kennedy a rating of two for his accomplishments and for his ability to make the nation feel good about being Americans. I do give President Reagan the same credit for making people feel good about America. President Kennedy also did a good job with job creation.

President Kennedy handled the Cuban Missile crisis about as well as we could hope for. The Peace Corps has been a good program for the country. He gave us the high tech space and computer industries!

1963-1968 LYNDON B. JOHNSON, DEMOCRAT
36TH PRESIDENT

President Johnson had a Democratic Senate and Congress for all of his 5 years in office!

1. May 22nd, 1964. President Johnson announces the creation of the Great Society. It was an honest attempt at bettering the lives of millions of Americans. However to be honest I would guess that many Americans including myself probably believe had he started a "Work Fare" program rather than a Welfare program, he might have had better acceptance with the middleclass.

   Of all the programs Democrats have come up with, Welfare has been the hardest to accept due to inherent problems of how it was originally structured. Democrats are not perfect. But please remember President Clinton did re-structure Welfare.

2. July 2nd, 1964. Johnson signs the Civil Rights Act of 1964.

3. April 11th, 1965. Lyndon Johnson signs the Elementary and Secondary Education Act.

4. July 30th, 1965. He signs legislation creating Medicare/Medicaid supplements to Social Security. How many of us, and how many of our parents and/or our grandparents have benefitted from these programs?

5. August 5th 1965. President Johnson signs the Voting Rights Act into law.

6. President Johnson has the highest Job creation rating of all post WWII Presidents. At 3.9% job creation, each year of his Presidency that was an excellent number for him.

7. President Johnson also gave the nation a balanced budget, one time!

I combined a couple accomplishments to give President Johnson and his Democratic Congress a rating of five for the things he accomplished for society and America. In my mind I feel the Great Society did lead to some problems. President Bill Clinton did modify Welfare to correct some of the deficiencies.

President Johnson gave us good Civil Rights Legislation, Elementary and Secondary Education Act, Medicare/Medicaid, Voting Rights, High Job Creation and Balanced Budgets, all were good things!

1969-1974 RICHARD M. NIXON, REPUBLICAN
37TH PRESIDENT

President Nixon had an all Democratic Congress and Senate to work with for his entire Presidency. He also knew it would only take a couple Republican votes to override his vetoes should he make them.

Back in those days politicians were more likely to cross over Party lines on issues. Congressmen and women were more likely to vote for what they felt was best for the nation. That is a situation which does not exist in America today.

1. December 29th, 1970. President Nixon signs the Occupational Health and Safety Act of 1970. Known as OSHA Laws, this

set down rules for businesses to follow ensuring the health and safety of workers.

2. December 30th, 1970. He signs the Clean Air Act for automobiles, bringing us catalytic converters.

3. December 9th, 1971. President Nixon vetoes a Bill providing for a national daycare system.

4. March 16th, 1972. Nixon dismisses bussing as a means of achieving racial integration.

5. October 21st, 1972. He enhances EPA to regulate the use of pesticides, in an effort to protect the environment.

6. October 10th, 1973. Vice President Agnew resigns and pleads no contest to election fraud.

7. December 21st, 1973. President Nixon increases Social Security Benefits.

8. April 3rd, 1974 President Nixon is forced to pay back taxes on improperly reported income!

9. April 8th, 1974. He increases the minimum wage to $2.00 per hour.

10. July 24th, 1974. President Nixon is ordered to turn over the White House tapes which confirm his involvement in the cover up of the Watergate Scandal.

11. July 27th thru the 30th, 1974. Three articles of impeachment brought against Richard M. Nixon.

12. August 8th, 1974. Richard M. Nixon resigns the Presidency.

13. During his Presidency President Nixon begins the process to establish a working relationship with the Communists in Red China.

Now the first chance I had to vote in an election was in the November 1972 election. I did proudly vote for the re-election of President Richard Nixon. But Nixon had avoided paying income taxes. Vice President Agnew had to resign. President Nixon expanded the Vietnam War into Cambodia. Then the whole "Watergate Affair" happened.

Looking back, it is easy to see I was not yet a very wise voter. I quickly found out politicians were not always honest. I began to learn I must be careful with my vote, or you will find that you may not get what you voted for. At that time I was still an idealistic young man.

This along with other Republican issues taught me some lessons. In the big picture, it all added up to a desire on my part to try and not be taken advantage of ever again by any politician, Republican or Democrat! Since then I have always taken my vote seriously.

As I said before, I was young and I did not know many things at the time. I was still in a learning phase of life. It took me about 20 more years to begin to see things correctly.

I give President Nixon a generous rating of three and a half, and I give two and a half points to the Democrats. Nixon's rating really should be seriously lower considering his many negatives. I do not know what kind of a price or penalty you give a President for trying to cheat his way back into the Presidency.

President Nixon was against bussing. He was against day care. He had avoided paying personal income taxes. President Nixon had a dishonest Vice President. Then that whole Watergate Affair and cover-up happened.

We must not forget what the Watergate Scandal was all about. It was basically about a President of the United States cheating his way back into office! He was doing illegal surveillance and bugging of his Democratic opponent's party headquarters.

This was almost like Nixon ordered, CIA surveillance of Democrats! This is just the kind of thing we all want to see from our Presidents, right?

To me, with the office of the Presidency, there should be the highest level of integrity expected in that office. How would you Republicans act if President Obama were to do such dishonest things today? You Republicans would rightfully explode!

1974-1976 GERALD FORD, REPUBLICAN
38TH PRESIDENT

President Ford had to work with a totally Democratic House and Senate during his years in the White House.

1. November 21st, 1974. The freedom of Information Act passes into law, over President Ford's veto. He was dealing with a strong Democratic Congress and Senate.
2. January 1st, 1975. President Ford signs the Privacy Act into Law.
3. April 4th 1975. Unemployment reaches 8.7%, highest since 1941.
4. June 6th, 1975. Unemployment reaches 9.7%. It was rising as we were nearing the election.
5. October 6th, 1975. President Ford asks for 28 billion dollars in tax and spending cuts.
6. April 20th, 1976. GNP is at 7.5%.
7. September 13th, 1976. President Ford vetoes development of the electric car.

It is hard for me to give President Ford a positive rating since most of the things accomplished were over his veto. I have to give President Ford a rating of one half since nothing to major benefitting the middle-classes happened during his Presidency or because of him.

I give Democrats one and a half points for the things they pushed through. The one thing that did pass during the Ford Presidency was offset by his many vetoes. Was President Ford a nice man? Yes, both he and his wife were very nice individuals.

1977-1980 JIMMY CARTER, DEMOCRAT
39TH PRESIDENT

President Carter had an all Democratic Congress to work with.

1. With a Democratic Congress and a Democrat President, we had the return of very good job creation. President Carter gave us 3.06% new job creation each year of his Presidency. That was second best amongst all post WWII Presidents.
2. May 22nd, 1977. President Carter announces support for Human Rights in communist countries and de-emphasizes importance of Communism in the world community.
3. In 1977, President Jimmy Carter pardoned all Vietnam War draft evaders, to heal the country.

4. August 4th, 1977. He creates a cabinet level position of the Department of Energy.

5. Carter signed the new Panama Canal Treaty of 1977.

6. February 2nd, 1978. President Carter makes remarks on the Camp David Accords. This has kept the peace between Israel and Egypt since it's signing.

7. 1979 U. S. Officially recognizes the People's Republic of China.

8. 1979 The Three Mile Island Reactor has a major incident.

9. 1979-1981. The Iranian Hostage Crisis engulfs the Carter Presidency. President Carter attempts a rescue mission in Iran, which ends in failure and loss of life.

10. October 17th, 1979. He forms the Department of Education.

11. President Carter bails out the Chrysler Corporation, saving thousands of jobs, and a good American auto manufacturer.

12. He signed the SALT II accords with the Soviet Union, but he could not get Senate approval.

13. Later in 2002 former President Jimmy Carter is awarded the Nobel Peace Prize for the Camp David Accords.

All in all, I give President Carter a rating of 6. Not for the stagnation or for the un-employment he inherited, that was unemployment he had to deal with. But rather for the jobs he saved at Chrysler, for his accomplishments with the Camp David Accords and the Peace Treaty plus the Salt II agreement with the Soviets.

Also I am giving him credit for his recognition of China, his creation of the Departments of Energy and Education, as well as the Panama Canal Treaty, and several smaller accomplishments. President Carter accomplished several good things.

He also did create a lot of jobs in America. He created 10.3 million jobs in his four years. That is an extremely important accomplishment. He was third best in actual numbers and second best in percentage gain of new jobs. Those are all important issues.

Some of these positives are offset by the unfortunate high inflation he had to deal with. He also had the Iranian hostage crisis and failed rescue mission. I believe those issues combined to make Jimmy Carter a one-term President.

1981-1988 RONALD REAGAN, REPUBLICAN
40TH PRESIDENT

President Reagan had a Republican Senate for his first six years. He had a Democratic Senate for the final two years. The House was Democratic for the entire eight years of the Reagan Presidency.

1. March 30th, 1981 John Hinkley attempts to assassinate President Reagan.

2. August 5th, 1981 President Reagan orders the dismissal of 13,000 air traffic controllers.

3. August 13th, 1981. He signs a Republican tax cutting law into effect.

4. January 26th, 1982. He calls for less spending in the future. He also calls for less national government and more spending by State and Local governments.

5. March 4th, 1987. He takes responsibility for the Iran Contra Affair.

6. January 29th, 1988. He prohibits Federal funding of Abortion Clinics.

7. 15 to 17 million jobs are created during the Ronald Reagan Presidency. That is a very good number, but we should keep in mind where his policies were actually taking us.

8. He put great pressure on the Soviets in the arms race. This was very good and helped lead to the collapse of the Soviet Union. He did worry them a great deal with the Space Defense Initiative.

President Reagan no question was a great public speaker. Without a doubt he did make people feel better about the country. Aside from that, he really did very little for the people. He did not help the economy in the long run.

His successor George H. W. Bush had to pay the price for the collapse of the economy that Supply Side Theory had caused. President Reagan did create around 15 to 17 million new jobs. Of course that was a short term positive.

As I told you before, Supply Side Economics will give you a short term boost in the economy. Democrats knew that was a policy that would not last. Unfortunately they were only able to slow down the implementation of Supply Side Economics until President Reagan's second term!

It was late in the second term where the economy finally began to be affected. President Reagan did pass some tax-cutting laws, which were beneficial to the corporations.

Once the middleclass collapsed, the economy became weak. As I said that did not happen until the George H. W. Bush Presidency. President Bush had to suffer the results of a weak economic structure.

President Reagan did try to disarm and outspend the Soviets. That was a very important and correct thing to be doing. In my view that was the one really good thing President Reagan did for the country!

Sadly, I can only give the great President Reagan, a rating of two. And that does include giving credit for making American's feel good about their country!

1989-1992 GEORGE H. W. BUSH, REPUBLICAN 41ST PRESIDENT

President George H. W. Bush had to deal with an all Democratic, Congress, and Senate for his entire Presidency.

1. February 6th, 1989. One month after assuming the Presidency, President Bush had to bailout the Savings and Loan Industries. A huge problem which was caused by President Reagan's excessive deregulation of those industries!

   Do you remember how Republican deregulation was supposed to be a positive thing for the country? Do you remember that it was President Reagan who promoted it? Corporations will abuse their freedom with deregulation. I believe even though Regulation is disliked, it clearly is needed!

2. November 17th, 1989. President George H. W. Bush raises the federal minimum wage to $4.25. But Democrats wanted it raised to $4.55.

3. June 1st, 1990. President Bush signs an Arms Reduction Agreement with the Soviet Union reducing nuclear arms by 25%.

4. June 26th, 1990. He has to renege on his no new taxes pledge. During his administration he had to raise taxes a total of three times.

5. July 26th, 1990. President Bush signs the Americans with Disabilities Act, an act forbidding discrimination against the disabled, and instituting and mandating reforms dealing with access to public buildings, transportation and the like.

6. November 3rd, 1990. President Bush signs the first of three new tax hikes into law.

7. November 15th. President Bush signs the Clean Air Act of 1990.

8. January 10th, 1992. Unemployment reaches 7.1%.

9. July 13th, 1992. Unemployment reaches 7.8%.

I give President Bush a rating of three for: his raising of the minimum wage his Arms Reduction Treaty with the Soviets, his bailing out the savings and loans industries, the Americans with Disabilities Act, and for the Clean Air Act. I give Democrats a rating of two for their part in the passage of those laws since there was a majority of Democrats in both Houses of Congress when that all passed into law!

Democrats knew Supply Side Economics was not a good policy. But they also knew that if they openly opposed President Reagan on it they would be voted out of office. It also was a time when more co-operation between the parties happened. Again not like the situation we have today.

1993-2000 WILLIAM J. CLINTON, DEMOCRAT
42ND PRESIDENT

President Clinton had a Democratic House and the Senate for the first two years. He was tied in the Senate in the last two years. Republicans had both the Congress and the Senate for the middle four years. Congress was Republican in the last two years.

President Clinton was dealing with a largely un-cooperative Congress in the final years. President Clinton did create a large number of jobs. We all agree he had a strong economy. We have to wonder if Republicans were more co-operative perhaps even more jobs could have been created!

1. January 25th, 1993. Was his first attempt to pass a National Healthcare Reform act! Republicans were successful at stopping it.

2. February 5th, 1993. He signs the Federal Medical Leave Act. Many of us have had ill family members where this Act has helped us to be at our family member's side in those tough times.

3. March 3rd, 1993. President Clinton and Vice President Gore pledge to re-design government. The goal was the cutting of Federal spending to a percentage of population and governmental growth.

4. September 22nd, 1993. He unveils Universal Healthcare Plan. Republicans are again successful at beating it back.

   What does this show to you about the Republican Party? It shows me Republicans wanted to keep the healthcare corporations in the driver's seat of providing healthcare to Americans and they do not care if many Americans have no insurance at all! Republicans wish to protect the profit structure for healthcare providers, rather than delivering proper health care to all of the people.

   Even though our medical system is already the most expensive system in the world, we are forced to deal with the corporations for our healthcare. Republicans are forcing us to participate in that for profit insurance based healthcare system!

5. November 30th, 1993. President Clinton signs the Brady Bill into law mandating minimum five-day waiting periods on gun purchases. Is that unreasonable?

   I do not understand where the law is now on background checks so I am not going to make a statement. But I do think some back ground checks are still required with licensed gun dealers. We may not have five-day waiting periods any longer. I am not a gun person but I do believe gun sales are way to free!

6. December 8th, 1993. President Clinton signs the North American Free Trade Agreement.

7. August 26th, 1994. He fails a 3rd time on National Healthcare Reform. Those darned Republicans.

8. Nov. 8th, 1994. Republicans win control of both houses of Congress. No chance of healthcare reform now.

9. January 23rd, 1996. President Clinton declares the era of big government is over.

10. April 10th, 1996. President Clinton vetoes a ban on late-term abortions, upholding a woman's right to get medically safe abortion procedures.

11. February 12th, 1999. Senate acquits President Bill Clinton on articles of impeachment in the Monica Lewinsky matter.

12. February 1st, 2000. The Labor Dept. announces the longest peacetime expansion of the American economy in history. President Clinton along with Keynesian Economics, (Consumer Focused Economics) created 21 to 23.5 million new jobs during his eight years in office. That is huge!

I am going to give President Clinton a rating of five for his many attempts at healthcare reform. He gets points for the very important strong and growing economy; for the Brady Bill, the North American Free Trade Agreement, plus the incredible four times he balanced our budget, as well as for paying down our debt. He gets credit for the longest peacetime expansion of the American economy in history. Everyone knows the economy is the single most important issue for the people.

He, along with an all-Democratic Congress, gave tax cuts to the middleclass and created seven million jobs in his first two years. This was the root cause for the expanding economy. President Clinton showed us the correct economic policies to use!

He did do the right thing by totally rejecting Supply Side Theory. He had massive job creation throughout his entire Presidency. I give Republicans one point for their part in legislation during his Presidency.

With his performance as President, Mr. Clinton did a lot of good for America. Whether you like President Clinton personally or not, you cannot say he was not good for the economy. America itself was quite healthy during those Clinton years. But you Republicans just love to hate President Clinton. You look right past all of the good things he did!

2001-2008 GEORGE W. BUSH, REPUBLICAN
43RD PRESIDENT

President George W. Bush had a Republican House for the first six years of his Presidency. The Senate was split 50/50 for the first and last two years of his Presidency. He had Republican majorities in the Senate during the middle four year of his Presidency.

1. January 22nd, 2001. President Bush's first policy decision was to re-instate a ban on aid to groups providing Planned Parenthood counseling, or aiding in abortions.
2. March 29th, 2001. President Bush abandons the Kyoto accords. How wise is that to abandon those international accords? What does that do for the word of the United States?
3. June 7th, 2001. President Bush signs a 1.35 trillion dollar tax cut into law beneficial to corporations. That does nothing more than to help corporations to book profits and just creates larger deficits for the nation! It does not increase commerce! It does not strengthen the economy in the correct way, and it just creates the illusion of a healthy economy!
4. August 9th, 2001. Bush bans stem cell research. This keeps America behind in medical research for the curing of various medical conditions. He limits research to the existing 51 Stem Cell lines. He basically was allowing religious values to override common sense and human values. I believe most Americans do not find stem cell research is a major moral issue!
5. September 11, 2001. Terrorists hijack and fly four jetliners into the World Trade Center buildings in New York. They then crash two more jets. One was crashed into the Pentagon in Washington D.C. Then a fourth jetliner crashes in to a field near Shanksville Pennsylvania.
6. December 2nd 2001. Enron Corporation files for bankruptcy protection. Later many ties to the Bush Administration are revealed. Enron Corporation made the single largest campaign donation ever made to any Presidential campaign ever.

That was basically money swindled from the public through Mr. Lay's dishonest corporation! Perhaps Kenneth Lay was of the mindset that the government would not go hard on him if, he had friends in high places in government. Was he buying favoritism?

7. November 5th, 2002. Republicans do gain control of both Houses of Congress.

8. January 7th, 2003. It only takes President Bush two months with full Republican control of government to reveal another 674 billion dollar tax cut favorable to the wealthy and the corporations. Supply Side Economics hard at work.

9. March 28th, 2003. Just two and one half months pass before another 350 Billion dollars in tax cuts for the wealthy are announced. My goodness folks this should not be thought of as help for consumers and/or aiding consumption! This was just lining corporate pockets!

10. February 2nd, 2005. President Bush tries hard to privatize Social Security. Republicans are trying hard to take that away from the people!

11. August 28th, 2005. Hurricane Katrina strikes New Orleans. The government's response was very poor and not very effective. FEMA and President Bush are criticized. Many families were permanently displaced from Hurricane Katrina!

12. July 19th, 2006. Bush vetoes a Bill that would lift the constraints on certain stem cell lines of research. This allows other nations to continue to take the lead on stem cell research. In my mind this was just holding American researchers and the world's human community back.

Helpful cures have been delayed because of President Bush! He was harming American lives and American companies with this veto. Damn those religious values!

13. November 7th, 2006. Democrats regain control of Congress for final 2 years of Bush Presidency. Now ask yourself, if Republicans are better for the American system, why would people turn away from Republicans? Maybe people turn away because they were seeing the economy and the American system going to heck again. Republicans always cause the economy to contract!

14. December 19th, 2007. New energy and fuels legislation passes after Democrats had regained control of Congress.

15. By the end of the Bush Presidency over 4,300 Americans have lost their lives in the Iraq War. So many lives were harmed for no good reason! This is no small thing!

16. May 22nd, 2008. The Democratic House and Senate have to override President Bush's veto of the 307 billion dollar Farm Aid Bill. President Bush's has no problem helping corporations but he will not help the farmers of America!

17. June 5th, 2008. After a five-year investigation, the Senate finds President Bush seriously exaggerated evidence that Saddam Hussein possessed weapons of mass destruction. Obviously no weapons of mass destruction were ever found!

18. September 7th, 2008. Federal Government places home lenders Fannie Mae and Freddie Mac under safe federal controls. That has ended up costing tax payers major money!

19. October 3rd, 2008. President Bush signs a 700 billion dollar bailout package for financial institutions at the onset of the financial crisis. This is just the beginning of the meltdown in the economy!

    Job creation was not happening at any time during the Bush years. Since there was no job creation, it was an indication the economy was on the verge of a major collapse! Business was generally weak and there was not enough commerce in the economy!

20. October 30th, 2008. G. D. P. drops to .3% for the first time in 17 years. That was the first time it was that low since his father, George H. W. Bush was in the Presidency!

21. November 25th, 2008. The United States Treasury buys 800 billion dollars of debt. from Fannie Mae and Freddie Mac. The wheels of the economy are really starting to fall off at this point.

22. December 16th, 2008. The Fed cuts the interest rate to 0% on loans by the fed to banks. This is so the banks can offer extremely low interest rates and mortgage loan rates to try and get the economy going!

23. December 19th, 2008. Bush issues 17.4 billion dollar bailout
     package of General Motors and Chrysler Corporations. But
     everything was just hunky dory with Republicans running the
     show. Yeah right!

President Bush has actually created the largest American government bureaucracy in the history of the United States. We all thought
Republicans want less government, right? We should remember
government Bureaucracy is what has led to excessive government
spending and high Federal Deficits.

The point I am trying to make to you is this, Republicans are just
as bad as Democrats in creating large governments. Do not think
Republicans are better for the economy than are Democrats in that
respect!

At the same time President Bush was creating larger government, he had been weakening government revenues by giving huge
tax cuts to the corporations. He was allowing taxes to rise on the
middleclass! His actions have harmed consumption, and ultimately
the profits of the corporations. That has all been bad for the economy. But Republicans are the better party, right!

He then added to the financial problems by starting two wars,
and funded neither of them! One of those wars was totally unnecessary. Today Iraq appears to be disintegrating in sectarian violence
because Saddam Hussain was removed from that government!

At least Saddam Hussein kept a lid on the various factions in
that country. Yes he was brutal and a cruel leader, I admit that! He
ruled with an iron hand and prevented entities such as ISIS from rising. Perhaps his iron hand was better for that country than the total
kayos and carnage we see there today!

What would you Republicans be saying if Barak Obama had
ruined the economy like George W. Bush actually did? I know
Republicans would be pointing out how bad he is. But President
Obama has clearly been creating jobs for years now. He is giving us
a better economy without any constructive help from Republicans!

Isn't destroying the American economy a huge issue for you?
Clearly Bush's economic policies failed. So with all of that government President Bush created, naturally he did set the all-time record

for the biggest spending increases in history. But Republicans only complain about how Democrats spend too much.

Why didn't Republicans become vocal about Bush's spending when he was doing it? Why did they not question the war spending? Was it an OK situation back then?

24. President Bush withdrew the United States of America completely from the World Court. What is that all about? Do you think it is right? The United States of America is not represented on the World Court?

25. President Bush did not allow access to the POW's at Guantanamo Bay. He allowed no access by international human rights groups. What was President Bush afraid those groups would see, or hear? Given what we know today, it is clear why human rights groups were not allowed access!

    Now we have seen in newly declassified reports America under President Bush did use torture on the prisoners. It was worse than reported. It was against our American values, and against international law. The important thing is it was generally not effective in the gathering of useful intelligence!

26. President Bush set the all-time record for receiving corporate campaign donations. In my mind, excessive corporate campaign donations can't be good for the country or for our political system.

27. President Bush had more convicted criminals, serving in administration positions than any other President in history. There were so many criminals connected to the Bush White House. I suggest you check out.

Suzie-Q's Truth and Justice Blog

There are too many people to name them here. It is almost a book unto itself. Do we want to have people who have run afoul of the law, with questionable morals in administration positions? These people have shown they have character flaws.

It is kind of like would you let a child molester baby sit your kids? Of course not, but George Bush was bringing these type of people into our government!

28. President Bush is the first President to have average Europeans believing the major threat to world peace was in fact the President of the United States! 71% of European's thought President George W. Bush was out of control, in foreign affairs and more likely to involve them in wars!

    Think about that, our friends and allies should love America and all that we stand for! However European's thought our President was the biggest threat to world peace. It bothers me greatly that my President was not trusted or well regarded by the rest of the world community!

29. President Bush has created the most divided and polarized political landscape in America since the Civil War. I cannot remember a time when Republicans were so uncooperative with Democrats. For Republicans party loyalty is more important than being good Americans! That situation is only surpassed by the Republicans and the Tea Partier's of today.

    In my view, progress cannot be made with Republicans in office. Republicans are literally opposing Democrats on every single issue! Even logical solutions are opposed by Republicans.

30. President Bush entered office with the strongest economy in the history of the world. He turned every economic indicator we had, upside down! He then gave us a financial collapse of huge proportions.

31. President Bush was the first American President in 51 years to actually allow for a federal military prisoner to be sentenced to death. July 28, 2008 He approves the execution of an Army prisoner.

32. President Bush was the first American President to actually enter office himself with a criminal record. See it yourself, here are my sources:

    "www.blogd.com/bushrecord.html"

    "pearlyabraham.tripod.com/htmls/bush-arrest.html"

    In a nutshell, they were crimes done in his youth. 1. Theft at a football game. 2. Disorderly conduct. 3rd, was a suspected DUI arrest. Specific details were not given.

    You may say, well it was not that big of a deal. Okay, but we know what Republicans would be saying if that had happened to President Obama in his youth! Then, of course it would become a big deal. Knowing Republicans it would probably be grounds for an impeachable offense!

33. As Governor of Texas, Governor Bush actually executed more prisoners than any other governor from any state in our country's history! Does it bother you at all that a President of the United States played such a role in the execution of more people than any other government official in history?

Well over 200 prisoners have been executed in Texas under Governor George W. Bush. I know there are bad people in the world. But do I want for my President to be a major figure in capital punishment? To my knowledge no Democrat President has ever executed anyone!

34. During his first year as President, President Bush set the all-time record for the most days of being on vacation. This is the same year of the 9/11 attacks. I am sure he used Air Force One to fly everywhere. Republicans incessantly give Barack Obama grief if he flies on Air Force One anywhere!

35. President Bush cut unemployment benefits for millions of Americans, just as the economy tanked. Good show there.

36. President Bush has ignored the constitution and signed or enacted more amendments to the constitution than all other American Presidents combined. But people like Michele Bachmann will call President Obama a socialist and a dictator. Check the links below. I am not seeing him stepping all over our constitution like President Bush actually has.

"www.inthesetimes.com/article/2868"

"tpjmagazine.us/jonas219"

"en.wikipedia.org/wiki/George_W_Bush"

Don't you believe our constitution is a sacred document? George Bush himself appears to have had little respect or reverence for it. Then Republicans will claim Barack Obama has ignored the constitution more than any President in history. Are you kidding me? Republicans just want you to think that because President Obama had the nerve to bring us the Affordable Care Act. Because he actually got something done! They have no choice but to label the good he has done as bad, otherwise if they do not talk him down he will look good to the people!

37. George Bush presided over the biggest energy crisis in the history of America, which included rolling blackouts in California and throughout the West. Enron Corporation was behind most of them. Enron was making loads of money off of us in the process. These are your big money corporations at work.

38. President Bush refused to get involved when close corporate ties between his Administration and the Enron Corporation were revealed. How wonderful it was for President Bush to have all of those campaign donations flowing in from Enron!

39. George W. Bush presided over the highest gasoline prices in history. At the same time, he did nothing about record oil company profits. He simply allowed oil companies to make record profits off of the American people during those high fuel oil times!

40. President Bush actually cut healthcare benefits to veterans. He lowered the VA budget for veteran's health. Do you like and remember that? President Obama has actually added at least 80% to the VA's funding and we still are having access problems for the vets. And that 80% figure was calculated before the recent VA problems came out. Their budget I believe was raised yet again!

41. With all of the controversies we are having today, George Bush was unwilling to bring universal healthcare to the people. Because he certainly did not try to do anything like that. He is not looking out for average Americans! In my opinion he did not give you a better government and country!

42. President Bush dissolved more international treaties than all other American Presidents combined. How does this harm the word of the United States of America? Throughout his Presidency, George Bush reverses positions on more International Treaties than all other Presidents combined.

What effect has this had on our relations with the world community? Will other nations honor the treaties they make with us or other nations when America is not honoring the treaty's we have already signed?

Seems to me this action can only show America is not dependable as a nation. No wonder Russia does not behave better? America has demonstrated to the world that treaties just do not mean much!

43. Now just to show you close ties between his staff and big oil companies, President Bush's national security adviser Condoleezza Rice was an executive with Chevron Corporation. She has actually had a large new Chevron super tanker named after her!

   Now I am sure Republicans are proud of her. I am sure she is a nice lady. I am just trying to show you there really were very close ties between big oil and the Bush Presidency!

44. President Bush had the wealthiest cabinet in our history. Big money people were running the show.

45. President Bush set the record for the most campaign funds raised by any President in history, mostly from corporate donors. These corporate people apparently still believe in the idea that a low tax environment creates a better business environment, as opposed to the benefits of having a growing and dynamic economy with full employment and lots of customers and commerce!

46. President Bush as President held the fewest number of press conferences in modern times. In my opinion, he simply did not handle himself or difficult questions very well in those news conferences. He constantly embarrassed himself IMO. He was not a gifted speaker, but he was the decider!

47. President Bush took the entire month of August 2008 off. When he came back from vacation, he then presided over the worst securities failure in our country's history. Remember this was when the economy actually collapsed big time. He did that just before leaving office. He left a huge mess for President Obama to fix. How responsible was his governance?

48. In the first two years of President Bush's administration, two million jobs were lost with many more millions to come throughout his Presidency. His job creation record was the actual worst job creation record since the Herbert Hoover Administration, and the Great Depression! Is that what anyone wants?

Had we waited another month or two at the most, his overall job creation numbers would have been in negative territory. President Bush received the strongest economy in the history of the world from President Clinton. Do you Republicans just switch off reality when observing your Party?

49. The National Debt tripled under President Ronald Reagan. Then it doubled again under President George W. Bush. We went from a relatively insignificant debt burden, to towering debts, long before President Barack Obama ever came to office. I tell you the tax cuts which have been given to the wealthiest Americans accounts for fully half of our entire National Debt! Do you think the wealthy really need those tax breaks? Are they suffering?

50. During the Bush Administration we had little regulation or rules of safe behavior in financial markets. We found ourselves dealing with large banks that were writing complex derivatives. These complex derivatives very nearly led our nation to a total financial collapse of the entire national banking system!

51. More bankruptcies happened under George W. Bush than under any other President. Both individual and commercial bankruptcies were happening left and right.

52. George W. Bush ran up the largest budget deficits in history through the end of his Presidency. He then left the nation in financial shambles for President Obama.

    After the Great Depression we did have a massive Democrat majority in government. That majority lasted for 12 years of the F.D.R. Presidency. Then we had eight more years of mostly Democrats in control with President Truman. President Obama has only had two years of cooperative Democrats since being elected!

53. Coming into office with the world's strongest economy President George W. Bush, went on to bankrupt the Treasury!

54. President Bush set the record for the largest dollar drop in the stock market in history. By contrast with President Obama the stock market has hit an all-time high. The DOW as I remember was around 7,500 at its low under President Bush. At this

writing it reached 18,000 and has now backed off a bit to the 16,500 area.

55. President Bush set the record for the most home foreclosures in history. He also was the first President to have all 50 states Declare bankruptcy!

56. President Bush lowered clean air and water standards. Allowing his wealthy campaign buddies to profit more from those lowered standards. How has that affected the air you must breathe and the water you drink? Today, Republicans are trying again to lower those standards. These actions are giving Americans poorer health through more pollution in the environment! Why would you support that?

The life expectancy of Americans has been increasing nicely because we have been cleaning up the environment. When people are living longer, it ends up creating more commerce for the nation and less in medical expenses. Maintaining the environment is good for the overall economy!

57. September of 2006, Republican Representative Mark Foley of Florida had inappropriate sexual contact with teenage aids. It was an embarrassment to the Bush Presidency!

58. George Bush designed a plan to help seniors on Medicaid buy prescription drugs at a supposed discount. You can be sure the drug companies were not hurt very much in this deal!

59. I feel President Bush has not supported women in having full access to contraceptives and birth control. In fact, Republicans are restricting those freedoms.

Now you might say that President George W. Bush did have his Faith Based Initiative. It clearly is a well-intended effort to aid charities doing good work. Something which we all feel is important but with the difficult situation of mixing government revenues with religious organizations. Was this the right thing to be doing? I am not sure on this.

Then we have the No Child Left Behind, Act. Has that act improved the performance at our schools? Again I am not sure on that. I know many people including Republicans opposed this program.

The only thing which might be categorized as a positive might be the Lower Cost Drug Bill for seniors I think on Medicare Part D. But that has been a relatively small plan!

Don't all of these negatives of President George W. Bush just turn your stomach? There are so many things wrong with the Republican Party. I do not know how anyone can lend their support to them after that. How can anyone support policies which bring us horrible economies?

I want you to understand Supply Side Economics will make things better for the corporations, big business and for the wealthy. And this is of course is a good thing. But Consumer Focused Economics makes things better for those groups too plus it makes things better for the middleclass and all people. We should want to improve the lives of all Americans!

Why on earth would you want to bypass the middleclass trying to get to prosperity? That makes no sense. Unless you have the mentality to be the one on top and you want to keep everyone else down. How kind, gentle and good is that? Do Republicans fundamentally view kind and gentle behavior as incorrect behavior in some way?

I feel it is fairly safe to say, the Bush years have been a disaster for the nation. But loyal Republicans will try to make you think he has been a wonderful President! I do not know how a reasonable person can think that way. With him you had a President who literally destroyed our American economy!

There were so many negative things about his Presidency I cannot in good faith even give him one half of a point. He really accomplished little and what he did do mostly benefitted corporations and businesses. He gave trillions of dollars in tax cut to corporations and to the wealthy over and over again! All of that just added to our deficits!

His actions were typical for Republicans. He attempted to strengthen America the Republican way. His Faith-Based initiative and the No Child Left Behind Act, plus the supplements to Medicare drug purchases were all small programs. They were far outweighed by his damage to other aspects of government and the total collapse of the economy. His many vetoes and policy changes harmed America.

You cannot give the man credit on one side, and then totally ignore the massive damage he did on the other side. He was literally taking away jobs, homes, livelihoods, work and incomes with the other hand. He came close to putting us in another Great Depression! Over all he did great harm to the nation! The only thing that saved the economy was the regulation which Democrats had put in place.

So many businesses went bankrupt during his time. That does not compute for me. We clearly know he has not been good for the middleclass. How can he be considered good for the middleclass when five to six million people lost their homes, their jobs and their incomes as a result of his Presidency?

Overall, he has harmed America. He broke our economy and he has harmed the word of our country. I believe that has had a effect on every aspect of our lives. After President Bush, Americans were not always welcomed in other nations because of his extreme cowboy-like actions.

He has also harmed our nation's good name. Do you people care about things like that? All the good that America used to stand for has been undone by President George W. Bush!

I have given the Democrats two points for passing several things without the support of President Bush. I honestly do not understand how anyone can support Republicans after George W. Bush. President Clinton gave the nation surpluses! President Bush did nothing to ensure that consumers remained strong.

Was President Bush a bad President? Well he did not do meaningful good things when he had the chance and he sure could have! He could have been the one to really improve the healthcare system in America. But he did not do that. No Republican wanted to change how healthcare was provided. He had a lot of chances to improve society but he did nothing!

What do you think? Did President Bush and his Party's beliefs do a good job with our economy? Remember I am trying to show reasons to stop believing in the Republican Party. I am looking at things in the honest light of hindsight!

Has this whole experience taught you anything at all? How many of you find that you still need to work in your retirement years? This is what happens when you do not take care of the economy or the middle-class. Republicans should not be supported at all!

OK, so now looking at the totals for the good accomplished by our Presidents.

Now we need to compare the two parties side by side. I will not count President Obama in my totals. We do need to consider all of the Presidents accomplishments. So it is possible to see the good which has been done. That is the whole purpose of this chapter.

By my calculation, Republicans have done 24.5 positive things for the middleclass and for the country in the past 105 years. That is the total number of good things done, or actions taken that have had a positive impact on average everyday Americans and also our corporations.

10 of those things came in the Pre-Truman era. 14.5 of them have come from Republicans in the post WWII era.

During this same time period, Democrats have done more than two and a half times more positive things for average people. Let's talk about that.

Democrats have a score of 61.5 meaningful accomplishments for the average American. Remember we are not counting any of President Barak Obama's record. However his accomplishments alone number well past 10 positive things done for the country!

Since the beginning of our comparison, Democrats have done 28 positive things in the Pre-Truman era. 33.5 of those changes came to us in the time from Harry Truman to the present.

I must ask Republicans, where are you? Why are you not doing things for all of society? If we counted the things which Barack Obama has already done we would be adding 10 more things to the Democrat side of this list!

Republicans why aren't you contributing to a better system for the masses? The answer is, Republicans are protecting the corporations! Republicans believe helping the corporations directly will strengthen the system and economy more!

Counting Republicans and Democrats accomplishments gets us to where, around 70% of the accomplishments have come to us during the times when Democrats are in power. Isn't this evidence which shows that Democrats are looking out for the whole system, not just acting for the corporations!

In fact the way I would say it is Democrats enrich the middle-class and the corporations equally. They are good for all and make our entire society and economy stronger. Since the entire system is healthy that creates a better business environment which means businesses do well too!

We should know Republicans are not the type of Party to bring about progressive or forward thinking policies. Republicans just view progress as weakening the corporations. In their Republican minds, if it makes life better for the middleclass, it must be costing corporations. Therefore if it weakens the corporations it will be weakening the economy on the whole. That is according to Republican reasoning!

Republican are hard at work turning voters against the Democratic Party whenever they can. Naturally they are turning you against Barack Obama even before you have had a chance to understand and learn all of the good things he has been doing for you. Republicans simply are against anything that comes from a Democrat.

I have found when you actually list or talk about Democrat accomplishments one by one, most people simply accepted them as being reasonable and beneficial for Americans and to the system. But when a Republican personality says its bad some voters go right back to agreeing with that. Perhaps you will begin to see the light. only after President Obama is long gone and regarded as just another good Democrat President of history!

2009 – 2016 BARACK OBAMA
DEMOCRAT 45TH PRESIDENT

Now just for fun let's take a quick look at President Obama. Though we will not be considering any of his stats for the book at this time, I do believe we can discuss some of his results.

His first term will not give us accurate information about him as our President or Democrats in general. That is because he was handed a complete disaster and has had to absorb all of the problems left to him by his predecessor. All most all of the problems he was facing came from Republicans!

In spite of all of that I believe President Obama has achieved numerous notable things. One of the biggest was just stopping the implosion of the economy!

Republicans naturally will only say negative things about the man and his Presidency. We know this because Republicans just flat out hate everything which Democrats bring! They view Democrat accomplishments as always costing corporations and the wealthy money, instead of viewing it correctly as improving society!

Some Republicans have even called him a socialist, or say he has not followed the constitution etc. Some have used racial slurs or miss pronounce his name on purpose calling him Osama Obama.

Some have called him a Muslim! As President he has only used executive action to act where Republicans refuse to move forward and take no actions at all. Republicans will not talk to work out compromises. Not co-operating with a sitting President is not governing, it is just obstructionism!

Yes I admit he does have a strange name but so what, in America we are a melting pot society! We all should know one day we might have a minority President and that person could have an uncommon name. It is not that big of a deal.

In the interest of not considering skewed economic statistics, we are not considering his first term. Doing so, though accurate would not show accurately what this Democrat wanted to bring America. His second term is only about ¾ over but I believe his second term will be fair game to look at since the economy has returned into a more normal state!

Some of the issues I am going to site have nothing to do with his Presidency, but go more to his individual character as a human being. He will not get points for his accomplishments at this time, but I do want for people to be aware of them and the type of man he really is.

For example, Barack Obama is the nation's first African-American President. That is not a bad thing at all, and I am glad that America can elect anybody including a minority person. It says good things about the country, and the progress we as a people are making in putting racial prejudices behind us! Hopefully you've matured to the point where you are not bent out of shape by his race.

He seems to be a fairly well-educated individual and I like him as a person. He speaks thoughtful clear English and that is a good thing. He could be someone who speaks with a thick southern or inner city accent, but he does not. To me he appears to be a moderate politician and a good person in every way!

As far as I can tell he has a nice wife and family. In my opinion politically he is not too far to the left, and of course he is not too far to the right, and that fits me well. I like a person who is in the middle on political issues. But I also know when I say that to some Republicans, they will look at me like I am crazy. They will shake their heads and firmly say oh yes he is far, far to the left!

I think he is a normal level headed moderate President. It is just that conservatives believe anything in the normal category is far left! I believe most average Americans will disagree with Republicans on this!

Republicans will say that about anyone who is less than a full blown conservative. Honestly I do not see any liberalness in him at all. But for sure I think of him as a progressive President who wants to make progress and move the country forward! I am not embarrassed by the progressive label at all.

I think he is very conscious of wanting to be both an effective and good President. He is very aware that he is a black man and does not want to give black people a bad name by being unreasonable with his actions as our President!

So I view him as trying very hard to be a fair man and honest President. He is trying as hard as possible to be "normal". In my opinion he has not been letting race over take his Presidency. He has not been to black in other words!

He really tries to reason with the people. He explains himself well, and is not overpowering or too assertive. I think he has been a very good and thoughtful man!

You could have been dealing with someone much worse. Imagine a progressive who sounded like Herman Cane!

But because Republicans will not work with him or compromise at all to make any progress, he must use executive action just to get common sense laws enacted! To make anything happen at all today unfortunately he must occasionally use executive action.

Because of that Republicans will just try to say he is bad and not following the constitution. How can you people say he is a bad president when he has frozen or lowered income taxes for people earning less than $250,000? He has brought us a public Healthcare System which is workable!

Is it bad for you that he has graduated of Columbia University and Harvard Law School? Is it bad that he has written two successful books and was elected to the U. S. Senate in 2004?

In 2009 he was awarded the Nobel Peace Prize. I believe he was embarrassed to have won the prize, given he has not had that much time on the world stage to impact society. But I also believe the Nobel Prize Committee was telling us Americans how relieved Europeans are to have this man as our American President. Plus I believe they felt he has common sense and it would be possible to work with him!

I will say I believe Europeans are ahead of America in general sophistication because we do have the problems of a melting pot society. Many of our citizens do come from very traditional societies and from all over the world. His perceived character as a man and as our American President is seen as being good in their eyes!

The world has a good opinion about him, and I like that. We must agree it is never a bad thing for people to like our President! That is always a good.

Now just for the heck, let's look at the record of President Obama. I have not counted his accomplishments in our final summary.

2009 PRESIDENT BARACK H. OBAMA, DEMOCRAT
44TH PRESIDENT

1. February 17, 2009. He signed the American Recovery and Reinvestment Act into law. This was a needed $787 billion economic stimulus package. This money was not used as a tax break for corporations. This money was directed at saving teacher, police and firefighter positions as local governments across the country were going through tough revenue times during the economic collapse.

   That money was used mostly to save existing jobs, rather than to create new jobs. Nobody wanted to do it, but it was an important part to halting the crash that was upon us. The first job which must be done when taking over an economy stuck in a downward spiral is to stop the slide and decline of the economy to the bottom. President Obama did do that!

2. March 23, 2010. He signed the Patient Protection and Affordable Care Act. That has been both important and good for average people. It has created rules that must be followed by healthcare providers. This was the precursor to the current Affordable Care Act. As Americans, we must get used to new healthcare rules. It is a process that will take time to phase in but we are getting there!

3. April 8, 2010. He signed a Nuclear Arms Reduction Pact with the Russian President Medvedev. Now keep this in mind. Republicans would not sign off on that treaty which was vital to our safety and security as Americans, until the wealthy had received a two-year extension of the Bush-era tax breaks!

   This is blatant evidence that Republicans are looking out for moneyed Americans. I felt this action has held the recovery back and added to our budget deficits. To me this has been counterproductive to the Nation's economy!

4. July 21, 2010, The Dodd-Frank, Wall Street Reform and Consumer Protection Act was enacted to protect average people, their investments and their money from unfair Wall Street practices! Do any of you oppose that idea?

   Though not fully implemented yet these are steps which are in the right direction. By the time you read this book I am not sure if the entire Act will have been implemented. Republicans have been blocking provisions of the Act. It is even possible provisions in it will be repealed. Republicans are trying to weaken anything President Obama has brought in!

5. April 20th, 2010. A BP oil well in the Gulf of Mexico blows out and creates the world's worst oil disaster. President Obama announces a moratorium on offshore well drilling until safer blowout preventers are developed. That to me seems to be a reasonable action to take!

   We sure do not want to have more of these accidents. We still have oil and the world has not fallen apart. In fact we have been enjoying the cheapest oil in a long time!

6. December 2010. President Obama signed the Tax Relief and Unemployment Insurance Authorization and Jobs Creation Act into law. That has been beneficial to the economy.

7. January 2, 2011. The 9/11 W.T.C. Health and Compensation Act is enacted to provide health benefits to emergency responders, recovery and cleanup workers from the World Trade Center tragedy.

8. September 20, 2011. Don't Ask Don't Tell Act was repealed.

9. October 12, 2011. Free trade agreements passed and were signed into law with South Korea, Columbia, and Panama. This will boost US exports by some $13 billion it is estimated.

   Of course Republicans voted for the trade agreement. But do you remember how 9 months after the agreement was signed on June 15, 2012 Mitt Romney actually criticizes President Obama for never signing free trade agreements? He had already signed a major free trade agreement with those nations. Geez!

This was something that was done to benefit corporations. President Barack Obama has done several things beneficial to both individuals and to corporations. How can corporations, Republicans, or even people like Mitt Romney have a problem with the man?

10. During his first term, President Obama was forced to set a time-line for withdrawal of forces from Iraq. That has now been accomplished. He has brought our troop's home.

   Our troops could not stay in Iraq without a Status of Forces agreement with the Iraqi government. The Iraqis were not will-ing to protect our soldiers from Iraqi persecution, so that is why we had to pull them out. If our soldiers are going to be in Iraq risking their lives they must be protected from unjust prosecu-tion by the Iraqis!

   Republicans will claim he has been at fault there. But the true fault lies with the al-Maliki government. We are glad to have our forces home anyway. Today we are seeing that nation fall apart.

11. He has now opened up the continental shelf off of the south-eastern states for oil exploration and drilling. Clearly, this was another action that will have huge benefits to our corporations. How can you think he is not a pro-corporate President?

12. He has O.K.'d parts of the Keystone oil pipeline heading to the Gulf of Mexico. Much of the pipeline is waiting on environmen-tal approval. Waiting on finding the safest and best possible route from the oil sand fields in Canada to the ports on the Gulf of Mexico!

   We should always consider the environmental concerns. That Canadian oil will be piped over our nation's largest under-ground water aquifer in the Mid-West which is absolutely vital to our farmers. We must use an abundance of caution there! Remember that Canadian oil is for export only. But corpora-tions want to transport that oil through our country!

   Additionally since the price of oil has fallen so far, oil sands oil is becoming too expensive to use at this time! It is not finan-cially viable to go after that oil. Of course Sarah Palin will say drill baby drill! If we follow Republicans we may end up building a pipeline that will not get used!

13. President Obama is now drawing our forces down and out of Afghanistan. At this writing combat troops are out. My guess would be that the government of Afghanistan has a chance of collapsing also! But this has been a long haul for America. The problem is those nations are locked in tribal loyalties over their own nationalism.

14. President Obama did get Osama Bin Laden. President Obama had the guts to make the risky call to go into Pakistan. It was by no means a safe military mission, and we were violating Pakistan's sovereignty. We even crashed a helicopter on that mission thank God we did not lose any servicemen!

15. President Obama has appointed two more females to the Supreme Court. We now have three women sitting on the court. How right is that? Are you so old fashion or conservative that you cannot accept women on the Supreme Court? I think women tend to be better decision makers than most men anyway. Especially when it comes to human values and family matters!

16. President Obama is working hard to bring about a raise in the minimum wage. Republicans have always been blocking that.

17. President Obama has brought us a Federal Healthcare mandate. He is just trying to pull our nation into the 21st century, like the rest of the civilized world already is doing.

18. He has been working for better our voting laws regarding access to the polls by all American voters, including the elderly, the poor, and minorities. I am not going to say anything about Republicans and their opposition on this issue except I think their opposition is un-American!

19. He has been dealing appropriately with the Russian incursion into the Crimea and the Ukraine. We are not embroiled in a war there, and we do not want that. He is balancing our foreign policy actions well. The Crimea fight essentially is not our fight. But perhaps we might help in some way if necessary!

20. President Obama has been strengthening relationships with Southeast Asian nations. He has worked out an agreement to

re-open several former U.S. military bases in the Philippines, Including Clark Field.

21. As to foreign policy, he has helped with the downfall of Mua-mmar Gaddaffi. Egypt has had the Arab spring, he is keeping us out of the Syria civil war, and he is keeping us out of the Ukraine. He is using drones to strike Islamic militants. I say overall he is doing a good job without fighting what rightfully is an Arab fight.

Some of my sources have been "Skymall.blogspot.com" and "third-worldtravelers.com"

If I were rating President Barack Obama I would give him a positive rating of perhaps eleven for his accomplishments. Though as you know I am not counting his accomplishments in my final totals!

He is bringing the economy back with no co-operation from Republicans though. You know it is really tough to govern and make progress when you have constant opposition from the other party. I would think Republicans say they are not co-operation with him too!

One of the first things Democrats did when they regained control of Congress was to raise the minimum wage. That was way back before we started talking about raising the minimum wage to $10.10.

How many times have Republicans raised the minimum wage when they were in power? They do not ever do that on their own and without outside pressure. Republicans never raise it or propose raising it! They just will not do that. Republicans do not stick up for the people at the bottom of the system!

To me Republicans are not thinking in the right way for the nations good. Raising the minimum wage will do much to keep the economy strong. It keeps people a little more in the money and able to take care of themselves. It helps keep consumption strong.

A livable minimum wage is a key component to a strong economy. As President Obama states, people who work full time should not be living below the poverty line, needing various forms of government assistance that cost all of us more money. Tax payers should not be subsidizing the big corporations!

I think President Obama has been a very good and wise President. He has been a levelheaded guy. He speaks clearly, carefully and with consideration. How would you like to be listening to Herman Cane all of these years?

What more could you want from any President, minority or otherwise? I just do not see him acting like a tyrant at all. I see him as the very good President he is!

The economy has been turning around now for years. This is much better for us than when Republicans were running the whole show. For four or five years now employment statistics have shown we are creating jobs at a pretty good rate! Things are moving in the right direction.

Democrat policies seem to be working in spite of constant Republican opposition. At this writing he has created around 14 million jobs on top of the millions lost!

OK so let's stop for a moment and talk about what we have seen up through this point in the book. So far we have seen that *every single time* a Republican comes to the Presidency we get a contracting economy at best, and sometimes a collapsing economy in the worst cases. I sight the George W. Bush Presidency and the Herbert Hoover Presidency as prime examples of collapsed economies!

Clearly when we look back through everything, taking all of history into account we do see Democrat President after Democrat President are giving us better economies! Be honest with yourself! Please look again at the job creation statistics. That is where you see the evidence!

We know Republicans take over healthy economies from Democrats because Democrats do have a lot of job creation. But then Republicans ruin the economies for their Democrat successors. Obviously that means Democrats receive broken and weak economies and then must rebuild them!

Remember Republicans get voted out of office usually because they are doing a bad job with the economy. Democrats on the other hand are voted out of office when they are doing a good job with the economy. Why, because Republicans successfully make the case with the voters that Democrats are somehow doing a bad job with government. Be it job creation, taxation, regulation, foreign policy or whatever! It is a constant negative drumbeat of all the things Republicans can dream up in their heads!

SO LET'S REVIEW
WHERE WE ARE AT!

Where are we?

1. Democrats are rebuilding the economy every single time they take over from Republicans.

2. Democrats always receive broken economies from the Republicans.

3. Job creation is not there with Republicans.

4. Republican don't take any actions which better society!

5. Our government is not funded properly under Republicans.

6. Corporations and the Wealthy get tax cuts with Republicans while the middleclass doesn't. This just adds to deficit spending and does not create consumption!

7. Democrats give us surpluses 2½ times more often than Republicans.

8. Republicans have a deceptive language that I call Republican Speak They will say what sounds like something good for you but they have a different interpretation of what has been said. They just suck you in with their deceptive language to get your vote!

9. Republicans have a history of telling untruths. They often use dishonest behavior which harms the nation!

I cite the Watergate Affair for you as one example of their dishonest behavior.

So we have had Nixon and Watergate, then Reagan and the Iran/contra affair! Even though he was specifically told by congress not to give aid to the contras he still did it. Republicans have given us Joseph McCarthy and the Red scare. Ted Cruz to come!

Ronald Reagan gave us that dysfunctional Supply Side Economic model which Republicans still love. In spite of that policy not working, Republicans want to return to that structure for our economy. Reagan fired 13,000 air traffic controllers. Do you think that made our sky's safer? I think he took a pretty big chance there!

10. Because of Republican economics we have seen massive bankruptcies, in insurance, in banking, in the brokerage houses, in our housing industry, we saw personal bankruptcies, and in automobile manufacturing to name just a few areas!

11. Republicans are working to make it more difficult for Americans to vote. Not all people have picture ID's. Having picture I.D. has never been a constitutional requirement but Republicans still want to start requiring it!

12. Republicans are keeping the nation tightly coupled too fire arms, rather than trying to dial the need for weapons down. We are a more gun crazy society because of Republicans, In My Opinion!

13. Republicans have not brought equal pay for women doing equal work. Child labor laws, the 8 hour work day and 40 hour work week did not come to you because Republicans were in the government!

This is just trying to review some of what you are getting under Republican government. This is a partial list of the bad things which come with the Republicans. Why would we want to have any of this?

Sure Democrats might do something bad once in a while, but nothing like Republicans. Democrats never give us Presidents who ruin the economy. Democrats try to enrich the consumer. Republicans try to enrich those who do not need it, the Wealthy and the Corporations!

I realize sometimes a Democrat President may have personal behaviors we do not like to see. I understand that. But their personal behaviors do not harm the public or me.

Unfortunately you should keep in mind it is the Republicans, not the Democrats who are trying to make political points by making sure a spectacle is made out of poor behavior when it is found! It is

Republicans who are exposing our youth to the in appropriate things which sometimes happens to everyone.

It happens to Republicans and Democrats. Of course they will only talk about Democrat miss behavior just to score political points in the moment!

Over all isn't it clear the economy suffers with Republicans. I am sure you would agree Republicans are less co-operative today than years gone by. Republicans are becoming even more conservative!

They are not allowing our current captain to lay his hands on the economic wheel for the purpose of steering the ship to stronger times. President Obama is in a situation where he must govern through executive action. Otherwise nothing at all will get done!

On December 2, 2014 it was announced that the nation created over 321,000 new jobs. The DOW has recovered from the George Bush low of around 7,500 to currently around 16,500!

Clearly Democrats are bringing the country and economy back. Why would anyone be thinking Democrats are bad for the economy? It is only the Republicans who are trying to make it look like it has been a bad economy!

I believe we must accept that the economy is not going to change overnight and without cost to the Treasury. We simply need to be patient and give Democrats the chance to rebuild our economy. Everything will work out fine!

What happened to the days when both parties thought more about helping the nation? Rather today, Republicans are thinking the important thing is to simply oppose the work of their political opponents. For them do not allow Democrats to make progress!

For me, there is only one reasonable answer. We need an overwhelming majority of Democrats in our government if we ever wish to accomplish positive things. Republicans are not in a compromising mood at all. They have no answers they have no workable positions or proposals of their own and I believe they are just simple minded obstructionists!

The Tea Party is totally nuts. They do not want for government to do anything! They do not want any progress or government at all. The Tea Party does not want to change anything! They only want less government on a massive scale!

I believe we would be wise to let this President bring us into the 20th century. Let him work on getting us out of this great mess Republicans have created again. We have to open our eyes and become wise!

HEALTHCARE IN AMERICA

Let's totally change subjects for a minute and talk about healthcare in America. I want you to think about this in a new way. Do not think of healthcare with a Democratic or Republican mind set. I will not talk about the Affordable Care Act. I would like for this discussion to be about what we could have had.

It is something which we still could have if we really wanted it. A version of what I am thinking of was proposed by many Democrats but there were not enough progressive Democrat votes to make it happen! We had to go with what the Republicans demanded through their non-co-operation!

We did miss the boat on a truly better system of healthcare. But as long as we keep the Affordable Care Act, the act can always be modified and improved upon. For that reason Republicans just want to throw it out.

There is nothing stopping the modification of the Act in the future. But if we get rid of it the progress we have made will be lost. Unfortunately what we got with conservatives in government was still an insurance based healthcare system!

Republicans were only interested in the health of their friends in the Healthcare Insurance Industry. Republicans were making sure insurance companies would still be at the center of healthcare in America!

But with the Affordable Care Act, it can always be improved upon. We are not locked into anything.

Why would any sane person want to pay for all of the operating expenses of a nonmedical industry to get your health needs met? That is the basic question?

Why pay for insurance companies and their expenses when all you want or need is to see a Doctor? This makes absolutely no sense to me.

If I have broken my leg why on earth would I want to pay for a very large nonmedical industry to exist just to fix my leg. I do expect to pay for the Doctor, the nurse and the hospital etc., but why should I pay for something that has nothing to do with medicine? Under the current system all of those other non medical industry expenses are added on top of my bill!

What I want to talking about is a single payer system! So what is a single payer system? A single payer system means the government will be responsible for paying all the medical bills of the nation. To me it also means everyone will pay a healthcare tax from their earnings to go into a fund to pay for healthcare issues of the nation. I will tell you how I envision this working! We will be paying for our healthcare, nothing else.

First the advantage of a single payer system is you are not supporting all of the expenses of the insurance companies! We know there are extensive costs associated with running the insurance based system of Healthcare! Let's talk about that.

With a Single Payer system (which is a government organized system) you are not supporting the following things. All of the local insurance agents, their secretarial staffs, their local offices and their overhead expenses! You also are not supporting the national corporate staffs, the CEO's, the executives, the headquarter buildings, the corporate jets and helicopters, their vacation plans, their advertising budgets, their employee medical expenses, their retirement plans, or their corporate profits or the corporate dividends!

Those expenses are huge. They add up to many billions and billions of dollars! Why would we want to support all of those expenses? This makes no sense. The single payer system is going to be more efficient at delivering healthcare because with that system we are not funding all of those other nonmedical expenses!

Do you remember when President Bush was speaking about healthcare to the nation and he said, he wanted to give you more choices for you healthcare. He said I want there to be competition for your business. However he did not mean you will be getting the least expensive healthcare! He was saying I want there to be many insurance companies for you to choose from.

Bush was talking about competition through the existing healthcare corporations and using the current system. He was talking about preserving the highly profitable healthcare industry. He was not talking about a single payer system where insurance company expenses are not a part of the equation.

Republicans are the ones working to keep the system in the hands of the insurance companies. They want to keep it as it always has been. That is the Republicans goal rather having the emphasis on delivering good, affordable health care to all Americans.

My system would be funded directly by the people through our payroll taxes. Yes it would be correctly described as a new health-care tax. You pay a smaller tax which will replace a more expensive health insurance fee! I still want that we pay for our healthcare just like we do when we buy health insurance. But I don't want that we pay for insurance company profits and expenses!

Yes you will be paying a new tax. But you will not have to buy private health insurance unless you want some kind of supplemental coverage. With a single payer system the level of your coverage will be determined by the amount of health tax you contribute.

But good basic coverage will come to you with normal employment. Some very expensive care may not be provided for some people as there might be allocation issues.

Of course we did not get a single payer system because there were not nearly enough Democrats in government with that goal. Many Democrats wanted a single payer system but not all Democrats were on board! So first we must have the votes to make something like that happen. On this issue of course there was no co-operation coming from the Republicans. It was a miracle we got anything passed at all!

The whole Republican position toward healthcare is another area where they create an illusion of wanting the least expensive healthcare possible to help the most people. But Republicans were really trying to protecting the healthcare industry not the people.

At least now we have organized health insurance which is better than what we had. We have told the insurance companies what they must cover. But it could have been so much better.

Under the new Affordable Care Act at least there is proper structure to the insurance, and the government will subsidize those who need a little help. Not the best system but a bit better than what we had!

I hate to say it bluntly, but Republicans were protecting the insurance companies and they were successful! Republicans were making sure the insurance companies would still be booking billions of dollars in profits. By the way the insurance companies have never been more profitable than they are today with the new Affordable Care Act. They are making good money!

What I am talking about is getting rid of the health insurance companies all together. We do not need them and we should be paying mostly for our actual healthcare!

The quality of healthcare you get with the government can be very good. I have seen how it worked in my own family and I will be telling you about that later.

The health insurance industry is a huge, huge industry. In most cases one dollar in every three goes to the insurance companies. In some cases we could be talking about 40% of what we pay in, does not go to actual medical care. These are expenses which the single payer system of healthcare would avoid!

I think most of you would agree America does have the most expensive healthcare system in the world. Well health insurance companies are the single biggest reason why that is! That just happens to be a fact.

I believe we need to modify how we *think* about how we get healthcare. I personally believe there is a responsibility on the part of government to provide the *best system* of healthcare that works for all Americans. Every life is important. The system itself can be organized better!

So this chapter is about what we could have had, and is not currently available. It is also about what we still can have if we only have more Democrats in control of the government. I guarantee you we will not get what I believe in as long as we have Republicans in there!

Our goal as a society should be to make healthcare available to as many good people as is reasonable. That healthcare should be priced fairly. I know we will never have 100% coverage for all people. But that would be our stated goal.

Now please pay attention as this subject can get a little complicated. There are important points here so please slowly and carefully read.

I am not proposing anything like unlimited healthcare for all people. Nor am I wishing for any form of free healthcare. We the people must pay for our healthcare! We all must get use to that idea. There is no other reasonable way to have it structured. I personally believe most of us expect to pay for healthcare and I feel that is correct thinking.

Common sense also tells us, when you pay more you should get more. That would be true in my system as well. Some people will pay in a lot, and they will get very good coverage. On the other end some people will only qualify for limited, good but basic care.

We know some people have less motivation in life, and they do fall into less lucrative careers. I am not overlooking that at all. You see my system involves us all paying a healthcare tax which is tied to our income!

But my system will have some generosity built into the system at the same time. Sometimes people just do not have high paying jobs!

Here are some examples. I certainly would make sure to take care of children! Working people and their families would qualify for normal care based on what they pay in. I would not bend over backwards saving unmotivated street people or those who do not seem to care about themselves or being constructive members of society. If people do not care about their own futures well then neither do I!

If you have done some bad things in your life, let's say you are a convicted criminal; I believe you are not entitled to good healthcare at all until you have become what we would call a constructive member of society. I believe you must generally be a normal American in good standing to receive that basic level of healthcare!

So we have many different situations here to consider. I believe it is reasonable that when you are employed you are entitled to receive a basic level of health coverage. Normal things can be covered, but where very expensive procedures are needed, such as transplants, or the like priority may be given through an allocation process!

What I am proposing is a good workable system with limited healthcare benefits. Under my system the government will not be on the hook for expensive care for the entire public. I do feel that certain simple rules can apply to the system.

Inevitably when we begin new forms of health coverage, doctors usually come out of the new system still making good money. That would be true in my system too.

They generally are not harmed. I do not believe Doctor's need to be concerned. In fact I have a niece who is a doctor and I have a few doctor friends and they all seem to be doing well even within the current system. I believe they will be doing well within the new system I am proposing also!

I also believe it would be a good idea to protect doctors from expensive malpractice lawsuits. My doctor friends have told me they often pay as much as 15 to 18 thousand dollars per month for mal practice insurance.

I prefer to think most Doctors are good people doing good work. In my system Doctors performance should be reviewed by other doctors and federal authorities. Our only expectation is for doctors to have normal and acceptable records. However I believe a great deal of money can be saved in the federal system by limiting doctor liability!

I am sure everyone understands sometimes patients are going to present difficult cases. That does happen and unfortunately it is normal. On the other hand, a small number of doctors do have bad performance records. I believe and hope the medical boards can work this out. I do think bad doctors can be identified!

I know it sounds a little embarrassing, but I would have doctors required to have random screenings for drug abuse. After all people lives are in the balance here. Doctor care must be kept at a high level. Doctors have easy access to drugs so we must use simple pre-caution. I understand it is a little hassle. Maybe just a little embarrassing, but I believe it should be done.

Good doctors should be rewarded with fair pay and financial security in the federal system. The occasional sad case should never cost a Doctor their career especially if it is determined the Doctor gave an honest effort!

Sometimes we need to recognize people's health is not very good. We never should punish good doctors who are helping patients who are coming to the end of their life. That sadly is also just a fact of life. We all live and we all will die!

Now one reason medical care is so expensive is because of the great deal of time and expense that is involved to train doctors and also because of the low number of Doctors. The first thing I would do to begin streamlining the system is change the education process for those wishing to become Doctors.

I know I sound like Bernie Sanders here but I would make medical school for doctors and nurses essentially free to them! Hold on now, just listen. I know that sounds extreme but let's talk about it for a second. The goal is to provide more Doctors to lower the overall expense of medicine to the public!

That education would have some conditions. First those future doctors will practice with in the new federal system for a period of at least 15 years. They will earn very fair but not excessive fees for their work!

Now to receive ones education for free, a student must first be American. Additionally in my system I believe our future doctors should be paid a small amount while they receive their education. That's right, help them to survive as they are getting their training!

I would start them off at only $400 or $500 so per month. But then raising their pay slightly as they become more valuable within the system!

So in my system medical school would be free for those students performing well and maintaining their grades. There would be no tuitions costs. Medical students would receive minimal existence pay. Once a student reaches internship they would receive a beginning wage for their work as they get their feet wet!

I would also weed out the bottom ten percent of medical students in that first year of medical school. The bottom five percent of the students would lose their support in the second year. Then maybe the bottom one or two percent of students each year after that would be flunked out. I guess I would have instructors monitored so there is no abuse of their position and power!

Simply weeding the lowest students out of the free health education system would be appropriate. If a student were flunked out for low grades they could continue their education on their own if they wish to arrange financing for themselves!

Now once a student becomes a new doctor, and when they have finished their internships, I would start them out getting around

$130,000 per year in their first year as doctors. Doctors' salaries would grow approximately $20,000 per year for the first three or four years becoming around $200,000 per year after about four years of being a doctor.

After that, their raises would be around $10,000 per year with the goal of reaching $300,000 per year after 15 years. At that point the Doctor would be free to enter into a private practice if they choose to do that, or they may continue on in the federal healthcare system if that is their wish!

New doctors will not have any student debt and will be protected from mal practice law suits within the federal system of healthcare! They will only be expected to work around 40 hours per week.

I believe existing Doctors could be compensated for the educations they have already paid for if they wish to participate in the federal system. The amount could be based on the amount of service they have left to give!

So I believe Doctors should receive compensation for their education. To keep the good Doctors we would sweeten their contracts in some way. I am not saying every detail is covered here. But the idea here is to keep care affordable by producing larger numbers of doctors, reducing their stress and their work load! Over time I believe we can transform the system and the occupation into a less stressful life style.

In my system Doctors would receive normal vacation time. They should only be expected to work about 40 hours per week. More doctors ought to give all of us a better system of care.

More established doctors would oversee the work of younger doctors etc. I would have Doctors collaborate on patient care. It should be seen as a normal way of creating patient care plans!

Please keep in mind the Republican Party is trying to protect the insurance company's presence in our healthcare system. I am not concerned about insurance companies at all. Basically I want them gone. But there is a place for them in the supplemental insurance arena.

We do give the government responsibility for our services and our protection all of the time. We organize as a nation for our military and national defense. We organize police and fire protection. We organize public schools, and even today we organize for things such as the fighting of forest fires, our parks services, and highway system are all government organized and controlled! It is normal for us to organize and have dozens of useful government services.

Why can we not extend that practice to basic healthcare protection? The healthcare system I propose would be paid for through our earnings and the income tax system. What difference does it make whether you pay for healthcare through a tax or through purchasing private health insurance which to me feels like a tax too? It still is money coming out of your pocket. We all want proper healthcare!

As long as you are an individual leading a productive life and even if you have a spouse and children, you and your family ought to be covered with basic healthcare protection. I will give you my tax rates and coverage in just a moment.

So I say there should be a new tax which goes to pay for your healthcare. Now the only ones this system might harm are those people who do work but will not buy any insurance at all. Then when they need attention they rely on government generosity giving them free or low cost care!

But I am sure we can keep the rates down by making the system larger, and having all people included automatically. Basically having a job covers you with some level of healthcare! Having more people supporting the system will make it less expensive for all of us.

We need a system where the profits of the insurance companies are not a consideration. I believe the responsibility to organize our healthcare falls upon us, through our government.

Government budgets will not be exploded. This is a conservative safe system of health coverage. The thing some people do not like about my idea is that it is more government and some people just love to hate that idea! Please read on.

I do believe there should be certain rules of coverage. First of all, children ought to receive good healthcare, regardless of how much money mom and dad make. As I have said all children ought to have a fair and reasonable chance at life! We should do everything that is reasonable.

Healthcare should come to all people automatically, regardless of where you work. Whether you work for a big company or small one it does not matter. I believe basic coverage comes with employment and it is a right of working people in America! With a federal system our coverage will travel with us automatically from job to job, state to state.

We will pay a percentage of our income for health insurance. It will start out at a higher percentage in the beginning and decrease as our pay increases.

It goes without saying this new health system will take a different way of thinking. No more insurance companies. No more searching for coverage. All medical conditions will be covered. No pre-existing condition clauses to foul your health coverage up.

What you are about to read will be my general version of a single payer system. Nothing is written in stone but this will be my vision for our healthcare!

So what do I mean when I say limited? Well for example, if you are a normal healthy person, and you have not even kept a minimum wage full time job for the majority of your working years, in my system you probably would not qualify for those expensive procedures should you need them. Organ transplants etc. may not be covered because you have not contributed very much! You would not have priority.

If you are a convicted criminal who has actually done prison time, in my mind you are not automatically entitled to good care. I believe you must live at least one month of trouble-free and productive life, on the outside of prison, for every year you were in prison before your status as a good citizen can be restored. You must demonstrate to society that you deserve proper care!

So as a convicted criminal you do need to be working and paying taxes into the system to get decent coverage. You cannot be what I call for lack of a better term, a worthless individual and still get great healthcare coverage. For me those are important requirements. Simply work, lead a minimally productive life, stay out of trouble and basic healthcare coverage will come to you!

It does not matter whether your spouse works or not. But couples must be legally married or committed to one another and file jointly for both individuals to be covered!

OK so here is how my system might work. If you are single or you have a spouse, I would have both of you contribute 11% of the first $60,000 of combined income to healthcare. I would have 7% of the next $60,000 of combined income, contributed to healthcare. Then I would have you pay 3.5% of the next $60,000, on down to say 2% of everything over $180,000 of combined income up to say 5 million dollars. After 5 million you would pay 1% of your pay or income for healthcare coverage!

Now, to help people get started in life, with the new healthcare expenses, I would also cut peoples income taxes to zero on let's say the first $20,000 of income for a single person, and maybe $27,000 of combined income for legal couples, increasing that by $2000 per child after that.

Though you may not have to pay income tax in the beginning, you will pay the healthcare tax on the first dollar and every dollar you earn. No exceptions to that rule.

This break point will help people to get started in taking care of themselves. Which I do believe should be the first priority in our lives for all of us. It should be expected that we take care of ourselves. That ought to instill some basic, proper human values into everyone's life!

I cannot say exactly what the limits might be. But let's say that if you earn less than $60,000 per year, perhaps limiting individuals to something like $250,000 of care in a five year time period. That time period begins when you start working or reach age 26 if you are in school. Each member of the family is calculated separately but once started your care goes in 5 year increments!

Most people will not need much treatment in normal years. But that would put a cap on very expensive treatments. As you earn more, your coverage credit will increase.

As I said before if you earn minimal money transplants and the like maybe out of the question especially if you are over age 26. Transplants can never be guaranteed anyway because of the availability of organs, and compatibility issues etc.

I am not saying what I have written is absolute. I know it is tough to not cover people. I would hope minimum wage earners would not be faced with large medical problems.

However ordinary medical care would apply to otherwise hard working people. My hope is that President Obama and Democrats will be successful at bringing in a national $10.10 per hour minimum wage. People working full time in minimum wage jobs will be contributing at least 11 % of their income to healthcare. They will qualify for pretty decent, basic healthcare!

Supplemental insurance would not be outlawed, so you could always buy more insurance if you wanted it. Insurance companies would still be allowed to sell catastrophic health insurance in that market as a supplemental insurance. I believe my system would basically self-fund.

Now here are some basic examples. If you make $50,000 per year, your health coverage would cost you $5,500 per year. Each family member would qualify for $250,000 of coverage once every five years.

With this system there would be no money wasted on insurance companies. You would be covering yourself and your immediate family.

Let's say if you make $110,000 per year your medical insurance would come to $10,100 per year. And your medical expense allowance would rise to $400,000 once every four years!

If your income is over $180,000 per year, we will just pick a number let's say it is $500,000 per year as an example. Your health tax would come to $19,300 per year. At $500,000 of income, your coverage would increase to $1,000,000 of treatment once every three years. That should cover most things!

The exact numbers would have to be left to the experts. I do believe there are limits for some treatments. I am not a doctor, but I am pretty sure there are in fact limits to the number of chemo treatments a person may receive as an example. As I said I am not a doctor. I am just saying as you contribute more into the system you will be entitled to get more out of it.

If you make very good money, let's say five million per year, your health tax would come to $61,100. I know that is a lot but you essentially would have unlimited healthcare coverage. You may receive as many expensive treatments as can safely be given. Medical decisions would not be hindered by the lack of funds at all!

Seems to me $61,100 is not a terrible hit on five million dollars of income by any standard. On the positive side, you are living within a system where all of your immediate family members are covered! There really would be no limits on procedures, and you would be able to see the best doctors.

With these rates it is not such a big deal. With $500,000 per year of income, you really will still have a small fortune of cash to spend and live on each year. Your Insurance is $19,000 per year. I personally know families who pay that much with the current insurance based system! So it is not out of line.

It is a small hit when you compare it to what income taxes are! But think of the safety and security it provides to all. For people earning less than $400,000 per year it should be a good deal!

So I say to you when we go to work, that healthcare tax will be collected. It will become an important part of our lives. We will learn to live our lives around that expense.

I am trying to make it so the system is a self-funding system as much as possible. It might be necessary to modify the numbers just a little. However I think I am in the ball park for what the system would cost.

I want to say beyond a shadow of a doubt in order to receive our healthcare we should not have to fund the profit and expense structure of insurance companies. Why would any of us want to fund them? Why would you care two hoots about insurance companies and their profits? I sure don't care about insurance companies!

I think what I have outlined is relatively simple to understand. Some of you may not be paying for your healthcare today. You are taking chances that you will not be getting sick So yes, with this new system you will automatically be paying for healthcare. There would be no easy way to avoid it, other than working under the table! Why would you take an under the table job and not have healthcare?

I think everyone would agree we should get regular physicals. I understand it will take time to get the system up and running. It will take time for us to get used to it. There will be a transition period I get all of that. But if we want what other nations enjoy it is we who must modify the system!

I can tell you Democrats had the absolute minimum number of congressmen and women to pass a deficient plan. We will need many more Democrats in office if we ever wish to create a plan like mine. We are very far from enacting a good system at this time. Keep in mind we will save 1/3 on medical expenses by going to a single payer system. It literally ought to be 1/3 cheaper!

Republicans hate the new Affordable Care Act for two main reasons. First because it has been proposed and put forth by a Democrat President and then passed by a Democrat government. Second, because it endangers the healthcare corporations as we know them. Because of its existence it still leaves the possibility for a single payer system to be brought to us in the future!

The Affordable Care Act can be modified as long as we still have it. That is why you will hear Republicans really want to get rid of it at all cost. Republicans are very afraid it will get modified in such a way as to take the insurance companies out of the picture. I honestly do not see how insurance companies can compete with a single payer system!

Republicans will try to convince you the Affordable Care Act is taking away from your personal freedoms. What the heck are they talking about?

They will say it is more government intervention in people lives and so on. It is easy to make negative arguments against something if you only want to kill it! But the reality is single payer does not have the expense of insurance companies so you definitely are saving. Do not be fooled!

The reality is that Republicans do not care about progress. Do not kid yourself, Republicans are protecting insurance company profits as well as a good source of their campaign funding! That really is what the Republican Party has been conceived to do!

Do you honestly think that if we get organized to create a better health system, we are magically going to all become a bunch of socialists? That we are somehow abandoning American values? That is the kind of language people like Michele Bachmann and others try to use on you. I know she is leaving, thank God for that.

Our neighbors to the north in Canada have already moved to a national healthcare system. According to my Doctor niece the Canadian system seems to be working well there.

She says it seems to functions better in Canada than what she was seeing here in the States! And she told me she believes we need to get the insurance companies out of the healthcare business. I believe her advice to me is correct thinking!

Yes I realize with my idea there will be changes. The healthcare system will be different. We will all have to get used to a few new things. But the system will end up working better, and it will be simpler to use. Once people experience it, I believe they will like how it works!

Republicans know the insurance companies cannot compete with a single payer system. So for Republicans this is kind of a life or death struggle.

The most important thing is that we keep the Affordable Care Act so that it can be modified however it needs to be changed in the future. I want the Act and I value it.

We never want to be stuck with a bad system. There is nothing wrong at all with having the ability to change the system anytime it needs modification. It is our system and we should be able to change it!

I would have very stiff penalties for any doctor who would try to cheat within the system. I would include jail time for cheating doctors. Throw the book at them.

Think of my plan as a multitier plan. All citizens must contribute to the system from their wages, salaries, earnings, or personal contributions. You will contribute an automatic amount from your paychecks. If you never contribute you will not qualify for much care!

Of course we would cover people who are disabled. We have to address mental illness and other problems too. The system will have the resources to be compassionate.

The new health plan has two parts. The first part is the mandatory part. It is how you get your basic coverage. The second part would be the optional supplemental insurance part, where you may buy additional coverage if you so choose. This would be the only part of the system in which health insurance companies would be allowed to participate.

With my system, I see no reason why you cannot see any doctor you may wish to see within reason. I would think many doctors will want to participate in the system as it will pay a fair and good salary and protect doctors from malpractice suites. Future doctors will receive their education for free, they will not have student loans to pay back, and they can expect to work fewer hours!

Most people will go to their ordinary doctors in most situations. I cannot say exactly how payments will be structured, but I assume the system would only allow for a set payment on normal procedures. Just like it is today!

I must ask, how wise is it for us to have for profit health insurance companies involved in our healthcare? At least now we are telling insurance companies what they must cover. Does it make sense to have a system where the provider of medical services has a vested interest in not providing care? Do we ever want for corporate profits to be a consideration in our medical decisions?

I do think government run healthcare does work! I have seen the quality of care you get with government-organized healthcare.

My brother was 64 years and about 8 months old when he was diagnosed with stomach cancer. From the standpoint of choosing your medical coverage it was pretty good timing. Because he was just months away from turning age 65 and where he could get onto Medicare. It really could not have happened at a much better time from that standpoint!

Once on Medicare, he had to decide if he wanted a supplemental plan. Most people will opt to receive Medicare with their Social Security. But many people do not make use of the supplemental plans.

In my brother's case he knew he would be facing large medical bills. So he opted for solid supplemental insurance coverage. Sure it cost a little but I thought it was still reasonable! My understanding is that Medicare alone will only cover approximately 80% of your medical bills. That is good but it is not complete coverage. The other uncovered 20% is up to you to pay.

Medicare coverage is taken from your Social Security checks each month, if you choose to participate. I assure you it is very reasonable health insurance.

About the time you get on Medicare, you are given the opportunity to buy supplemental health insurance. That is a separate additional medical insurance expense. My brother did buy supplemental insurance. The insurance he bought covered 80% of the unpaid portion of his medical bills. This was 8 years ago before the Affordable Care Act came in. That left him about 4% to pay out of pocket!

He had his monthly Medicare insurance fee, then his supplemental insurance coverage and his drug coverage. His total monthly insurance expense was not that bad. These are what the costs were about eight years ago!

He had been a truck driver with a Teamster retirement plan plus he had his Social Security. With both of those he got by pretty well!

In my opinion, his overall medical coverage turned out to be good. He did have to make it for about four months before he got onto Medicare. Yes he had to pay about $30,000 out of pocket before he turned 65. He had to pay for some chemo treatments. After age 65 he had his Medicare deduction plus around $140 per month for both supplemental and drug coverage plus he had to pay four percent of his medical bills.

Once he got on Medicare, he had no problem getting standard treatments. We even went to a major cancer center where he was able to speak with specialists. He pretty much got most of the available treatments and I feel he received good care!

Unfortunately, my brother's cancer was a bad one. We were not going to be beating it and I did lose him! However, all of my family felt the medical coverage he received worked well for him. Friends, it essentially was a government run medical plan. I was happy with it, and it was Medicare!

Social Security is willing to give you medical coverage, and it is called Medicare. It is a good deal. In my opinion, average people should opt to use Medicare. I say buy good supplemental insurance too, if you can budget for it; it is a good deal!

I do have another family member who is not participating in Medicare, just so they can get a slightly larger check each month. They believe in naturopathic medicine which is fine. I just hope that it all works out for them. But to me it is risky. They are turning their back on standard medicine!

We all should expect to pay for our healthcare. I believe in a small way that will contribute to responsible behavior. With the new system we will no longer have bad catastrophic plans to pay for. Catastrophic plans do not give you good coverage anyway. Plus plans like that just drain us of our wealth and do not provide decent coverage.

Additionally employers should like my system, as it should free them from the expenses of delivering expensive healthcare to their employees. That is a big deal to them too!

I would make employers pay to their employees what their medical insurance is currently costing them. So it would be a raise for workers.

So as medical expenses rise, that expense will no longer fall on the employer! Employers will see a more stable system of medical care for their employees. It ought to remove hassle from the companies. Plus all of their employees will be properly covered!

We as citizens will have peace of mind knowing that our families will be covered with health insurance. The system will function better. There is a level of security there.

What we got with the current Affordable Care Act was a pretty watered down healthcare system. Republicans certainly did not vote for any aspect of the system. Republicans were successful in making sure the system would not be a good system. There was no effort on the part of Republicans to create or help with an alternative system!

Republicans were successful in keeping the for-profit insurance companies at the center of healthcare in America. Thus I conclude Republicans by doing this were exacerbating some of the problems with the system. We need an overwhelming majority of Democrats to correct the problems we are now seeing!

With my system you will be covered more or less cradle to grave with health insurance. All you have to do is just lead a normal productive life and have normal constructive values. Those who avoid being in the system altogether, would basically have my most minimal coverage. Basically you would not be guaranteed of anything, nor should you expect much.

With regard to emergency care for non-contributors the system might be designed to stabilize the immediate problem with the individual until the patient is properly identified. I realize we do have to be humane about it. But we also have to figure out how to deal with those individuals who just are not motivated at all!

With a single payer system, my guess is it should cost less than 8% to 10% of a given medical bill to administer the program. Profits certainly are not a factor in the system.

Those of us who have unearned income sources may have to buy supplemental insurance on the secondary market if we want better coverage. Remember once you reach 65 your Medicare plan kicks in. You will pay into Medicare accordingly.

People will get out of the system more or less what they pay in. It is not free healthcare coverage at all. This system does not involve a lot of giveaway medicine and there is not a lot of paper work involved.

Government run healthcare under the Affordable Care Act would be complete insurance for the most part. Your coverage will be better with the government, because you have the government on your side. You are not fighting insurance companies for your coverage.

If your pay changes from year to year your insurance will adjust slowly. As an example, if you were out of work, your insurance would fall by say 20% per year until you are in the minimal category.

With a government run single payer system, you will need to have a rigorous and meaningful oversight mechanism. I get that. But other than that there are few expenses.

To find or get people or members into the system is simple. Simply put, all people are automatically in the system when they get their social security number and we all get one of those. The tax is removed from your pay and you are covered!

Everyone is entitled to emergency care. For indigent people we should fund at least a few days of emergency care in an intensive care facility. Or stabilize their condition before releasing them. But we have to draw the line somewhere. Society does not need to break the bank on none contributors!

I do believe it should be required that people have regular physicals. If you refuse to get a physical you could lose your coverage or it may be downgraded. People must take a physical for their own benefit and to minimize their total cost to the system.

I would have small co-pays for doctor visits, with the emphasis on the "small." This would be to stop people from frivolously using and abusing the service. These things will become an accepted part of life and of working. The majority of people will see their lives are better. We will quickly become used to it.

Republicans have no chance of making a better society by constantly making negative remarks about the Affordable Care Act. Republicans should be supporting the act and figuring out how to make it even better and not fighting it. How good and generous Republicans would look to the people if they did that!

Not one Republican would support any part of national healthcare for America. Not one! That should really upset you! Who in their right mind would not support improving the general health of our society, and the delivering of less expensive healthcare?

We have actually seen this behavior from the Republicans before. They do not want to give people anything. We know they do not support the middleclass. Republicans should be punished for their opposition by not giving them your vote!

I do not love everything about Democrats, but at least they work at bettering the lives of the people. Democrats generally are for all people, rich and poor regardless of their back grounds. Democrats try to organize the building of a stronger and better Society.

Health insurance companies are amongst the most profitable corporations in the country today. Do not kid yourself. You should not feel sorry for them. We the people are being forced to maintain those healthcare corporations, why should we do that?

We are maintaining the profits and the system of a nonmedical industry. At least with the Affordable Care Act we are telling the insurance companies what they have to cover, and how they must operate. We have set down some basic new guide lines.

But as long as we must go through the insurance companies we are going to have to finance their operating expenses and their profits. That does just not make sense to me as the best way to operate!

You must keep in mind, in the pre Affordable Care Act days it is very possible you may have to fight your own insurance company for the coverage you are entitled to! They are not going to be generous with you when it comes to expensive care!

We need to accept we will be replacing a voluntary insurance-based system that does cost real money, with a mandatory government plan which also costs money. But it is OK because it is better care at what should be a better price than what the insurance company can offer you!

Our system can be structured so much better with a little thought. Care could be about 1/3 cheaper just by moving away from the insurance companies!

I do not understand what the problem is. All I am trying to do is remove insurance company profits and operating expenses from the equation. Why is that not correct thinking? Why are you pro Republican voters fighting that approach?

My program will essentially pay for itself. If the tax rates I have stated do not quite work we might have to adjust them just a little. But I think I am pretty close.

It is possible that it will not cost as much as I say. It also has the side benefit of encouraging all of us to be productive people looking to make a decent living. Sometimes people need to be motivated a little. People will need to work in order to receive decent healthcare coverage and that is a good thing. We do want people to live constructive lives.

We, as a nation, are just beginning to join the rest of the civilized world in providing our citizens with public healthcare. I believe we clearly are on the right track. Healthcare is far too important to be in the hands of for-profit insurance companies. Finding an affordable way to provide the care is a responsibility of our government!

So what am I saying here? Once established, we will see in a short period of time government run healthcare will quickly become second nature to us. It ought to be viewed with good feelings and taken as a positive in our lives.

For those of you who feel you are being over taxed I believe you should be thankful that you are living and working in the land that offers you so much. If you do not like what this country has to offer, I say go ahead and live somewhere else. Because the American system is strongest when everyone is a part of the system and prospering!

OK this has been my views of healthcare for our nation. It is hard to have a complete discussion in a single chapter but those are my basic ideas. Because of Republicans what I have just written about does not have a chance of coming into being. I ask you to please start thinking and voting in the right way. We just need more Democrats and their progressive philosophies in government positions!

I am not saying Liberal politicians. I am saying sensible progressive thinking politicians. People who want to better the country and people's lives!

AUTO INSURANCE

Talking about automobile liability insurance is very nearly the same discussion as with health! Again why do we need to deal with insurance companies for our basic liability car insurance needs? How would you like to never have to deal with auto insurance companies or agents ever again? At least when it comes to basic liability insurance?

To my knowledge in most states we are expected to carry liability insurance on our vehicles. I say that is reasonable. But we also know that not all drivers insure their cars. The question becomes how can we prevent that dodge?

Under the current system if an accident happens, sometimes one owner is left with no recourse to resolve the damage other than trying to deal with the other party in a court of law. That is if you are lucky enough to track them down!

The uninsured can get around the law by not properly registering their car. Illegals often will have false ID's. If an accident is bad enough drivers of improperly registered vehicles might just abandoned their vehicles!

Do you people realize there are simpler and less expensive ways to have all drivers insured with liability insurance? We know people need gasoline to drive their car. So why not collect a small fee at the pump which automatically gives each driver liability insurance for the gasoline they have purchased?

Currently we have a system that is designed around people buying their liability insurance from insurance companies and through insurance agents. We rely on people having the honor, integrity, financial means and honesty to go out and purchase that insurance. This is in place because that is how the insurance companies seem to want the system to work. Insurance companies want to sell that liability insurance and get their cut!

How would you like for all of your fellow drivers to be insured properly and their vehicles registered and licensed? How would you like for liability insurance to be less expensive than what it currently is?

Well, it only involves some simple changes to the law and the way we do things. Covering people with liability insurance at the pump is a progressive solution to this problem!

The money collected at the pump will go into a general liability insurance fund usually run by your local state. Everyone who puts gas in a car will have $25,000 of liability insurance. As you know I have no loyalty to insurance companies. I do not want insurance companies in my life at all. For me they just represent an unnecessary expense when there are better ways!

So how would this new system work? Well, it is really simple. We probably would have to add around .30 to .40 cents per gallon at the pump in most areas to fund the insurance. That money will go into a general liability fund. Your cost will vary by the areas where you live.

Sure that will make gasoline more expensive. But you will never have to buy liability coverage ever again regardless of the kind of car you own. Unless of course you need some form of supplemental insurance!

I know that sounds like a large increase in the price of gasoline, which it sort of is. But let's say you tank up your car once per week, and you use 13 gallons of gas. That would cost you an extra $5.20 per week, for your basic liability insurance at .40 cents. That works out to $270 dollars per year, for $25,000 of insurance. I would think for most people $270 is a good savings on your insurance!

Even if you used twice that amount of gas per week, it still is not that bad of a deal considering the amount you would be on the road. Of course, we are not talking about collision insurance; I am only talking about liability insurance here.

If you happen to own your car free and clear, you may have no need to see an insurance agent ever again! The price added at the pump could be your only insurance expense.

Why on earth would you want to pay for all of the same expenses to get the insurance? Insurance agents, their support staffs, local offices, national offices, national staffs, advertising budgets, the adjusters, CEOs, corporate jets, corporate profits, retirement plans, medical plans and dividends? Why should we have to pay for those things? All we want is to cover our car with insurance. This is the exact same argument as with the healthcare insurance debate!

If you do buy a new car or truck on time, your dealer will require you to buy collision insurance. Or if you want theft, fire, and other forms of insurance you will have to buy those on the open market as well.

Now, I know 25,000 will not be enough to cover all accidents. But people who drive expensive cars usually have their own collision insurance. They have assets they wish to protect so they carry additional insurance. In the big picture I think normal people would be covered well, with this basic system!

Maybe we should adopt some form of no fault insurance. That is something that can be debated. However, the voters should decide it, not the insurance companies through Republican politicians!

I know the problem of bad drivers will still be here. But I believe if someone is a bad or irresponsible driver they can be taxed for their bad driving when they go to get their driver licenses renewed if nothing else. Nothing will stop those who would drive without a license anyway except mandatory jail time. But at least, they will have some liability coverage!

Those who drive more will pay more for their insurance, since they are buying more gas. They will also be on the road more and thus more likely to be involved in an accident. I feel that is a fair solution all around!

Imagine if you are retired, you may be gassing your car up only once a month. What retired people pay in insurance will be way less than what insurance companies would be charging you!

Those who drive heavy vehicles will pay more for their insurance. Since their vehicles are heavy they consume more fuel. They do more damage when involved in an accident. Again I believe this is fair and it will encourage people to drive lighter vehicles.

We can reduce the cost per gallon for insurance in areas where traffic is light or people must drive long distances to get to work. States like Montana, Wyoming, North and South Dakota, Alaska areas like that would have the least expensive insurance fee. Big cities would probably have the most expensive insurance fee.

Yes I admit it is a new tax. So what, it would give less expensive auto insurance to the vast majority of drivers. It should save most of us money and it will also be less hassle!

This will protect us automatically against the uninsured motorist. Every driver will have at least a basic level of liability coverage. It would be hard if not impossible to get around the fee. We all know a huge problem in the system is people often do not carry insurance at all, but they still drive on the road.

I am not sure how we will deal with fraudulent claims, other than to have severe penalties when people are caught. This is where having integrity in life works. If someone is found to be involved in a scam again I say through the book at them! Show no mercy!

I believe one way to deal with fraudulent claims would be to reduce compensation for back injuries. Perhaps if we pay only for operations, hospitalization, meds and rehabilitation etc. with no pay for unseen pain and suffering. I know there will be a few individuals who really do receive serious back injuries with lasting pain in accidents! But this new system would only pay for hospitalizations and actual medical expenses.

We can deal with the problem of irresponsible drivers by not being afraid of handing out hefty penalties for irresponsible driving, drunk driving and excessive speeding. Fines should be large. I say even jail time for bad accidents caused by drunk driving or speeding would be reasonable!

But the very first thing we need to do is get the insurance companies out of the basic liability auto insurance business. Insurance companies are not needed for that!

If you drive an average car that gets 20 miles to the gallon and you drive 16,000 miles per year (which is probably more than an average amount), at $.40 per gallon that would be about $320 per year for your liability insurance. To me, that seems like it would be a good deal.

Of course this will cause the price of gas to go up at the pump. However you may never have to buy car insurance through an insurance agent ever again. No one can be refused insurance!

The added cost of gasoline will encouraging people to buy lighter, smaller and more fuel efficient cars! This will help with our nation's trade deficits concerning oil imports. With more expensive gas, we will see less consumption of that fuel. There might even be fewer cars on the roads, easing congestion!

We all know Republicans will oppose this idea because Republicans wish to protect the profits of the insurance companies. Buying insurance at the pump will automatically put liability insurance on every car on the road. Do you expect Republicans to support this idea? I don't because it is too simple!

You may have assets you wish to protect from lawsuits. Supplemental car insurance would be for all those purposes. That is why we would still have the supplemental insurance market for autos. That is when you will need to go see an insurance agent.

Several accidents in a short period of time will cause you to start paying more for your driver's license when you go and renew it. When you have multiple accident fines may increase. We just need to be progressive and think outside of the box.

I know we will never solve the problem of irresponsible driving and perpetual idiots on the road. But at least insurance at the pump will provide a little help. Everyone will carry that basic liability insurance. There will be basic coverage for all drivers!

Laws like these can always be modified when needed. Nothing is ever written in stone. People will be more likely to register their cars properly since they do not have to worry about basic insurance! Again I view this as an improvement to our system!

WOMEN'S RIGHTS, GAYS
AND EDUCATION

Now we will quickly touch on a few different subjects. I am sure our personal rights are important to all of us. Everyone feels different about what should be allowed and or restricted.

However it seems odd to me because Republicans are supposedly strong on protecting personal freedoms. But the reality is Republicans will often try and take them away! Some freedoms are not protected by Republicans at all.

When it comes to woman, Republicans will not support things like equal pay for women doing equal work. What is with that kind of thinking? Do Republicans believe women are second class citizens?

Republicans will not stand up for a woman to have control her own body. Republicans do not stand up for women's abortion rights. Things like daycare, the right to be at home during family illnesses, and other types of family leave matters historically have not been supported by Republicans. Basically I say Republicans do not support women at all!

Sometimes Republicans will not even stand up for access to various forms of contraceptives. Republicans will not stand with women when they are using family planning or if she is using a clinic that is helping with the abortion process!

Listen abortion is not a pleasant thing for anyone to go through. It must involve a lot of troubling thoughts for the woman involved. It is hard to think about ending the life which is within you. I do not envy anyone facing that!

But for many Republicans Religious values trump women's rights and personal freedom. However I do feel women know their personal situations better than anyone else. So I do not understand the logic behind taking that individual choice away by not helping women who need the help!

We all think Republicans are staunch defenders our individual rights. To me this is another one of the illusions Republicans create. I do not see how Republicans are protecting women's personal freedoms at all. What Republicans really are protecting is getting the religious minded person vote! Just so they can attract more of those antiabortion voters!

For many American's religion is a consideration which must be taken into account when it comes to family matters and our personal lives. However in the end, these matters fall under our individual freedom of choice. Every ones situation is a little bit different. Every woman should feel it is OK to make the proper and sometimes difficult choice that is right in her circumstance.

No religion or party should ever be allowed to trump the individual's personal freedoms. Women must be given the freedom and support they need to make important family decisions. I guess you could say it is their God given right as women, to have the ultimate final choice to make these decisions!

I believe we men correctly have less consideration in pregnancy matters than women have. We must defer to the woman we love. We must have unusual trust with her. I believe woman will usually discuss their pregnancy with their partner, but in the end the final choice rests with her!

If you are a man and a woman wishes to have your child that is a wonderful plus for you. You are a lucky guy. However if the woman in your life is feeling this is not the right time for any reason, then I say you may be out of luck. That is just the way it is.

After all it is her life not yours and she must mother that child through its upbringing. Her decisions are the final word.

But it seems to me that Republicans are more of the mindset that men should have a bigger say in pregnancies. Or Republicans are more apt to believe that Religion can say what should be allowed by our society! Well who is going to determine which religious value we live by?

I believe if you are a man and you want your wife or partner to have your child, you need to make sure that person loves you. Make sure you are a stable person, who can provide for your family properly. You should make sure you create a warm and loving atmosphere. It is just that simple.

Republicans should be on the side of supporting wholesome relationships while religion should be thought of as a secondary support system for the family. Religions are good at providing moral support!

So what is right for one person may not be right for the next. That is why we always have to give the final word to the woman. Her future and health is on the line. That is a primary concern, and comes first over what men may want.

If I was a young woman, or I had daughters this Republican attitude would bother me greatly. Men are not here to control their families and have the final say. They are not here to lay down the law. Men are here to lend support and be a constructive part of a loving family.

Personally I like the idea that government should have the role to stand up to church organizations or religious thinking individuals! Government should let churches and all people know what is acceptable. Even if it runs against particular religious beliefs, government should support women!

Having said all that, I certainly understand there does come a point where ending a pregnancy becomes an issue. You may have a well-developed fetus in the womb. Then the debate rightly becomes where should society draw the line on abortion procedures?

Again I feel this is a highly personal matter. At least in my mind we may have gotten to a point when it does not seem right to abort the fetus. It is now clearly an unborn child.

For some people life begins at conception. For others it begins at birth. I guess for me, from a legal stand point it would be at a point near where the fetus can survive on its own outside the womb. But I am just an ordinary guy and my feelings do not mean that much!

Not being a doctor, I cannot put into words exactly where that point is. I would prefer to be very conservative about this issue. I know fetuses have been born quite premature and they have survived. I am sure they all are beautiful children. I realize aborting life is never going to be a pretty thing to see or easy to do or even just think about!

From a totally different legal angle another factor is this: is it clear the future child is wanted by the mother? Has she has gone to see her doctor about the pregnancy and so on? That is a good indication she wants the child. In a legal sense the woman appears to want the child and she is progressing with her pregnancy normally. We are kind of straying off topic a little. But I believe intent becomes a factor.

Churches ask people to practice religion they do not dictate religion to followers. We should always conduct ourselves within an atmosphere of love and acceptance. We must practice religions values to the best of our ability! Government should support women just like society supports them!

We must acknowledge that the individual, her values and her life are important. In this day and age we are blessed with modern medicine. It is a different time for people since we now have options. It follows we have some control of our future and that is a good thing. Continuing with or not continuing with a pregnancy has become a choices. They are all important decisions for the mothers!

Discussing abortion is a topic where strong feelings are on both sides of the issue. I personally believe most pregnancies usually are wanted. But I also recognize sometimes pregnancies are not wanted. It is not the right time. There are situations where it just is not right for the mother!

Perhaps rape, incest or age, are consideration. Financial or physical health can be factors. The ability of the mother to support herself is a factor. Prospects for future relationships all feed into these decisions. For me as long as the ending of a pregnancy happens early I can accept it for what it is, which is the choice of the mother!

How one person chooses to live their life may not be my way. But I must accept that. People and society must conform to certain norms. We should not try to control others. We can best support freedom by absolutely giving it to others!

None of us really knows for certain if there is a god or not. Some people are absolutely sure there is a god, while others do not know. I do know for sure there are mothers. We all understand there are basic moral values, rules and feelings even if there is a god or if there is not. So this is a very complicated subject. I believe we have a responsibility to maintain personal freedoms.

We men should love our wives and put real effort into seeing all sides. I believe we should not be thinking about ourselves first, we should think of those we love first!

As to church's, if you wish to practice religion and have that tax-free status, you must conform to basic values protected by the government. You are never entitled to control people or deny them their freedom. I honestly do not care that you feel your religious values are more important than my freedoms!

Republicans give just enough lip service to religion to be perceived by religious minded people as the more moral party. The party of Christians and of Christian values. I hate to sound corny, but I personally believe Republicans are not fulfilling people's lives at all!

I feel women's rights are in jeopardy with Republicans. If these issues are important to you, you must remember this. Presidents have the power to appoint justices to the Supreme Court. We are seeing the battle for our freedoms today in selecting a successor to Justice Scalia. Republicans want to keep the court as conservative as they can!

If you women value your personal freedoms, then you want Democrats to be appointing those judges. Nobody is saying a woman must have an abortion. Democrats are simply preserving the freedom to choose and to receive a safe abortion if that is her choice. It may be an unpleasant thought but it is her life, her body and her fetus!

Can you imagine if Mike Huckabee were President? Or, what if Pat Robertson, Rick Santorum, Mitt Romney and even people like Rick Perry were elected to the Presidency? These people openly have restrictive religious values. They will work to take away personal freedoms through conservative justices!

We have just seen the impact which conservative justices have had with recent Supreme Court rulings. In the Hobby Lobby case five conservative justices there ruled it was OK for Hobby Lobby to not purchase contraceptives for their female employees within their medical insurance plans!

The conservative court was saying it is OK for a business own-er's personal beliefs to be imposed upon their employees whether you agree with them or not. Hobby Lobby is bringing their beliefs to the work place!

The owners of the Hobby Lobby stores are very religious people, I get that and they do not believe in contraception, I get that too! What you do in your personal life is your own business. But denying commonly accepted insurance to others does not seem right for any reason that I can think of!

You do not vote for Democrats because you love Democrats. I vote for Democrats because they do not have overly conservative values. You should keep in mind Democrats are not pro-abortion at all. You should not think that. But they are 100% pro-choice. Dem-ocrats want you to carry your pregnancy forward if that is what *you* want. I believe that is correct thinking!

When it comes to pregnancy the two parties seem reversed from their core values. Republicans do not want government interference in our lives. Yet as you can see on the most important personal issues they are promoting that very thing!

We can never give the option of providing birth control or not providing it over to the corporations. If they have the choice they will opt to save the expense and not provide it to their workers. For me it does not make sense to lose a trained employee to save a cou-ple bucks per month on employee contraception!

As an American you need to stand up for the sensible values. I Say Hobby Lobby should give a raise to their employees in the amount of about $12 per month to pay for contraception or what-ever. Sensible values should preserve personal control of your own life.

We must protect everyone's right to control his or her own life. That is the first priority and first job of government. Society will be stronger when we protect those values.

Now onto the subject of gay marriage. Like the abortion issue Repub-licans are a little more inclined to want to have a say on what sort of relationships a person may have. Some states do not allow gay marriage, but I am pretty sure today the majority of states do. It will not be long before the vast majority of states allow what we call gay marriage. Times in America they are a changing!

How would you like for the government to suddenly say interracial relationships are not permitted. Or that Jewish people may not inter marry with Christians, and so on. This is a totally crazy way of allowing ourselves to think. Love is always the controlling factor in these matters!

I am not going to talk a whole lot on this subject. But I do not like the idea of government having that kind of power. Once you allow government to restrict one group, it becomes possible to restrict as many groups as you may wish. America is supposed to be the "land of the free." Not the "land of live your life according to my values!"

Though I myself am a heterosexual male, I personally believe people should be free to make legal commitments with anyone they want if that is their desire. I personally believe it would be wise for the gay community to come up with acceptable language which both politely describes these relationships and also does not offend anyone.

We should do this so everyone knows how to talk about these relationships. I believe general openness and honesty is constructive for all in this case!

I am sure many gays would like to use the term of marriage for the description of their relationships. But I also understand traditional married men and women sometimes have problems with that word describing same sex relationships. I personally believe using that word sort of hides the relationship being talked about because for many marriage means a man and a woman. So I do think language should be found.

I am becoming an older person. I admit I might sometimes have old fashioned values. If gays want to be accepted, I believe they should come up with terms which are both accurate, polite, and not confusing! I think that would benefit all!

My personal feeling about this is, we should not make a big deal out of these relationships. Everyone is entitled to his or her own way of living. Sometimes it needs to be talked about but USUALLY there is no need for it to even come up.

We do not want for people to feel uncomfortable when talking about their personal relationships. Yet on occasion, in some situations we want to properly describe a relationship. We do not want for people to be surprised. We can be welcoming to all people with just a little effort on our part. Having consideration for others and using simple respect works well!

If society were left up to me, I would give homosexual couples all of the same legal protections that heterosexual couples enjoy. It is not my thing but again everyone can practice his or her own values. I have known gay people and for the most part they seem pretty normal to me!

Since I believe heterosexual couples generally are not embarrassed with their relationships, in the end it should be that way for gay couples too. The homosexual community should not wish to hide their relationships behind unclear or deceptive language. We do need to be more accepting of these relationships! It is we who must grow up and accept these relationships without making a big deal of it.

So we should be able to give people the knowledge of what we are describing, without it being awkward, or making an embarrassing comment. We certainly do not want to put our foot in our mouth. We always want to have consideration for others.

Perhaps my feelings are not up with the times. But for people like me there are situations where correct language is helpful. Let's use an example. If you are having a social event and you are welcoming all people, make that clear in your invitation. You should invite individuals, spouses, their children, friends and partners.

Perhaps if you are only comfortable with heterosexual couples at your event just omit the word "partners" from the invitations. Then gay's might understand your feelings and at least keep their lifestyle quiet, if they choose to attend. I don't know for sure maybe I am all wrong on that!

Now is that correct language, I cannot say I am just throwing out ideas. But I do feel it pretty much tells everyone in honest language who exactly is welcome to come to the event! It makes sense to have language which works and I believe language can be found.

I am only trying to give you my idea of how society might deal with these issues. According to the dictionary marriage is between one man and one woman. I know I sound like Mitt Romney there. But I guess that is my definition also!

So, maybe the word "partner" or "committed relationship" works better in some cases. Sometimes on the TV show modern family they use good language for this issue! Seems to me anyone at all can enter into a committed relationship!

Committed relationships could refer to same sex relationships, or it could refer to couples who prefer to be in a heterosexual relationship but not be married in a church as an example. Anyone should be able to make a legal commitment to anyone else. But I am open to any language which is thoughtful and works.

The other big part of this is: we as individuals all need to grow up. We need to be OK with all types of couples. In this modern day and age we need to realize normal couples are sometimes gay people, sometimes they are interracial and sometimes conventional too! Love is the important thing!

Finally, I would like to talk about the subject of education in America. Wouldn't you say education in America has some major problems? Too many kids are dropping out of school way too early. They just do not value their education. Especially when we are talking about young people living with in the inner cities of America! They miss the value in getting that education!

As a result our schools are not producing mature young people for society. We have too many dysfunctional people who can barely speak clear English or think out and understand problems. Society is suffering with too much unemployment, drug and crime problems. Kids are not learning adult skills!

I know it is crazy, but some inner city communities actually have dropout rates as high as 70%. Don't you think that situation does not serve the nation very well? You are producing a generation of under skilled individuals. How well will they contribute to society?

Now to counter this I do believe strongly in motivation. You would be surprised but relatively small amounts of money can motivate young people. Kids like anyone need real reasons they understand to adopt adult behavior. So society performs an important role, society needs to send a strong message to people as they are growing up. That is we expect you to mature into an intelligent person!

I would actually compensate kids for proper attendance and getting good grades. I would think we do want our kids to make the most of that which is provided to them at no cost, for their own benefit. I would reward those kids who stay out of trouble and keep their grades up with compensation. Pay them for going to school and only pay that money upon graduation!

I would not pay much for C averages, maybe a few hundred dollars or so. But you could pay $1,500 for averaging B's throughout your entire High School years. Then if kids were straight A, I say pay them $4,000 to 5,000 upon graduation! They are kids who deserve to get off to a good start! Hopefully they will create fewer problems as adults.

I also believe there are other things we can do. First it is important that we keep in mind what teenagers want most! Then we will know how to better attack the problem of kids dropping out of school and turning out badly.

Teenaged kids essentially want to be adults themselves. That is the big thing they are looking forward to. This is a normal situation. It is very important for us adults to understand that. We can make use of those desires. We adults need to understand that having our kids reach adult behavior is an important goal. We want that for them and we must embrace it!

When you are young, you just want to get out on your own as soon as possible. Kids want a car. They want their own apartment and they want income so their parents will not have control of their life and so on! We all get that!

It should be understood we all go through a learning process in life. That process is not about becoming 18. It is about becoming responsible, thoughtful, well mannered, educated and considerate. What we call would call maturing. Young people need to see the value of having a good work ethic, coupled with skills.

So what can we do to help that situation become a reality? What am I talking about here? What types of positive changes can we make which will be good in our kid's lives?

Well I believe we need to make simple changes in our laws and to our society that kids understand it is a must for them to get that diploma and stay in school. Putting value on education is not just preaching about how important education is, like anything else, I believe kids need to be motivated!

Our entire system needs to work together and attack the whole problem. We basically should show to our kids that if you get your education, desirable things are going to come your way.

We can start by saying "if you want to drive you need to have passing grades in school just to get the learners permit." Permanent driver licenses should come only after graduation. Learner permits expire at age 19. We need to create a reality where there are going to be problems for you when you do not have that diploma!

I would use the simplest solutions I can think of. I would make it law that people without high school diplomas or the equivalent cannot ever enter into legal contracts. That is pretty simple to do. It would become a new law for society to live by. I know Republicans hate any kind of a new law and they do not like any change!

Basically we would be saying to all people, without a high school education we do not believe you are intelligent enough or mature enough to sign contracts or agreements of any kind. This would affect many areas of a young person's life. We could grandfather in older individuals who are adults and exhibited responsible behavior!

Think about this, we must sign contracts all of the time. We must sign a contract when we purchase a new car, and sometimes even when purchasing used cars bought on time. Before getting your diploma, signing a registration form for the ownership and the licensing of your car would be illegal.

You cannot sign rental agreements, or purchase homes. Sometimes you can't even buy furniture and appliances on time, because that involves signing a contract.

You could not get a credit card, because again that involves signing a contract. You could not even get a cell phone since that involves signing a contract! You could not sign a cable or internet contracts. Kids may not even be allowed to open a simple bank account unless their parents are there to sign.

Simple changes to law would create a situation where it is important to get that education. We have to make it a nuisance for kids to drop out. It is not expensive to do these things either. These are simple changes to society. Our goal is to help our kids become responsible adults with proper adult behavior.

Much like credit card databases, we ought to be able to set up high school databases concerning the progress of students. There is little involved to set this up, but the benefits will be important to society!

Simply have an office worker at all schools where one of their duties is the responsibility of logging student grades and progress. It probably would be a part time position. Then up load that information to a state wide data base once per quarter. Overall it is a good thing and fairly simple to do.

I realize there will always be a few young people who are coming from very difficult situations. We can have counselors and programs designed to help those kids out. Help them to become both secure and educated. We never want to make it impossible for people to get ahead. We just want to direct them toward correct behavior!

We know it costs much less to educate kids who are in school than it does to deal with them after they have fallen into a life of crime. Prisons, courts, police, and Welfare are all expensive. Lives generally are ruined or unfulfilled and unhappy when they are not educated!

Perhaps it might be wise to have two minimum wage laws. Minimum wage shall be paid to all kids leading constructive lives. As long as you are in school and getting educated with passing grades, you may have an after school job. The normal minimum wage will apply to all people who have received their diplomas, the equivalent and/or are actively in school!

Maybe there should be a lesser wage for kids who are dropouts. That may sound cruel but it creates a pretty good incentive. I would also prohibit companies with more than 50 employees nationally, to hire kids who have dropped out of school. These things are not that difficult to do! It just becomes our national policy!

It will be a positive thing to create these new realities for young people. I want it to be a hassle for kids to not get that education. That should be our attitude!

I believe publishing student's high school grades would also be helpful to society. I think it might create pressure to be somewhat educated and acceptable in the eyes of their community, and to not embarrass their family name. There would be a little pressure there for kids to push themselves a little bit in school.

Businesses ought to be rewarded with slightly lower taxes when they hire kids who are living the right way. I definitely am talking about pizza and hamburger joints. It takes a national effort to make our society better.

Education is the key to constructive lives. Educated kids should be more strongly valued in society. If you have a high school diploma it should be recognized as a solid first step in a young person's development.

Credit card companies should require a diploma before they issue a card. Apartment houses should be strict about not renting to non-grads. Better kids, will lift all of society!

We do not need more dropouts from our schools. Our system of laws should be constructed around the idea of getting your education. This is all a small but important part of creating a stronger society.

The first thing is for us to support the idea that government will have this role in the development of kids' lives. The Federal government should be supported in the monitoring of kids through high school.

Do you think Republicans would support this? I do not think it is that big of a deal but it is another change. Typically I would expect Republicans to oppose the idea, because it represents interference in our lives, another hassle and a small expense!

Merely following young people's individual accomplishments and progress as human beings does not require tight monitoring. Our goal is to reward people who exhibit proper behavior when it is found. We need to preach this information in the classrooms from the early grades onward.

I also believe it would not be a bad idea to have mandatory classes on social skills and correct behavior. That is a subject that to my knowledge is not addressed that much in schools today. Teachers will tell you kids often do not have basic manners. Kids are not learning proper behavior!

Yes that might be considered a new subject matter. But I feel it needs to be taught and it would not hurt. I would begin teaching it in the youngest grades then touching on it off and on throughout high school.

Businesses can perform an important link in the development of young peoples' lives. It should be hard to get a job if you are not in school!

Young people today are not guaranteed of much at all. At least we could guarantee them they will have a tough time in life without that education. Is that unreasonable?

Now if having these laws does not help kids from dropping out of school, I do not know what will. As I have said most kids just want to be out on their own. Kids actually want to be adults and live in a self-sufficient ways. But the message should be first thing's first. Get that education!

These relatively simple actions in a small but important way will lead to more constructive lives. It will end up giving us a stronger economy with fewer social problems. It should be a normal thing that the majority of people will want to have an education, normal skills and average intelligence!

As I view Republicans coming back into power again, I doubt a high school diploma bill would have a chance of passing under a Republican Congress. Republicans just want the simple reality: of keeping government out of the individual's life.

Republicans often have the view that any government at all is just bad. I view Republicans as holding society back. They are living with unfounded old fashioned beliefs.

There are constructive actions to be taken here. We should always be working for the betterment of society! We can make progress if we are not too hung up on old ineffective values. Our society still has problems and we must take action to correct the reality!

REPUBLICANS, RELIGION AND GUNS!

It seems to me if you really where a Christian with true Christian values, and you loved America you should be supporting the best Democrat you could find. Why do I say that? I say that because it is Democrats who are the ones who are bringing meaningful Christian values into our society! You must stop and think this out.

Perhaps not absolutely every religious value has come in but many very good ones have. They came in because of Democrats.

How many of you appreciate that your mate comes home from work at a reasonable hour? Democrats are the ones who brought working people the 40 hour work week and the 8 hour workday! That happened with Woodrow Wilson. Isn't that a good Christian value?

Most Democrats believe that each woman should have the final choice of abortion in her personal life! Too me this is just common sense! It is that person's life, not mine!

If the mother does not have the resources to obtain an abortion on her own, and she is not helped the tax payer may have to fund the delivery and possibly pay for the upbringing and care of that child. The mother may be locked into a motherhood situation when her heart is in a different place!

What if a day comes when government can tell you how many children you may have, like they had in China. Do we wish for our government to have that kind of power? Do we really want for government or religion to have powers like that over our Citizens?

I thought religious freedom was something people wanted! Historically that is why people have come to America in the first place. In the old days many came here to escape religious persecution back home and have that full freedom here!

I know for some of you, religion and God are 100% totally real. You live your lives with great consideration for religion. As a religious person you are OK with more religious values in your society. I am OK with that also. But I also understand my values may not be your values, so you know where this is going. Our individual values only work well in our personal lives!

When you get right down to it, everything about religion is based on our individual feelings. No one person's belief has any more weight than anyone else's. Some people feel strongly that religion is not good. I understand that too.

I believe Democrats are the true party of Christian values. How many of the following things would you say are your basic Christian values?

Isn't it Christian to have child labor laws preventing children from working? Of course it is. They came to us because of Democrats. OSHA health and safety laws also came in because of Democrats. What about equal pay for equal work? The Lilly Ledbetter Act came to you because of Democrats! Wouldn't you have to say that is all religiously correct legislation?

What about the laws protecting equal access to buildings and transportation for the handicapped? Surely those are all proper Christian values. Don't Christians want to help those who are having health problems and/or mobility issues? How about all of the civil rights laws which Democrats have passed? I think we all would say Civil Right laws follow basic Christian values!

Certainly the Affordable Care Act is here because of Democrats. Republicans have been "VERY MUCH" against the Act. That does not seem very Christian to me. How does the Republican position of hindering access to affordable healthcare line up with your basic Christian values? Was it better when we had preexisting clauses in health insurance? Geez folks please think this out!

The G.I. Bill came in because of Democrats. Then look at how Republicans will latch onto an issue like hindering reproductive rights for low income women. How is that in any way Christian? Many Republicans are openly against gay marriage! Evolution is the best non-religious explanation for life on earth. Creation is not based on any true science or evidence that I am aware of.

But for some reason religious people do not seem to appreciate what Democrats have done for our society. Somehow Republicans and their values seem to take the day with many Christians. The few changes that Religious people want today are not constitutional according to the Supreme Court! Gay marriage has become legal in the majority of states. For the time being abortion remains legal!

However the changes which Democrats have successfully brought into society are your basic religious values too. Democrats are successfully bringing society proper values!

I always thought Republicans were supposed to be the party preserving our personal freedoms. But Republicans seem to forget that when it comes to preserving a vote for themselves.

Christian people should remember that Republicans will do some very non-Christian things at times. Is it a Christian value to support any American, being able to buy assault weapons when you do not even know what they are going to do with it? Even when you know nothing about them personally?

I ask you what other purpose can there be for assault rifles other than for the killing of human beings? How is that Christian? Do we want more of those type weapons in our society? Aren't our police officers risking their lives enough for you? Isn't America violent enough for you?

Yet Christian's are the ones who seem to support Republicans. Republicans are the ones supporting free access to weapons. Republicans do not even want short waiting periods, or reasonable background checks to be performed! Is that logical thinking amongst you Christians? Christians if they were worth anything should demand that background checks are performed!

Can you believe Republicans are even in favor of allowing weapons to be sold over the Internet, and of course sold without those back ground checks? How in tune with religious values and common sense is any of that?

What religious person would think that is the right way to sell weapons? If you are a criminal having trouble purchasing a weapon, you will look for these alternatives paths to get what you want!

Why didn't Republicans ban abortions when they had the entire government in their hands under George W. Bush? They could have tried to do something like that, but did they? They didn't even try to

bring it about! Republicans are not doing anything for religious people except making sure there are plenty of weapons in your society!

How many thousands of Americans must die each year because
of gun violence or lack of proper access to decent healthcare? Just
look at the problems with the VA. Democrats even increased funding
for veteran healthcare before the access issues became a problem! I
always thought you Christians cared about things like citizens and
public healthcare!

My wife and I recently lost a dear friend to her husband's hand.
They both were really nice people. We were in shock when we heard
the news. The woman had worked with my wife and they were
friends! I met both of them several times.

The husband was able to go out and buy a handgun, with only a
very short waiting period. He shot and killed his wife and then took
his own life. Within their marriage I believe they were going through
a rough time. But we all agree murder is never the answer!

They both were very good people, even he was a nice person.
I liked him whenever I met him. Somehow I think he began having dark thoughts. His actions were totally out of character. To me
he seemed like a normal person! He could not have been in his
right mind. I believe he must have been in some sort of a severe
depression.

Having a total lack of sensible gun control laws, has cost society
two more very nice productive people their lives. They had young
children who have now lost their parents!

I believe if only he had been forced to wait a month for his gun
permit, or had he been required to have a face-to-face evaluation
with the police, perhaps he would have been prevented from getting
the weapon! Waiting a month might have given him time to think
things out!

Buying a weapon is a serious matter because it is a tool or device
that can take a life. It should be harder to buy a weapon than it is to
get a driver's license or just buying alcohol!

If only his separated wife had been informed of his intent to purchase a weapon, and had she been given the opportunity to express
her concerns about that, perhaps this tragedy might not have happened. Authorities may have known since the marriage was in
distress they could have restricted him for a while. He may have

returned to sensible thought with a little time. Life for all would go on.

We must understand, there is very little impact to a corporation if a life is lost. Corporations and Republicans do not care that much about the small things like individual lives. The gun lobby supports free access to weapons of all types for the sake of business, and making a buck.

Of course Republicans lend support to the gun lobby because of their deep pockets! They support politicians who will protect their freedom to sell weapons in America. That is sort of the American way. But if we wish to move our country to a more peaceful way of living please elect Democrats!

Republicans can only hope they or their loved ones will never become victims of these weapons! I do not understand Republican thinking at all. Don't they wish to live in a country where we do not have to worry about gun violence?

Gun manufacturers make millions and millions of dollars each year via gun sales. I totally realize the process of removing guns from society will be a long process. I would think it will take several generations to remove most of these weapons! But if we never start, we will never get to where gun ownership is uncommon.

I would much rather have these very nice people back in my life than to have those dammed destructive weapons. I truly believe people need to become more like Europeans in their life styles. I certainly would never remove classic guns, revolvers or hunting rifles and shot guns from the people!

Republicans portray themselves in one way to Christians and the public, but then will act in ways contrary to their stated peaceful values. Those two things, religious values and gun ownership do not seem to go together as natural partners. For me it is an un-natural fit and another illusion of Republicans!

However as long as you Christian people continue to support Republicans we are going to have these weapons in our society. You know the margin between Republicans and Democrats is so tight that Christians alone can change our country. You should not buy Republican arguments!

Why should Republicans ever stop supporting and promoting gun ownership laws, if they will still get Religious peoples votes? You Religious people need to stop and think things out. You need to consider what is good for society.

If you Christians wish to accomplish something constructive for society, work to remove easy access to weapons by not voting for Republicans. That is the most constructive thing Religious people could do today!

In my opinion, religious people do not seem to demand proper Christian behavior from their Republican politicians. I believe it is because Christian people are so focused on the abortion issue or gay marriage that they are not looking at the things which they could change and are really important!

I am trying to tell you, it is Democrats who have been the ones who are bringing proper values to society! Democrats wish for a more peaceful society.

No other country on earth behaves like America! Owning a weapon is a serious thing, we should be very careful about this subject. Honestly, I believe it should be pretty difficult for anyone to get their hands on many of these weapons!

People do not have to deal with these problems in Europe. Most countries have managed to keep weapons out of their societies. People are happy and well-educated there. I have lived in Germany for many months, and know what I am talking about. We could learn a lot about correct living from them!

Do you remember the Gabrielle Gifford's shooting? Do you think that was right? Of course that was not right. The young man who shot her and others was not mentally fit. Yet he was able to easily put his hands on weapons. That cost society multiple lives. There were no simple checks in place to judge that person and determine their mental health!

If Republicans cared at all about society they would encourage gun ownership through responsible gun laws, not through reckless gun ownership. Republicans are only thinking about being friends with the gun lobby and manufacturers. Republicans need the votes of both Christians and 2nd amendment lovers to be in office. Christians really could make a difference if they wanted to!

Christian People could bring the country to the next level by supporting the one peaceful party. Christians could help make America a great and peaceful nation by abandoning Republicans!

DIRTY WORD

Now we know Republicans are not about to think in progressive ways. Even though Teddy Roosevelt was a well-respected progressive President, somehow Republicans today have come to reject progressive thought. They view progressive thought as always changing perfectly good laws. Meddling with things which do not need to be changed!

For Republicans, "progressive thinking" is a kind of dirty word. They believe liberal and progressive have more or less the same meaning. One is just as bad as the other it is not conservative!

I do realize liberal thinking can be in line with far left thinking. But for me I do not identify too much with the liberal side of the Democrat Party.

As an example, liberals might think we need to share the wealth or tax the wealthier more heavily. Liberals may believe we should provide ridicules levels of aid to average citizens with no concern for what that average person has given back to society! This for me is over the top and not correct thinking.

But progressive thinking is very different and has nothing to do with liberal thinking. Progressives are not about wild left wing thinking at all. Progressive thought is only about making the best choices. It is about making progress as a society!

The word progressive is a form of the word progress. Progressives just want to move society forward in the most progressive way to benefit the most people. Progressives are not against people being wealthy and they are not against corporations!

So, progressive policy is about make society work better through sensible changes. It is about making progress and definitely is not about being stagnant or unchanged. Progressives are looking to use smarter techniques. So we simply should be learning and adapting ourselves to our changing world!

In our society we constantly are faced with a change. Everything about society is changing and we tend to be progressing pretty much all of the time!

Don't you think Republicans have had their chances at controlling and structuring government? However they rarely bring anything new to society. They usually stay with older time tested values and the stability it brings. Republicans believe in keeping things unchanged and as they were!

They also are constantly trying to have less government to shrink the need for taxation of the wealthy and our corporations. But I do not know how you have a strong society without having good infrastructure and strong consumers? This is where Republicans are really going wrong. The values our parents and grandparents used may no longer work very well for us today!

Things are changing on a constant basis. Everything from cell phones and electronics, to cars, highways, and transportation, to occupations to the economy and healthcare or whatever, things keep progressing. Things are constantly changing around us, all of the time!

Now listen to this, if you have agreed with anything I have written about in this book then guess what, you yourself in some way are a progressive person. You probably live conservatively like I do, but you still want to move ahead. Well that is totally OK and it is essentially progressiveness!

For example, if after hearing how single payer provides medical care and avoids all of the expenses of the insurance companies, and if that sounds good to you, you are a Progressive person! If that makes sense to you because you see no reason to support a non-medical health insurance industry, to receive healthcare that is what progressiveness is!

If liability insurance coming to you through a small fee taken at the pump sounds good you are progressive. Or if you would rather fork out big money twice a year to insurance companies you are being a stubborn conservative Republican. So what are you?

If you believe Europeans live better than Americans and if you believe Europeans are a bit more sophisticated than the average American is, you probably are a little more of a worldly person! If you see the wisdom of supporting the government to better society through some structure rather than through ruthless commercialism and freewheeling behaviors, you probably are a progressive type person!

If you want proper screening before selling weapons that is progressive. If you believe supporting consumption rather than supporting corporations for a strong economy to exist then guess what, that is all progressive thinking!

If motivating kids with small changes to what they will get from life with an education makes sense that is all progressiveness. You really are a modern thinking person. You want to move forward!

I basically am a conservative person in my personal life. I watch what I do. But I believe conservative policy in government can be pretty backward thinking. Please do not support that when you find it!

WAR ON THE ECONOMY

I think we need a greater effort to pull the nation from the Great Recession of 2008. WWII helped the country get out of the Great Depression. FDR had fellow Democrats supporting his policies.

But that war represented a lot of government spending. Because of FDR, the new deal and the war we spent our way out of the Great Depression. We could spend our way out of the Great Recession by starting lots of infrastructure projects. We could improve our military and provide healthcare to our citizens!

Other nations have all improved their societies and their countries by modernizing. For example Europe, Japan and China all have high speed rail systems for their citizens to use! America does not!

The point I am trying to make to you is this. Massive government spending has pulled the nation out of numerous Recessions and Depressions! Today I believe we need to do now what we have done successfully in the past. We should not be afraid to spend our way out of this recession! We need a lot of government spending on a massive scale. We need to put people to work and we need to modernize the country! We also need to maintain our country.

I absolutely understand nobody wants to do deficit spending. If we are going to try it I believe we should be careful with how we spend our resources. Today we need an economic policy and a recovery plan but do not stop spending. That will only continue the contraction of the economy and would be the wrong policy to use!

The economy will just languish without government spending. I believe providing good healthcare to people would be one way to improve our economy, plus obviously improving the health of the nation along the way! That coupled with various infrastructure projects are what is needed!

Some Republicans believe the system will be able to self-correct. That would be the same old policy used in the Hoover administration.

Just hoping that the economy will come back rather than actually taking action to make it so. But with Republican inaction, while we wait for the economy to self-correct, we are going to lose a lot of good people! The economy will be bad.

So there I go again, talking just like a typical Democrat. We must do whatever we can to create consumption. We essentially need a war like effort on the sluggish economy! Lord knows we have tons of infrastructure problems to solve. We need to create jobs that pay well, but do not cost the government a fortune.

I am not in favor of the government spending $200,000 for each $50,000 dollar job we create. Our spending must be done with great care. We should not be wasteful.

In any kind of a recession or depression cutting spending is exactly the wrong policy to be doing! That policy would just add to un-employment, add to the cost of modernization and the expense of our social programs. In addition as we waist time our highways, bridges, power and water systems will just be declining further!

I am sure you realize unemployment actually costs us money too. Unemployment checks can run into a lot of money and you do not receive anything much from it. Businesses and contractors will be languishing when there is a lack of consumption.

As to tax cuts for working people, there little expense to giving tax cuts to working people. It is an efficient way to put more money into the economy. Just collect tax at a lower rate. That leads to more consumption and more commerce! The economy immediately improves!

Those lost tax revenues will usually come back to government a short period of time. They will end up getting collected by government from greater business activity. Greater consumption will ultimately create jobs in retailing and manufacturing.

All of this new business activity represents increased profits at the corporations and revenues for government. All because people, have more money to go out and consume.

So just do it. Either put people to work in efficient ways in make work projects, or allow working people extra cash in their pay checks by cutting there taxation! In my opinion, our problem is not that we are spending too much it is that we are not being very progressive when we hold back on lowering middleclass taxation!

Thanks to the Tea Party and Republican thinking, we are becoming too timid about taxing corporations and the wealthy at fair rates. As the divide between the wealthy and the middleclass continues to widen, why are we so afraid of taxing corporations just a little bit more to improve the overall economy?

I am not calling for a big increase on anyone. Perhaps only 1 to 1.5% is all that is needed. Get taxation back to the rates used in the early Clinton years makes a lot of sense to me!

Voters are smarter than you think. If we explain things, people will support the correct action! Corporations will more than make up for the cost of increased taxes through increased commerce.

A great example of progressive action was how we ended up putting great pressure on Middle Eastern oil producers through developing our own oil sources! I assure you fuel will stay down in price as long as we have the ability to produce oil cheaply here. This will benefit the economy greatly as we keep a cap on the cost of fuel!

We need so many things. We need roads and bridges and we need to rebuild schools. We need all sorts of improvements!

I believe we could be delivering fresh water to drier parts of the nation from the wetter regions. There is much water in the northwest; we could build water pipelines to Southern California as an example. Why just let that water flow away! We literally could have a war like effort on water supplies.

It could be any type of a large project. Simply identify the problem you want to solve and go after it.

If we wish to have a great nation, we must be willing to fund its operations and develop its recourses. We want to create the strongest economy we can create. We want a good and strong nation for our children!

Having said all that, low tax rates are naturally a good thing too! That is a secondary goal when it can be done responsibly.

I really want a strong and vital economy versus an under-taxed, lethargic and slow economy. I understand that a government supported by the people is what makes America the greatest nation on earth. We should not view government as being fundamentally bad?

I cannot say this enough to you we do need an overwhelming number of Democrats in government to make progress and improve the nation! Just give Democrats the time to correct the problems.

It takes dozen of years to solve ingrained problems. They are not going to go away in 4 years. It takes years and years of hard effort to correct problems.

We have very good economies *every single time* Democrats bring their policies to the government. Changing government policies does take time, exhibit a little patience and stay calm!

BEING HONEST
WITH YOURSELF!

For the purposes of this book I am trying to show you we all have to step back and think before we vote. We have to think about what really makes the nation better. Strong feelings can completely lock you in to incorrect thinking if you are not careful! So I had to ask, how can I convince people that the party they believe in and love is somehow flawed?

I know I must be truthful with my arguments. I know if I am not honest some Republican out there will catch me in something which is not accurate. I also know how hard it is to change someone's thinking. If they are really set in their beliefs can you change them? Is there any chance to get through to them? That really is what this book is all about.

Now I know some people are really set in their feelings. I know nothing I say will get through to people like that. If there is going to be any chance at all, readers must be 100% honest with themselves!

If impartial evidence is showing you that your party does not deliver good economies for America shouldn't you stop supporting them? It takes a very strong person to be able to change party loyalty. For Republicans, it goes against every belief they have to vote for a Democrat!

So now I am going to start on you. I am going to ask you, can you sight for me just one long lasting strong Republican economy? Simply ask yourself that very simple question. Was the economy ever good in a lasting way under any Republican Presidents ever? Simply and honestly answer that question. Was it ever good? Have Republicans ever given us lasting growth? Think back... Hmm? Well, if we did have a long lasting good economy, please name it for me!

Now, I know the one good Republican President you Republicans love to sight would be Ronald Reagan. Of course we will talk about him, but I want you to also be thinking about all of the other Republican Presidents too?

But first, did Reagan give us lasting growth? He did give us one term with good job creation. That represented a good economy. We also know Democrats blocked Supply Side Economics from coming in during his first term they controlled the House and Senate then. But when Reagan won re-election Democrats allowed his Supply Side Economics to come in because the people wanted to try it. President Reagans first term only created 1.43% new jobs!

We also know George H. W. Bush succeeded Reagan, and do you folks think he drastically changed economic policy from what Reagan was doing? Of course he was a fellow Republican.

I think the first President Bush continued President Reagan's Supply Side policies and his job creation numbers were very poor! The economy pretty much collapsed for him.

His new job creation number came in at just .62% new jobs created. That is a very bad job creation number and it indicates a collapsing economy. So we really did not have lasting growth with Supply Side Economics!

In President Reagan second term he had job creation averaging 2.69 percent new jobs created each year. I admit that is a good number for one term but to be regarded as a good economy shouldn't that go on for a while. In your mind does one lone 4 year period indicate lasting growth?

So I would have to say Reagans Supply Side Economics was not a good model for a strong LONG LASTING economy! Either the model was in fact flawed, or President Bush himself believed it was bad and changed policy. But I don't think that happened.

Either way he did not have a good economy based on the job creation statistics! I think George Bush Sr. was trying to use Supply Side Theory!

Since WWII Democrats have never had more than 8 years in a row in the Presidency. But their economies are always strong and growing economies.

Looking just at the statistics Democrats give Republicans growing strong economies every time when they are in the White House. Then Republicans bring policies in which are too conservative and it leads to contraction at best!

We know anyone can say anything. So I ask you to review the job creation charts from earlier in the book. We know commerce at Corporations, job creation and revenues flowing through to government are strong indicators of a good economy!

So you must have statistics like that confirming your party is good for our economy. You cannot blindly love your party simply because they carry the correct label. Your love for the party should be based on economic facts!

I do not see how you can love a party when they have only given you a onetime momentary pop in the economy! All of the other Republican administrations have been more than 4 times worse at job creation than Democrats!

We need more than love! There must be other indicators telling you that your Republican party gave us a good long lasting economy!

Did Ronald Reagan's Supply Side Economics in the end leave George H. W. Bush a healthy economy? I do not think so! So we must ask ourselves, did Supply Side Theory lead to the collapse of our economy? Well President Bush had such a bad economy that businesses saw no need to add jobs!

Additionally ask yourself this, if the economy were good why did voters leave the Republican Party after President George Bush's first term was up? Why would voters go to Democrats if Republicans were giving us good economies?

He had won the first Iraq war that alone should get anyone re-elected. Why would voters turn away from Republicans Hmm? You have to agree George H. W. Bush was a one term President. Why was that?

After Clinton came in the economy recovered, now why was that? He used Consumer Focused Economics! But when George W. Bush came in the economy went bad again. He was using conservative economic policies. Supply Side Economics! Hmm!

Now for President George W. Bush 17 of our nation's biggest banks, were on the verge of bankruptcy. GM and Chrysler were within a few weeks of going under. Housing was dead. Every aspect of the economy was in the tank with six million job losses to come!

Personal and commercial bankruptcies were happening left and right. George W. Bush had no job creation while he was in office!

So Hmm, did Republican President George W. Bush leave us a good economy that time?

So we would have to say looking at those two presidential runs, they both delivered weak or broken economies, right? President's Clinton and Obama have both brought the economy back! I must wonder how many Republicans out there are still thinking Republicans are good and Democrats are bad for the economy!

Let's talk about the Nixon/Ford economies. They ended very weak in job creation, and they both had high inflation too. Just look at the job creation statistics! Their economies declined badly based on those numbers. So now we are talking about three bad Republican economies right their!

Much as I hate to say it even President Eisenhower was not that good. He did balance the budget twice which is good but he did not have job creation in the end. This means he left us another weak economy!

His second term only had .9 percent new job creation. Nine tenths is again very bad job creation. When the evidence is staring you in the face; are you going to deny the truth just because you believe in Republicans?

Do not get mad at me I am just giving you the federal statistics. Please just be honest with yourself when you are looking at the statistics! They are what they are.

Will you continue to keep supporting a bad party regardless of the reality of what you get with them? When you are hit over the head with Republicans repeatedly making a mess of our economy is that never important to you?

We know Herbert Hoover had 8 years of Republican Presidents preceding him. In the end Republicans left us the Great Depression! I have not seen where any Republican President or run of Republicans have ever given us a good long lasting economy!

So now you know what the answers have to be concerning Republicans, but you are still going to be loyal to them, why? Why on earth? Don't kid yourself, please just be an honest person. You have to be honest about what is going on in the economy, in your country and with your party! It is all important stuff!

If Supply Side Theory and/or more conservative policies really work, how come we have never had a long-lasting strong economy when Republicans are using it? If Republicans are good why would we see they always cause the collapse the economy?

If Republicans were good, the economy should become stronger. People would see that happening and Republicans would be getting re-elected again and again. Republicans would win re-elected because they were doing a great job, and they had proper policies. But that does not happen for them!

If we are not supposed to tax the job creators to have a strong economy, then why have we not seen any job creation when George W. Bush and the Republican majority gave them tax cut after tax cut? The logical thing to do is look at politics with a critical eye. You might change your thinking!

Why was the economy in a near depression situation after eight years of George W. Bush? He had a Republican government helping him all the way.

The only thing Republicans ever said they wanted was to have complete control of the economy and of government! Well they had it with him?

Reasonably speaking how much evidence do you need to see? After watching politics for years now, I have learned Republican rhetoric talks to growth, but their policies actually bring us the opposite. We do not get growth with them! So why would you keep returning them to power?

How long are you going to believe in them? Basically until we see Republicans using Consumer Focused Economics we must not vote for them! Have we ever had a strong economy under any of the Republicans? It is just a very simple question for you to ponder. Honesty on your part is very much a requirement here!

Is what I am saying basically the truth? I know for some of you, voting for a Democrat is just a stomach turning and unacceptable idea. But considering all of the information with open eyes, don't Republicans deliver us contracting economies based on the fact there are no jobs being created?

If Republicans are doing harm to us and to our economy, shouldn't we hold our nose and vote for the best Democrat we can find? We vote for Democrats not because we like them, but because Democrats use policies which businesses like and it builds a strong economy.

You must vote for Democrats until such time Republicans adopt Consumer Focused Economic policies. They must abandon Conservatism!

Aren't 23 million jobs created by President Clinton a very good thing? President Johnson gave us the highest new job creation rate in the post WWII time period at 3.9 percent new job creation! President Carter gave us the second highest job creation rate. President Truman gave us the third best job creation rate.

President Obama has stopped the Bush collapse in the economy and is now adding jobs at a good rate. Several hundred thousand jobs are being created every month! Some have said they are not the best jobs, but at least we are growing. Everything really is negative when Republicans are in there. Those are just the honest and sad facts.

Democrat's good results have nothing to do with them being Democrat. It has everything to do with Democrats using correct economic policies!

Republicans could use the same policies if they wanted to. But I must ask why would you still be loyal to the Republican Party when they have such a bad record? That makes no sense, and honestly it fits more with ignorant stubborn Republican loyalty!

WELFARE

Now I hate to talk about welfare, because I know that is or was a Democrat inspired program which I feel had problems. Yes it was a well-intended program but I admit, it totally ignored human nature!

I do want to remind you right up front Welfare was reformed during the Clinton Administration. I think today it is a much smaller program than it was under President Johnson. But this is an example of how Democrats began a well-intended program with less than great results!

Under the current system I believe people are limited to five years of support. My understanding is they are allowed no more than three consecutive years in the system. I believe today it is more of a true safety net program instead of being just free checks forever!

I do not think society was served very well by having Welfare queens. Unfortunately we did have people just living off of their Welfare checks with no real incentive to find work. So those were the problems!

People should never think they are entitled to limitless monthly checks just because they are a woman in need. I believe a better solution, would be to move to a Workfare solution. I know there are literally millions of jobs that can be done. These are jobs which need to be performed and we taxpayers are already paying to have many of them done for us anyway!

Instead of just giving checks to people, give them a job to do. I would only make this type of work available to drug and crime free women with children under school age. I would ask people to give an honest day of work for an honest day of pay. Recipients should be expected to work at least three or four days per week, at the minimum wage, and only receive pay for the days they actually have worked!

If we did have a Workfare system, women with children might need daycare services for their own kids. If women have dependent children they will qualify for five days of free daycare being provided to them. With the goal of giving the recipient four days of work and one workday per week to look for a better job or take care of personal matters, etc. Workfare should not be a cushy living!

So what type of jobs might women on Workfare do? Well, we would start by trying to identify the motherly types to work at delivering daycare services to other Workfare recipients. But that is not the only thing these women can do. For every workfare recipient actually working in daycare, that will free up at least one other and maybe two women who can then work in other jobs!

Yes some jobs might involve daycare services to government employees, military families, or other Workfare recipients. Generally speaking, I would not allow recipients to work where their own children are in day care, unless it is a very small community with few options.

Those Workfare recipients not involved in daycare could be put to work maintaining parks, zoos, schools, Universities, hospitals, painting government buildings, directing traffic etc. There are hundreds of jobs which can be done by normal women and we do have the need! Pay them properly.

Each community will have its own particular localized jobs and needs. But why pay people, or contract for government services when you already have an available workforce? We could be killing two birds with one program!

People could work in hospital laundries, or they could work on maintenance in government facilities. Those women with better educations might help out in elementary schools, shadowing kids. Giving good one on one attention to kids is often needed for better results! Workfare jobs should feel like real jobs! Recipients must be good people themselves before they work with kids!

We know our schools are underfunded, poorly maintained and are always in need of maintenance. The schools need grounds keeping and general cleaning! Simply be creative with your ideas. People could work at just about anything!

Welfare as it was originally structured was not one of the Democrats' greatest creations. I personally believe society will always have women with children who do need help and a job. I believe we citizens should be willing to pay for and support a better society!

Giving people a job will build character into the person's life. It will show their children how life is supposed to go. It should show children that we all are expected to lead productive lives.

People ought to get used to getting up in the morning, cleaning themselves up and leaving for a job. I believe kids will be less likely to vandalize buildings and property if they see their own moms working with these properties?

In a nutshell, I believe Welfare should evolve into Workfare for the needy. Give people a job any job. But that is just my opinion. Those who will not work, I say simply cut them free. We do not need to be generous with the terminally unmotivated individuals.

USING OUR WISDOM

I believe we should use some of our acquired life's wisdom before we vote. It is very important to vote the correct way, and with full knowledge of what you are voting for. You should only vote for someone because you know beyond any doubt, that they are better for your country! Too often people just vote for who they like.

I think that is advice we all should take to heart. I personally believe as we age we usually do gain wisdom! So logic says you will support policies which lead to a strong America.

We must understand there is another very important part to wisdom. It is something which I can't transfer unto you magically. Correct thinking and true wisdom is very much a part of being able to *reason* correctly! You must be able to reason things out.

It is through the reasoning process, where we learn to take life's puzzle apart. We examine it and then reconstruct that puzzle into a picture we understand. We formulate our views. We adopt logical positions!

I believe that reasoning process is something which more concisely could be called the process of *deduction*. It is through reasonable deduction we form our beliefs. It is through reasoning and deduction we reach to our own level of wisdom!

With my years of life and time of watching people, I can tell you there are people out there who do not have the gift of reasonable deduction. For whatever reason some people are drawn to strange or backward thinking. It just seems to happen and I can't explain it. That is a situation that often exists with humans.

If I tell you about Republican or Democrat legislation or their positions, I typically will sight evidence in the public record backing up what I say! If I tell you a particular administration gave us a weak economy that will show itself in job creation, and in tax revenues generated to the government as well as high earnings at the corporations. It may be checked by doing internet searches, should you wish to check me!

I hope my book is not considered Democrat propaganda. I believe essentially the book is full of common truths, facts, and public information all coupled with my views, and an admittedly critical eye on Republicans. I assure you I am only interested in a strong American! I want what is best for the nation.

Unfortunately one reality seems to be, Republicans feel they must be totally different from Democrats on every single issue. It does not matter what the issue is it just should be different from Democrats!

Often Republicans wish to be so different that they will do absolutely idiotic things or doing nothing at all about a given problem. All done just to be seen as different from those hated Democrats!

Doesn't it make sense to you that sometimes there is a best policy? Not saying Republican or Democrat just a best way to address a problem? You would think both of our parties would occasionally agree and co-operate on fixing a given problem in the correct way.

But it seems to me regardless of what the issue is Republicans will always take the extreme opposite position for solving the issue. The two parties do not need to be totally different from each other 100% of the time. Sometimes we should be able to agree on what is right for society, the country and economy!

We know Consumer Focused Economics will give you a strong economy, because we have actually seen that under President Bill Clinton. We saw it under Presidents Carter and Johnson too. We had pretty good economies with Truman and now Obama.

I remind you the name of the game here is to create wealth for all people including the corporations. We want for everyone to be making money. Making money is a good thing.

I must now ask you this question? When was the last time you saw any Republican or Democrat point to federal job creation statistics? I never have seen very much of that. I do not understand why Democrats don't sight those statistics? They are good for Democrats.

Are Democrats embarrassed by them? Maybe there is a rule or something about not campaigning on job creation statistics that I am not aware of!

However, I am not restricted by any such rules if there are any. I am simply an author. We are all trying to find our political way here. We are all developing our loyalties and political beliefs. But job creation statistics show when you have a good economy and when you don't!

I did start life out as a fairly strong Republican. I am to an extent still a conservative person. But I also discovered there is much more to politics than just liking a party. I found that Republicans often do have mistaken values. I found they give us poor economies and sometimes they will even venture into dishonest behavior. It took me about 20 years to figure these things out!

I must ask you, if Democrats use a policy which clearly creates a strong economy, then Republicans want to do something totally different? That is simply nutty thinking! Why undo a policy which is working?

So I will say even though we may be conservatives at heart, I believe we usually want to be somewhat progressive by nature. In my case I think that is a normal way to live. We want to approach problems with the most effective solution possible!

Again today I do consider myself to be a strong Democrat. But it is more out of necessity than for any other reason. I would love to vote for Republicans. Democrats are not without their share of problems. I have learned I must accept that Democrats are not perfect, however they are better. They deliver better economies!

It probably took me 20 years to figure this political stuff out. It took me a while to learn that **"helping the middleclass helps the entire economy"**! That is the way you make the whole economy stronger. That is the reason I had to turn to Democrats; Republicans do not understand that the middleclass is the key!

Please do not think that I am in any way a blind Democrat. I do recognize the type of liberal thinking people the Democratic Party sometimes attracts. But what else can a person do? Democrats are the only ones interested in improving the lives of all Americans across the board. I am talking about the rich, the corporations and the middleclass!

All Americans ought to be able to enjoy peaceful and productive lives. At the same time I want you to know I do not believe at all in the redistribution of wealth philosophy. I also believe that tax burdens should fall more so on those who are not living near the edge of failure.

I am someone who loves that we enjoy the most freedoms of any people, anywhere. Teddy Roosevelt would love today's America for all of its freedoms. I believe he would be more in tune with current Democratic values rather than Republican values since he like Democrats was very progressive!

Keep in mind enriching the middleclass does not in any way limit business people from reaching greater success. In fact it creates a situation where business people may become even more successful. Businesses will have more customers with money in their store. That is always good for them.

Now any sensible economists will tell you it is easier to regulate the economy from the consumer side, rather than trying to control the economy from the supply side.

Simply allow people to keep more of their earnings, and then let them decide where to buy merchandise! Those vendors with the popular products will thrive. In a sense it still is a survival of the fittest economy but in a healthier way!

That is the primary differences between Supply Side Economics and Consumer Focused Economics. More money in circulation will heat up an economy. Less will cause the economy to slow down. I want to remind you if you need to slow the economy down simply raise taxes on the consumer!

That is the approach which was taken by Democrats and promoted by most economists. We have already seen how cutting taxes worked under President Clinton. It was successful. Then we saw what raising taxes on the middleclass did under George W. Bush!

Supply Side Theory is just that, it is a theory which to this day is still an unproven model for a successful economy. We have never had a good economy trying Supply Side Economics!

Actually Supply Side Theory has demonstrated it will bring collapses in our economy. As evidenced in particular by the George W. Bush economy as well as the George H. W. Bush economy and a whole host of other Republican administrations!

By contrast Consumer Focused Economics has easily used tools to slow down or heat up the economy. Giving tax breaks to the massive middleclass is like giving aid directly to the corporations. The profits from ongoing sales will exceed the income from momentary tax windfalls.

I don't agree with Republicans' and Tea Partiers' beliefs that any government at all in society is basically bad for America. I do not buy that. Unfortunately that issue has almost become a core belief for the Republicans, and especially for the Tea Party. For them government is always going to be bad!

So while Supply Side Economics might lower the price of a product in the market place which is a good thing, with that policy you usually are taxing the middleclass more. You are cutting the legs out from under the consumers with those additional high taxes. You end up creating tougher times in the economy and nobody wants that!

With Supply Side Economics you have no tools to control the economy. You are not dealing with consumers at all. You are only dealing with the manufacturers and the retailers. I say simply producing a product does not automatically give you people capable of buying it!

Simply the act of practicing Supply Side Economics will cause contraction in the economy. I guarantee you that you will get contraction when you stop supporting people's spending power!

With Republican economic policies the beginnings of a slow and lethargic economy are now in place. It does not happen immediately. It takes a few years to kill off an economy!

Voters did do the wrong thing for the economy by supporting what was considered popular Republican logic. Supply Side Economics just seemed like it should work!

You remember during President Clintons second term he was losing popularity. This was partly due to his personal morals, and partly because his tax rates were being portrayed by Republicans as being a little on the high side. Even though the overall economy was doing great!

The misguided public genuinely wanted changes and felt Supply Side Economics would be good. But the public was not correct in that thinking.

America you must be careful when you support tax cutting. You have to be careful because you might support the wrong kind of tax action. You might just be ruining the good economy we were enjoying!

Have you forgotten during the first two years of George W. Bush's Presidency, he and his Republican Congress had turned all of the positive economic indicators we had at the time, into negative indicators! All of them, GDP, interest rates, corporate profits, job creation rates, trade imbalances, our balanced budgets and inflation rates, etc. to name a few had all become collectively worse!

Do you remember how President George W. Bush pushed something called the Economic Growth, Tax Relief and Reconciliation Act of 2001? Do you remember that one? That basically was corporate and wealthy tax relief! What did we get from that? We got contraction in the economy and larger deficits!

450 economists opposed the George W. Bush era tax cuts in 2003. And there was never any job creation! I would say their opposition turned out to be accurate. Check the following links.

- http://en.wikipedia.org/wiki/Economic_policy_of_the_George_W._Bush_administration

and

- http://en.wikipedia.org/wiki/Economists%27_statement_opposing_the_Bush_tax_cuts

The exact same collapse which happened for George W. Bush happened for Presidents Reagan and George H. W. Bush. The time line was slightly different because of moderate Democratic opposition in the early Reagan years. Democrats knew it was a wrong policy for the long run!

You see, it was Democrat opposition which slowed President Reagan's Supply Side Economic policies from coming in. Ultimately his Supply Side Economics did come, and of course it did kill the economy. But it was George H. W. Bush who had to pay the price for the Reagan failed economic policies!

The situation with President George W. Bush was a little different, because he had a cooperative Republican government helping his Supply Side Economic efforts all the way! Hence Supply Side policies came in much faster.

We also had 4 additional years of bad policies compounding problems in the economy. The collapse happened quicker, and lasted just that much longer. It all ended up being much much worse! We got a near Depression out of those policies!

Now, Ronald Reagan's predecessor, Jimmy Carter, created jobs a full half percentage point faster than Ronald Reagan's best term. And Jimmy Carter was not even the best Democrat at job creation!

President Reagan's second term was his best term for job creation. The inflation Jimmy Carter had was already high and rising from Presidents Nixon and Ford. Do you remember how President Nixon actually had to use price controls on the economy to control inflation?

Here are my sources, search:

Economyinperspective.com/inflation

Yet in spite of all that, President Carter still managed to create 10.3 million jobs during his 4 years in office. That was because he was using correct policy! He had the second best job creation record in the post WWII era. We had job creation because President Carter made good changes in economic policy!

Now I realize we never want high inflation, I know that. But at least people had jobs and they could put food on the table etc.

President Carter's per year job creation rates were much higher than those of Presidents Nixon, and Ford whom he took over from. He greatly improved the strength of the economy!

So you cannot try to say his job creation rates were somehow due to Republicans because they gave him a poor economy! The economy was steadily collapsing with Republicans. Plus we had to deal with persistent high inflation.

So your beloved President Reagan did not create jobs as fast as President Carter did. Still you Republican supporters pretty much hate President Carter. Certainly not for the job he did on the economy.

President Carter added 3.06% new jobs each year of his Presidency. That is a very good number. While Ronald Reagan's best 4 years was at 2.69% new jobs created. That is good job creation but not as strong!

Ronald Reagan was the best Republican at job creation. President Reagan's worst term of job creation was only 1.43% new jobs created per year. That was in his first term.

In President Reagan's first term he had a lower job creation rate than all Democrat Presidents in history. All of them combined, clear back to 1920! How can you think Republicans are better for the economy?

Again these are easily checked figures with regards to job creation. Simply Google:

Job Creation by U.S. Presidents

As disliked as President Jimmy Carter may have been by some, his job creation percentage was far better than the master of Supply Side Economics! Now what does that say to you? Might you possibly believe Democrats are not that bad for the economy?

People you must be honest with yourself on these economic matters. You must admit Democrats are pretty good for the economy!

Well I would agree most Americans think of President Reagan as a good President. I do believe he was liked. He did do some very good things for the country. While President Carter is often disliked, I have to scratch my head because I really do not know why people would feel that way!

I hate to be harsh but what President Reagan ended up giving us was what turned out to be a flawed policy and another economic disaster. It was simply a version of financial suicide. He did not understand and appreciate the importance of having a healthy middleclass!

By the end of the George H. W. Bush Presidency, job creation had come to an effective end. The economy was again collapsing, just as it collapsed under Presidents Eisenhower, Nixon/Ford and how it collapsed for George W. Bush!

President George H. W. Bush had little job creation success. There was only 0.62% new job creation in his entire four-year Presidency. He created only 3.4 million jobs over 4 years. Then President George W. Bush had no job creation at all! My source is the same source.

Job Creation by U.S. Presidents

We have gone over the job creation statistics. There is a very strong job creation advantage for Democrats. Did you hear that Newt? Job creation is stronger under Democrats than under Republicans. That hardly is indicative of food stamp societies!

Government must use correct economic policy and voters must think correctly before they vote. You should support parties who understand how economics really works.

If the consumer is feeling more in the money, that consumer is more likely to go out and purchase the vehicles, the appliances, cars, furniture, clothing and vacations etc. the things the middle-class needs in the course of living their lives. They will keep on consuming!

One also has to wonder whether or not corporate tax cuts will be used for expansion of their businesses. Possibly it will, but maybe not. Just as often that money flows to the bottom line of the company's books in the form of profit which is where it can stop!

At any rate, corporate tax cuts are a poor way to create jobs. That money may not do anything at all other than to inflate the profit picture for the company. It kind of creates a misleading picture of a strong company! A corporate tax cut will not be close to 100% efficient.

Now, listen to this we know businesses will always have the fewest number of employees on hand as is possible. That would be a natural thing for businesses to be as efficient as possible. That is a normal reality of operating a business.

Another way to think about it is this. If I give businesses a tax cut have I done anything to increased their commerce or add to their business model, of course not! How has a corporate tax cut increased the buying power of the people who are your customers or stimulated your business?

By giving out corporate tax cuts, I have just given the corporations a way to stay profitable, without having to actually work for it. This basically is a windfall tax break. This is what Republicans always want to do. I understand they want to help the corporations and the wealthy but that is not helping the middleclass or any other part of the economy!

If your business was sick before, in all likelihood it will still be sick tomorrow. Even though you have gotten a tax cut, and you can stay more profitable in the poor economy you are still sick. That hardly is the best use of tax cuts!

So from the cost to government stand point, tax cuts given to the middleclass will allow them to have better lives. When the middleclass is spending that ought to benefit the corporations and add to commerce as well. More entities are helped!

Increased commerce creates the pressure to hire still more individuals. Jobs are created. Ever increasing commerce equals more money chasing products. It makes the overall economy stronger in the process. Commerce is our goal! You see, Consumer Focused Economics creates natural forces to move the economy forward. This is the right way to grow the economy!

We Americans must stick up for proper policies when regulating the economy. We should always work on building the economy up.

Do we have a really good economy today? The answer is not really super good. Do we have full employment? Not even close. Do we wish to have more commerce in society? Yes more commerce is what we need. President Obama has been creating jobs and shrinking deficits, even though Republicans constantly oppose and hinder his efforts!

Current Republican economic policies do not match very well with what Teddy Roosevelt's economic approach would have been. Voters should be wise and not support Republicans as long as they are trying to help the job creators over helping the middleclass! They fundamentally do not understand economics.

Fortunately for Democrats, the Bush collapse came while George W. Bush was still President. There basically was no way to blame the Democrats for the collapse. Which they surly would have done if they could! Republicans created the collapse completely on their own.

Republicans had to delay as much of the collapse as was possible to put more of it on the new Democratic President. Then Republicans actually said the recession should be fixed in just 12 months! Are you kidding me?

Bush gave us a near Depression economy. You should remember it took seven years for FDR to turn the economy with the help of the outbreak of a World War helping the economy. The George W. Bush collapse has been a huge problem, affecting core parts of the economy!

President Obama had to ride the George W. Bush's sick economy all of the way down. He literally had to completely rework the economy. He had to restructure and support the banks. He enacted Wall Street Reforms. He gave loans to auto manufacturers. He did many things. He spent government resources funding the economy!

President Obama did not create the crash, but he has had to deal with problems. I think he has been doing a pretty good job! But Republicans will try to tell you President Obama botched the recovery.

My god, have you already forgotten how Republicans put our economy in the tank? Then they have the nerve to blame Democrats for a slow recovery?

Republicans know if the economy remains sick, they will have an easier time winning in the next election. So you need to see through these things! You need to know what Republicans are working for.

I believe the best way for us to solve this sick economy is we need an overwhelming majority of Democrats in government. Democrats always do a good job with the economy even with the small number of Democrats they have.

Not having obstructionist Republicans to deal with would be helpful! I hate to be blunt about it, but that is reality. Those Republicans are not co-operating at all.

Obviously with an overwhelming majority of Democrats that will then put them squarely in a position that they are responsible for the recovery and the economy. Democrats will not be able to blame Republicans for lack of co-operation. I believe that would be a good situation too!

Sometimes I think a parliamentary system might work better for America than the Democratic system does. At least we would have one party in total control of government at any one time! And that party can use their policies without opposition. Majority rules!

Today, even while the economy is still a little sick we are improving. But we have a long way to go. Shouldn't Democrats have an unrestricted chance to improve the economy using their own policies?

We know Republicans really need the one thing that the average American has. They desperately need the people's vote. I can tell you they will do anything and say anything, to get your vote away from you, regardless of how outlandish it is! Please do not allow yourself to be take advantage of.

Here are examples of Republican misleading misinformation. Do you remember when Newt Gingrich said he can bring us $2.50 cent gasoline? Well guess what that has happened without his help. Do you remember how he said he wanted to build a moon base?

Michele Bachmann said she could give us $2.00 gas? That has happened too! Are you going to give them your vote for just saying things like that?

Listen, I am not telling you to love Democrats at all. You do not have to agree with me or Democrats! You do not have to become a liberal person. You only have to love America, and want what is best for our country. We must look at politics with open eyes!

Everybody wants a strong economy. Above all, you should not tolerate a party that places their party or any corporation over the good of the nation!

We do need to have decent livable wages being paid in America. We need safe work places and reasonable labor laws. The system should be structured. It should be fair and it does need to be controlled. We know corporations will take advantage of the little guy if they are allowed to run free!

We should understand the wisdom of having government. Things like public education, police departments, fire departments, libraries a strong military and so on are what makes a nation worth living in. We should have a good constructive government creating jobs, commerce and generating revenues for the country!

We should have a good workable healthcare system in this country. Developed nations all around the world do have national healthcare systems! Having a strong government is normal and we should be OK with supporting it.

When the overwhelming evidence shows you Republicans always leave us declining commerce we must remember that. When Democrats give us a growing economy with lots of job creation we must appreciate that. When profits at our companies and corporations have never been better you can't deny Democrats have better economics. When the government is better funded, we want that too because as a nation we do want to be paying down our debt. That all is correct and responsible!

We really need to look for and then support conservative Democrats who believe in protecting the middleclass. Doctors, Lawyers and professionals of all types, will make more money if there are more well off middleclass people to be served.

That is all there is to this discussion. I do not know how else to argue this. We should love our American system not hate that we have a government. We should help the government and support policies which have a record of being successful!

We must be behind the idea, that it is totally OK for businesses to make good money. I have no problem with that. It should also be O.K. that the people who work in a company have good lives too! Everyone understands that working people are not going to have as much money as business owners. We all understand businesses are operating in a competitive environment!

Don't you think we want people to be happy, earning enough money to enjoy a good life and support the commerce of the nation! I believe we have a responsibility to ourselves and to the nation to develop the proper perspective about politics and economics. Don't waste your vote supporting policies which just weakens the nation! You really have to pay close attention to the political system!

Donald Trump is just spewing comments about what he does not like. Well there are tons of things none of us like! But explain to us what you will do for America. Anyone can gripe!

The focus in life should not be about being on top and holding others down! Rather it is about building the prosperous society we want to live in, and where we want our companies and our employees to be tomorrow! How can we maximize that experience? How can we better the system while not sacrificing our own life, or any ones business at the same time! How can we preserving every ones happiness in the process!

PROPER POLICY

It really has been due to Republican policies that we have acquired so much of our debt! Have you ever stopped and thought about that?

Believe it or not President Obama and the Democrats have not given us that much debt! Not only did Republican policy ruin the economy under Presidents Reagan, George H. W. Bush and George W. Bush. Republican policies pretty much have ruined the economy for President Obama too!

Can you believe Republicans are proudly saying how they are not co-operating with President Obama! Why would Republicans be proud of not co-operating with a sitting President when he is creating Iobs and a stronger economy? Why are Republicans proud of creating gridlock?

Republicans keep hoping they can make Supply Side Economics work again. They are hooked on that policy!

You see Republicans actually saw how the economy improved with their own eyes! They saw an improvement with President Reagan and thus they are sold on that policy as a working model for the economy.

But what Republicans are not thinking about is Supply Side Economics only lasted for a short three years or so. They are not thinking about the reality of what that policy brought! It delivered a pop in the economy on the way to serious collapse.

Republicans have fallen in love because it gave the momentary illusion of a strong economy. I say the illusion is so strong it has even fooled most Republicans!

I feel I must be honest with you and say, while I do not love everything about the Democratic Party I do pretty much dislike everything there is about Republican methods for the economy.

They really do not stand up for the middleclass! They refuse to do the correct policies to bring growth to the economy.

When you have a strong middleclass, you will have a healthy business and professional class. Everyone does better when average people are doing well!

Those two things go hand in hand! According to Consumer Focused Economics, you do tax the middleclass more when you wish to slow the economy down. We know taxing the middleclass more does slow the economy because that is exactly what George W. Bush did with our economy!

OK I feel I have argued this enough. Reality has shown us that Democrats really are good for the Economy, while Republicans cause the economy to contract. Friends this subject is not rocket science.

Everyone clearly sees the ups and downs of the economy in the job creation statistics! Economic policy will always remain an important issue to the nation.

Teddy Roosevelt knew the middleclass was the reason the trust had become powerful. Just like the corporations in today's world are very strong. President Roosevelt knew a strong middleclass would build the strength of the entire economy faster than a weak middleclass.

Republican Teddy Roosevelt knew the trusts needed to be limited for the good of the trusts themselves. We must control them for their own long term good.

After the trusts were broken up they created even more wealth for the people at the top. We want corporations to be both powerful, responsible employers, long lasting but always in a constructive way!

Therefore I see no value in allowing corporations to buy our elections. There ought to be rules that prevent corporations from excessively funding campaigns. I see no good reason for that. I personally believe the corporations should be content to not have much of a political voice as long as they are not being taxed out of business!

I am not necessarily a Sanders supporter but in some ways I think Bernie Sanders has the right idea. Corporation must be limited for the good of the nation and for the corporations themselves!

Another reason to not support Republicans is this. They will use the weak economy, which they have created as an excuse to remove government programs and services from the people. In fact Republicans view weak economies as a good situation!

When you think about it, a weak economy provides a great reason for the removing of programs from the government and the people! This is the unspoken rule Republican tacitly live by. It is one of the few ways Republicans see they can give the corporations a little less expense and a little more profit.

We always want strong economies. I say, hold your nose and find the most conservative and progressive thinking Democrat you can find. I am not saying Liberal Democrat I am saying forward thinking Progressive Democrat. Changing for the better is always good policy!

I do not care that Democrats are seen as regulating the economy too much. A strong economy with proper regulation is more important to me. I believe overall regulation strengthens the entire system!

Democrats have given the country balanced budgets two and a half times more often than Republicans! That is also just a hard fact! So I think this is another illusion Republicans would like you to believe. They want you to think they are more responsible!

I will tell you Democrats always take over weak economies from the Republicans. Then they restore the economy and giving us strong economies in their place! Imagine that, those hated Democrats are giving America more job creation than Republicans according to impartial federal statistics. But Republicans will still tell us, Democrats are bad for the economy.

Folks please believe the federal job creation statistics. It is good honest information!

Could it possibly be that Democrats have growth policies that actually work? They give us policies which the economy itself reacts well to. That is not a bad thing is it? Democrats just happen to be giving us strong economies!

In my opinion Republicans do have an unreasonable hatred of President Barack Obama and the Democrats. It is really unfounded in the facts and statistics surrounding the economy. Most of our allies have very positive feelings about President Obama and the way he is doing things!

I for one believe President Obama has been a very good President. I thank him every day for bringing us the Affordable Care Act.

I know he is well regarded in the world community. I am proud of that also and I am not embarrassed to have him as my President!

I understand Republicans believe corporations are carrying too much of the burden. Republicans are sure corporations and the wealthy are paying enough as it is. Republicans feel the corporations will not survive a higher level of taxation. All of that is untrue! Corporations will prosper more with higher taxation because the economy thrives when the middleclass is supported and taxed less!

Until Republicans adopt policies which work how can we vote for them? Republicans give federal money directly to the corporations and the wealthy. I want to give the corporations more commerce so they can earn their place in society!

THE POWER OF
THE ECONOMY!

O K, we need to look at how big money really is affecting American politics. Some people understand Corporations make more money when the middleclass is doing well. While other individuals are so focused on what they must pay in taxes that they completely lose sight of how much money can be made when we are enjoying as strong economy!

Business people often have very short-term views of the economy! Business people do not look ten, five or even just two or three years ahead. They look mostly at current profits. For they are not sure if they will be employed if results are not good in this fiscal year!

Corporate leaders must answer to share-holders today. Current profits often take precedence over long-term stability. I think Republicans totally understand the thinking which many corporate executives have!

I believe Democrats are looking out more for the *long term* well-being of companies. Safe existence in the long run takes precedence over immediate short-term profits amongst most Democrats.

Those executives who feel the pressure of performing well right now will support the politicians who can give us an immediate kick to bottom line profits. Those who are thinking about stable growth will be more concerned in having dependable structure to the economy and customers with money. For some companies it becomes a situation where they need tax cuts on a yearly basis just to continue to deliver strong profits!

We need to look at where corporations are putting their money in the campaigns. Well according to published statistics, I was somewhat surprised to see both parties appear to receive corporate support!

Microsoft for example is a company where ongoing computer and software sales lead to repeatable business activity and profits! Microsoft has supported mostly Democratic campaigns in the Pacific Northwest. I think Microsoft is planning to be around for a while!

Phillip Morris (A.K.A. Altria) on the other hand is not sure of it has a future? Altria is to my knowledge a company involved in the tobacco industry and the selling of cigarettes. They are donating primarily to Republican candidates. The executives at Altria are more interesting in current and immediate profits!

Mitch McConnell of Kentucky, Richard Burr of North Carolina, Roy Blunt of Missouri, and former congressman Eric Cantor of Virginia are good examples of those politicians receiving corporate support from Altria. Given all of the information surrounding smoking, those corporations need friends in congress!

So where do you want to come down on this. Do you believe in playing for the long term good of industries and the country? Or do you play for the short-term killing to be made today?

When I started researching this I thought I would find more Republicans getting money from corporations. But what I found was a somewhat even split between the parties. I often find that corporations are covering their bases by supporting both parties.

One thing that is still disturbing to me is the amount of money being spent on lobbying. Recently we saw how Big Money is responsible for the lobbying of the FDIC in the guaranteed exotic derivatives which have been prohibited under the Dodd/Frank Wall Street reforms but Republicans are trying to bring this craziness back!

Both parties are lobbied. However Republicans definitely want less government regulation. Republicans want less oversight with fewer rules and restrictions. I say this is unhealthy for the little guy. Wealthy Republicans can and will make money easier when there is little regulation. With less regulation you and I will be responsible for bailing the big banks out again!

Bernie Madoff's famous Ponzi scheme found fertile ground when there was no oversight. This is the kind of thing that the Dodd/Frank Wall Street Reforms was trying to catch. Republicans are all about loosening the system up. While Democrats are trying to keep the system on the up and up!

Doesn't it seem odd to you that Democrats are the conservative people when it comes to business activities, operations and oversight! This is another of the many Republican illusion. Republicans want you to believe they are bringing us stable government and safe laws! But they really are not, that is an important thing and it comes with Democrats!

Keep in mind the big money people are the people who do have the money advantage, obviously. They have more resources and connections to other wealthy people. So we have this constant battle between those who believe we need more oversight, and those who want less. Republicans want to bend the rules and make more money today, usually by taking advantage of what the system offers!

This is where the old saying, "the rich will get richer" comes from. With Republicans you will often get business activities, which can get out of control!

In reality it is Democrats who are the ones that are trying to create opportunity and preserving fair play. Democrats want for all people to be able to make money! Keep in mind it is also Democrats who are giving you growing and expanding economies. Democrats are not hindering commerce at all.

I believe wealthy people figure they can still make a killing today with Republicans, while at the same time they know Democrats will come in and maintain the system when they gain power. So because of Democrats there will in fact be a long term future for the entire economy. In effect the conservative Democrats with long-term conservative policies and practices are giving the greedy, short-term Republican players a way to survive and then abuse us all more in the future!

The little guy maintains the system at their expense, while the greedy take advantage of loopholes around the edges and make a killing when Republicans gain power! So that is how the system works. It is the little guy who keeps the system functioning with their Republican created tax payer guarantees!

Now as more evidence of the wealthy supporting Republicans we have people such as Sheldon Adelson (Las Vegas casino owner) Harold and Annette Simmons, Bob and Doylene Perry, Joe and Marlene Ricketts, Peter Thiel, Jerrold and Margarette Perechio, Robert Mercer, John and Marlene Childs, Foster and Lynette Friess, Paul

Singer donating to Republicans. These wealthy people have vested interests in seeing Republicans elected!

Collectively according to the article I read about big campaign donors, these 10 Republican donors have contributed 134.6 million dollars to Republicans and their causes in the 2008 election. Then you have the Koch Brothers who everyone knows are also mega donors to Republican causes. They do their contributions and work through numerous Republican PAC's, or Political Action Committees.

Did you hear how the Koch brothers announced they will be donating about 900 million dollars to Republicans causes this election! I cannot believe this kind of campaign donations would be allowed. But that is what the conservative Republican Supreme Court is allowing!

I do not like naming people. But the information I used here is available off of the Internet. Simply Google "Republican mega donors" the information is right there for you too!

By contrast, the ten largest Democrat donors only contributed 46.1 million dollars. That is about a third as much. I do not even like to see big money contributions to Democrats. "In My Opinion" there is no place for large donations in politics! But I know the Supreme Court has ruled on this.

Now as I have said, I am not against the wealthy at all. I believe in helping all people, but always in the right way. You help the wealthy more, by keeping the middleclass strong. We help the middleclass so those wealthy individuals can make even more money! For some reason people are not understanding that the big money is made when you have a strong economy through a strong middleclass!

Businesses really need to appreciate how strong the business environment has been under Democratic administrations. They need to understand how weak it has been under Republican administrations. My God just look at and appreciate what happened in America after George W. Bush and his Republican Congress were in there. We know they completely destroyed the economy for everyone!

I feel we need a major education effort directed at all Americans and especially at corporate America. We need to educate the people about the big economic picture! That can be accomplished best by showing the facts.

If businesses did great under President Clinton why are businesses not supporting Democrats today? If business was terrible under President George W. Bush we should learn from those mistakes!

Many corporate people and the wealthy are buying into the Republican arguments lock, stock, and barrel. The economics I'm talking about is not just adding and subtracting dollars, it is the process of understanding how money moves around within the economy. It is understanding human nature!

I will prove to you that what I am saying about Republicans is in fact true. Wouldn't you hate to be getting life's voting decisions wrong for all of your adult life?

For example, you cannot deny Republicans recently destroyed the economy. That is just a fact of life. But I know there are Republicans out there who do not acknowledge anything bad happened under President Bush!

We could call it the George W. Bush economic recession. Republicans must take responsibility for what their governance has brought! Republicans had the White House and both houses of Congress and ran the economy off a cliff. They had no excuses for the economy!

You may complain about what President Obama is trying now, but honestly the economy is not collapsing either. So your hatred of President Obama is just more thoughtless hatred of Democrats. It is not based on poor economics or any factual information or bad policies! It is just unsophisticated hatred!

Sure, President Obamas actions may not be perfect in every respect, but at least he is bringing us a growing economy. It could be much worse.

My intent with this book is to show you how Republicans do not act on behalf of anyone. They do not bring the country a more prosperous America! Nor do they act with consideration for the long-term wellbeing of the business community.

Please learn how Republican Supply Side Economics is harming America. The hard evidence is in the job creation statistics.

Ten years of Republican policy is plenty of time for Republicans to bring us a stronger economy if they had the right policies. I say ten years because Republicans were in control of the economy from nearly half way through the Clinton Presidency to year 7 of George Bush's stay in the White House!

Remember first we have to be able to recognize the problems. If you can't see problems with Republican governments you are not paying attention! We also have to be able to recognize the truth when it is right in front of us. Just be honest with yourself, and look at the facts with open eyes.

How many of you lost your jobs, your homes and/or your businesses or commerce activity under President Bush? George W. Bush was a disaster for our economy. I hate to be critical of the man because who am I compared to a former President of the United States but we must admit that is the history of what happened!

The point I am trying to make is Republican rhetoric will win elections for Republican candidates. I completely understand that. I recommend that you not listen to their rhetoric but focus on what they actually have done or accomplished and what the future direction is likely to be!

My simple view of Republicans is this: come hell or high water, they will keep selling or trying Supply Side Economics as long as they can. They are determined they can make that policy work again! But we should keep in mind we have never seen lasting growth with that Supply Side Economics.

If people are not working, but corporations have profits, that is all that is important to Republicans. Hey, not having work is your problem, not Republicans and not the corporations either. Are these the type of leaders our country needs!

I think now is a good time to add, I am not against building a better business environment. I am 100% for prosperity! Having strong profits and being responsible employers are all important to me. I just happen to believe those things happen better when correct policies are being used.

Supply Side Economics is based on misguided principles, which then become coupled to misguided policy! Do not fall for it.

Under George W. Bush we did have a total collapse of the economy. He was lowering taxes for corporations as much as he could get away with. Are you starting to get this now? Low taxes does not equate to profits. A lot of commerce is what equates to large profits!

So as a business person would you rather have a small percentage off of your tax bill, coupled to a lethargic economy? Or would you rather have customers in your store where you can be making another 15% to 50% in profits from those sales! Not to mention the benefits of conducting business in a strong economic environment.

A growing business environment creates an inherent need for additional hiring, because businesses are more active. It stimulates and maintains manufacturing. For government it reduces the need for unemployment, for food stamps, for school lunch programs and other services.

It takes burdens away from government. It is how we got to surpluses in the economy! All of this increased commerce and hiring eventually makes it possible to cut back on taxation.

When you want more commerce, all you have to do is lower the tax burden on the middleclass. If you should ever need to slow the economy because it is over-heating, simply place taxes back upon the middleclass. That is how Democrats control the economy!

I feel the retired wealthy are more affected by higher taxes. So the moneyed donors are still supporting Republicans. However if your income sources are affected positively with a strong economy, you really should support Democrats. Even though Republicans might cut your taxes a little, you will have greater income with Democrats and the strong economy which they bring to us!

Understand job creation closely mimics the strength of the economy. In my opinion, it is the single best indicator of where we are at, with our economy. When we see job creation it directly says we have a good, strong and expanding economy! Or when there is no job creation it tells you the economy is not good. The statistics are real, and they are not an illusion!

Job creation statistics are literally the pulse of the economy. We do want to have a healthy pulse rate don't we? We do not want a pulse rate so slow we are wonder if our economy is dead or alive? If we want to feel that pulse in a strong and healthy way we must use Consumer Focused Economic policies! That is all there is to this discussion!

REPUBLICANS NEVER HELP THE MINIMUM WAGE EARNER!

Do you remember how for seven years when George W. Bush was President, Republicans did not raise the minimum wage even onetime. It was not until Democrats regained control in the house when the minimum wage finally was raised!

President Obama has stated that full time minimum wage workers should not have to live with federal assistance, and below the poverty line! Does the last 2 paragraphs say anything to you? Democrats are trying to help those earning minimum wage?

I also believe President Obama was trying to make the point that people should be able to take care of themselves in a minimal way, if they have a full time job. He was not saying it would be a good life, but at least living without government assistance!

Think about this for a moment, many Wal-Mart employees receive food stamps and other forms of government assistance while working their jobs? Why should tax payers subsidize Wal-Mart's low pay? Wal-Mart is one of the wealthiest corporations on earth. The Walton family is worth well past 100 billion dollars! They also do not need to employ as many part time positions as they do.

Most of us have worked in minimum wage jobs at some point in our lives. We know it is difficult to make a go of it at that wage level. Today many mature workers are stuck in minimum wage jobs! So the question becomes should we really allow our system to subsidize America's largest corporations?

Republicans had total control of government and they could have done something, but they just did not want corporations to pay workers a proper wage. We know the cost of living did not stop rising during those Bush years! Minimum wage workers would never get a raise under Republicans if they were not removed from office, once in a while.

I wish to say we do have corporations like Home Depot and Costco who will pay their workers better than minimum wage and they are very successful companies. If a company like Wal-Mart will not allow their employees to organize then I believe it is up to government to do something! There should be a law that states as you gain employees certain minimum pay standards must be met.

Perhaps raising the pay for minimum wage earners by .50 per hour above once you have 500 employees? Then by .75 when you are over 5000 employees and so on! I do not feel I am being hard on the corporations here. Once you employ 50,000 employees you would be at least $1.00 higher than minimum wage and so on!

I believe health care should be provided to all employees and it would be with a single payer system! If you are a part time worker your health care will be based on the hours of work you perform. If you are half time your healthcare benefit will be half the size of a full time employee.

Having that law would remove any incentive for the employer to hire part time workers. Two half time workers will still cost you the same amount of money for medical coverage as one full time worker!

Paying minimum wage workers better are key ingredients which create a booming economy. Additionally when Wal-Mart pays better they will attract a higher quality employee! Every time we have a higher minimum wage being paid we see more commerce. Wal-Mart will benefit from the additional commerce!

President Clinton warned Republicans to not change tax policies and start deficit spending. But Republicans did not listen. We were right back to the same old policies of massive deficit spending!

Had President Clinton's tax rates and surplus's been left alone, I am sure we could eventually have seen tax cuts for corporations. Our national debt would be much less today!

In the final years of the Clinton Presidency voters were putting Republicans back into government in larger numbers. Republicans were campaigning on the issue of trying to cut taxes since government was collecting more money than was actually needed. But Democrats were doing the responsible thing, by trying to pay down the national debt!

Doesn't it go without saying if we wish to pay down the debt we do need to run surpluses? We need to collect more than what is needed just to run the government. How can you support a party when it does not look out for the long-term wellbeing of the nation? Isn't guiding the nation to prosperity the primary function of government?

I do not want for anything to be given to me. We all should expect to be responsible in our own life. I only want that we get organized for the collective good of society. Before you give your vote to Republicans please be aware of what they are doing to the economy. Republicans are not looking out for the little guy they are just trying to enrich the corporations, and they are not achieving that goal!

REPUBLICANS AND
THE UNIONS

Now, let's give a quick look at the relationship between the unions and Republicans. I believe it is pretty common knowledge Republicans work against the unions. Republicans view unionization as troublesome to the economy! They view unions as demanding too much from Corporations!

So this is another area where Republicans are not on the right side of middleclass working people! The illusion is they want you to think they are with the people and for stronger commerce! But they are protecting the corporations!

I wish to remind you it is because of the existence of unions, that workers are treated fairly! But I also admit unions need to be somewhat controlled. Unchecked unions can literally break our corporations! Likewise corporations will take advantage of workers if unions are without any power. So I believe we must find a proper balance here.

Republicans have always claimed union demands are unreasonable. Yet here we are today the corporations are still making money, and unionized workers for the most part are still earning fair wages. The system and our country, has not collapsed because of unions.

The system does seem to work better when the unions do have enough power to not be taken advantage of. But by the same token, not so much power as to cripple their employers. That is not good either!

I do believe Republicans try to take away the power of the unions. I am convinced President Teddy Roosevelt would have been more on the side of workers in preserving their bargaining power and maintaining fair employment practices in this argument.

Democrats do side with the unions where Republicans side more so with the corporations. This fact clearly says to me Republicans are on the side of business and not interested in the little guy!

President Teddy Roosevelt completely understood the wisdom of maintaining a strong middleclass. That is my goal also! In my view the one thing you should never do is completely take away one sides power to negotiate or over empower the other side's strength!

Republicans do miss a key point. What good does it do for businesses to have a low tax environment or less labor expenses, if they must then deal with weakened consumers? That is a huge problem for any business! Having fewer customers weakens business activity and Corporations ability to make a buck.

I do think state and federal salaries pull the rest of society along. Our pay becomes better usually because state and federal worker pay improves. Better pay throughout society leads to greater commerce. You end up with a good and strong economy. The trick is to not let inflation get started nor over tax corporations!

So we do not want to be antiunion and we do want to be pro-commerce! We do want to protect the Corporation's capability to be profitable. The proper stance is not to be against or for either side but to work for fair wages!

Taking collective bargaining powers away from state workers in Wisconsin was an unreasonable power grab by Republican governor Scott Walker in Wisconsin. That will have a negative effect upon that economy there. Everyone's salaries will drift lower, and commerce at corporations will ultimately weaken if this becomes widespread.

You should remember weakening the consumer or the union in this case will not be felt in the economy for several years. It takes that long for people's savings to be tapped out!

The Tea Party is very much behind this assault on government programs and worker rights. Governor Walker of Wisconsin is a Tea Party Governor. He is trying to take America backwards to the bad economic times.

He claims we need to reign in state workers in order to balance the state budget. Even though state workers have already agreed to give back many things that were in their new contract, to make the overall economy stronger and not weaken the state government.

Governor Walker just wanted to remove collective bargaining from the equation. He wants to weaken all unions and in his mind strengthen the profitability of Wisconsin corporations in that way.

This is what Republicans want for the economy. Seems to me unions in this case were being the responsible ones. The state workers were well aware the state was in a huge budgetary bind. They were willing to give back some of their salaries to help the state survive!

I tell you the Tea Party and Republicans wish to weaken the unions and lower living standards for all Americans. I do not see how moving in that direction benefits commerce, the economy or job creation!

Remember that the state employee unions include police, firefighters, schoolteachers, some hospital workers and various department workers such as highway dept., utility and office workers. Those state workers are being told it is they who must balance the state budget on their backs.

State workers are actually a large part of the economy. Scott Walker was not asking corporations to pay anything at all. In fact he was cutting their taxes!

If a Democrat dares to say anything about Republican actions Republicans will claim Democrats are promoting class warfare. Democrats are trying to stick up for the little guy and maintain the economy!

I certainly realize times are tough for businesses. The unions know that! Everyone knows unions have to control their side of the bargain. But having basic collective bargain protects all workers.

I believe we will never see unionization at the nation's largest employer Wal-Mart, if the public through our government, does not require Wal-Mart to unionize. Wal-Mart is making many billions of dollars each year off of the backs of low-paid workers and they will not allow unionization.

Wal-Mart employees are not being paid a livable wage. Wal-Mart should take care of their people and their employees properly. The world largest corporation should pay their workers more than the minimum wage allowable in each state!

Government policy should always be with creating more commerce. That is the target we all have. Taking collective bargaining away has an element of unfairness to it and does not strengthen commerce. Collective bargaining ensures certain minimal standards are maintained!

Republicans desperately need your vote but they do not stand up for the average worker. They will portray themselves as conservative people with sensible views, policies, and values. I say that is not accurate. I consider this book to be a fairly thorough examination of the Republican Party. I am trying to lay it out for you in plain English.

I consider myself to be a conservative person, and I love America! But at the same time, I am also an American with a heart. I have compassion for all people. I know that a strong economy is way better for the nation and for corporations than low taxes are!

I stopped voting for Republicans because of the honesty and integrity issues. However by the time I matured their economic policies were the bigger problem. It all added up to incorrect policies for me. *Every single time* Republicans come to power they ruin our good economies!

If you will never abandon your party, why should your party make any effort to behave correctly? Shouldn't there be some consequences for bad behavior? Don't you want for your party to behave up to your American standards? You do not want to be embarrassed by Republicans in the future do you?

I want you to learn just one important thing about Republicans. They are in office to shift tax burdens over to the massive middle-class and away from the corporations when-ever they can. That can be achieved much easier if workers do not have collective bargaining power!

Now, of course Republicans cannot publicly admit any of this is going on. But that is their quiet agenda. The focus should be on more commerce for everyone. That is where the real money is to be made!

REGULATIONS

L adies and gentlemen, I we need to talk about regulation. Regulations are important to our economic system. There is a proper way to be thinking about regulation. Think of it as if it were a vaccine to maintain a healthy business environment and economy!

Instead, Republicans are more than willing to take chances with the health of our economy by not wanting any regulation at all. Recently Republicans have been bringing back the bailing out of investment banks and brokerage houses by the FDIC if they lose money on complex derivatives. That is a very dangerous policy for us tax payers!

This is a sweet deal for the big banks. If those risky investments go up in value the banks will make money! But if the investment collapses, you through the FDIC will guarantee the loans when the banks can't pay. The tax payer will have to pick up the pieces once again of the mess the bankers have created. Of course the bankers will still have their fortunes even after the bank has gone under.

I realize having no regulation would seem to be a more efficient way of doing business. We all understand that but if there is no regulation even business people can fall victim to these schemes.

Few people understand the risks they were exposing themselves to. They all collectively relied on the advice of those who were selling derivative instruments! It turned out to be very badly thought-out policy.

When those sophisticated mostly American conceived derivatives collapsed, they pretty much brought down the entire economy. That was one big reason the stock market collapsed. But ultimately the system survived only at great tax payer expense. Government should never allow derivatives to be guaranteed by the government ever again!

Republicans are responsible for the stock market crashing. They were responsible for the broken economy! This is where I hope to help people like you to see some light.

Government should not be thought of as our enemy or bad for our economy. Government provides useful structure to the economic system. Our government is needed. It should be looked at as a partner in our lives, rather than some sort of an oppressive entity; a partner which is looking out for honesty!

I myself am thankful for my government. I am thankful for things like Social Security and the Affordable Care Act. I am thankful that when I invest my money, it usually is not a scam. I do not feel I am being overly controlled by the government.

Whenever big money is involved in anything, someone needs to be checking that everything is on the up and up. If no one is watching out for you, your funds may get swindled.

My problem with Republican supporters (or voters) is this. They just naturally gravitate toward incorrect and sensational anti-government thinking and comments. They agree with Republicans because Republicans gripe about having to fund this or that! Nobody likes doing it but the government basically protects us all. We should be supporting that.

I say Republicans are harming businesses because they do not seem to get that honesty is a basic component to the system. Helping the middleclass through fair business practices builds a stronger economy for the entire nation. Everyone can prosper when we have basic regulation!

Republicans will get you thinking Democrats are somehow anti-business. Republicans will not give Democrats any credit at all for the stable business environments they have created!

Democrats have supported business whenever it makes sense to do so. Democrats will bring the economy growth and expansion. Jobs are being created with Democrat policies!

I am not saying you have to start loving Democrats at all. I am just saying keep a close eye on politics. Really understand which party is giving the nation, a strong economy. Then support the party which brings us the growth and proper policies!

Look how President Obama is bringing the economy back yet again after another Republican crash. We had a monumental collapse this last time. We have seen what George W. Bush did for the economy! How can any of you excuse that?

Job creation is the holy grail of all things we want in the American economy. For when we have jobs being created, lives are better. People are buying things to better their lives. They have an easier time keeping up with their obligations. Everything about business is good!

Republicans should adopt their own version of Consumer Focused Economics. They should be focused on taking care of the middleclass. That is how to keep the economy strong!

Let me tell you a quick story about the benefits of regulation! Some people I know inherited a sizable amount of money from an aunt. It was multiple millions. The aunt's money was held in a trust fund. The aunt originally had the trust fund set up to produce income for herself and then was intended to be passed on to her family upon her passing.

She did pass roughly around the time Barack Obama was elected and the trust did pass to these people. But because of the Wall Street Reform Act it was later discovered the trust had been mishandled. Numerous inappropriate stock trades had happened which the elderly aunt was not aware of. I believe the trading had happened at the Aunts brokerage house in conjunction with her bank!

The individuals I know were essentially swindled out of tens of thousands of dollars. But because we had regulation these inappropriate transactions were discovered and caught!

Now President Obama plus Senators Christopher Dodd and Barney Frank have been working hard to bring in regulation called the Wall Street Reform and Consumer Protection Act. It was first enacted in 2010, then a different improved version in 2012, and still a third version in 2013. These reforms are sometimes collectively called the Dodd/Frank Wall Street Reform Act.

The Wall Street Reform Act began looking into brokerage house dealings, along with the banks. The investigation found the brokerage house associated with this aunt had essentially cheated this person's trust.

Well because of the Wall Street Reform Act it all ended up being caught. A nice settlement was obtained for that family. Several tens of thousands of dollars were returned to the beneficiaries.

Thanks to a little oversight and reforms, the person I know and her family received that money. In that case the new Dodd/Frank reforms protected the little guy who never would have known they were being taken advantage of.

What makes me mad though is this. These people are confirmed Republicans and they do not even appreciate how Democrats and the Wall Street Reforms discovered these problems. It was because of President Obama and his policies they got a good settlement! They got money back that was rightfully theirs. President Obama saved these people money but they will never appreciate it!

They like all Republicans just hate President Obama even though he is doing so much good for them in a very personal way. These people are so unaware of what is going on and how lucky they are!

Just like the banking reforms that were made in the thirties, the reforms taking place today protect the average person too. Regulation is needed and is good for the system.

Look how Bernie Madoff scammed so many billions of dollars from good, honest and hardworking Americans. Many of them were ordinary investors like many of us are.

It is my current understanding approximately 17 Billion dollars was stolen there! Later I heard a different figure. I am not sure of the exact number but again this is where the Dodd/Frank laws could have helped had they been in existence. All decent sophisticated financial societies have and use regulation!

In that case there was no one watching what was going on, Madoff was able to pull it off. No oversight and no regulation provided fertile ground for such a simple scam to reoccur and thrive again.

These are all perfect examples of exactly why we should have a healthy level of government, not less government. Government should willingly be given the necessary resources to perform the duties we need, want, expect and hope for.

Of course we do not love everything about government, who does? But I do believe a reasonable level of government is OK. Would you want to get on a plane, if no one has checked the plane for airworthiness? Or whether the pilot has enough experience? I am sure we all agree that would be foolish!

If we had proper rules of behavior for banking throughout the Reagan Administration, we probably never would have had the huge

Savings and Loan collapse we had. That cost the public Billions of dollars again! Because of a lack of regulation and President Reagan, the Savings and Loan industry collapsed!

Regulation both caught and protected the system and us all from an even larger total collapse. A little Regulation in that case worked. But the system was allowed to weaken under President Reagan!

Do you remember when the banks and George W. Bush were talking about self-regulation? We have seen what happened with our economy when banks try to self-regulate. They gave us complex derivatives and poor banking practices. The economy collapsed because of President Bush and the other Republicans!

Today we are supposed to trust Republicans again even after Republicans have taken the nation to another depression like situation! Would you trust banks with your money if we had no oversight at all or if we did not have the FDIC? Use your heads folks do not be foolish about this. This is just common sense!

How many of you understand derivatives? Even large banks like J. P. Morgan/Chase with all of their analysts recently lost many Billions of dollars for the second time on those derivative investments. They actually announced they will not invest in them in the future. They are too complicated for even the biggest banks to use and understand. This is the type of thing Dodd/Frank is trying to help with.

America has the largest economy in the world. Large economies should operate with high levels of honesty built into the system. In this day and age that is done through regulation.

We should have safe places to put our money. The cost of government oversight is minimal compared to the possible losses to the public. And it does make the entire system operate better. Use your heads folks this is not complicated!

REPUBLICANS AND THE
FOX NEWS NETWORK

Now I must talk about the FOX News network and their relationship with the Republican Party. I know I must choose my comments carefully but by the same token I have to try to call it like I see it.

So now for my disclaimer! The following chapter contains my personal views. My views should be taken solely as my opinion with regard to the FOX News Network. In my opinion the FOX News Network is a legitimate news organization following conservative beliefs!

I wish to say I love the FOX Network but I can't understand their failure to recognize that conservatism when practiced in national economics only brings you slow, sluggish and even collapsed economies. We must be wiser than that. We must know conservatism has no chance of working when you remove consumption from the economy!

In my opinion the people over at FOX News are basically paid to both push and popularize a specific conservative point of view. They believe if they say something on mass it then becomes believable by the uneducated! Voters can be swept up in the frenzy.

FOX News will successfully promote tax cutting for the wealthy and the corporations as good policy for the entire economy. Even though the evidence clearly shows strong economies come to us when government policy supports the middleclass!

I believe FOX News is a powerful network, with many resources. They employ analysts who understand the economy and politics. They know what they are doing when they promote the Republican Party and conservatism to the nation. They also know it is just putting lipstick on a pig!

As a media organization their success is tied closely to their ability to attract viewers. Having large audiences is what advertisers love to see and that equates to advertising. We all know they are the primary news organization in America catering to "quote n quote" conservative values.

FOX claims they are the most popular network. I do believe FOX News literally has 100% of the conservative segment. The other news organizations must share the remaining moderate, progressive and some liberal viewers. So those viewers end up being spread more thinly across more networks! Thus their audiences will be smaller.

Naturally with that situation FOX can rightfully call itself the most popular news organization because they pretty much have 100% of the 40% of people calling themselves conservative voters. With that situation FOX News will have the largest percentage of viewers!

Anyway just like any other news organization operating in American don't you feel FOX News has a responsibility to the country to be honest when performing their service! I would say it is pretty much understood they occupy a position of responsibility!

Certainly it is OK for them to cover the news. I have no problem with that and they do cover the general news well like all other networks do.

However I do not feel it is OK to knowingly misguide the public through willful twisting, slanting or skewing the facts concerning politics. We know Republicans have a long record of not creating jobs and only giving the nation weak economies! When FOX News covers the news (especially on the economy) they create the illusion everything is fine with Republicans!

As a news organization, if all of your analysts are aware of the poor economies which conservative policies bring, integrity says you should be reporting that in order to do your job correctly. Good news organizations would report the facts correctly and not ignore the honest facts. We know every time Republicans come to the Presidency they bring contracting economies at best!

So how does FOX News justify providing an honest service when they are promoting a Party which has such a terrible record of delivering good economic policies to the nation? I am talking about bringing one contracting economy after another. How is that seen as performing a useful service?

I certainly do not believe FOX News is good for me, or good for the nation when they are popularizing flawed conservative Republican policies which in effect are leading to the collapse of the economy. Job creation is an issue which both parties, along with most economists will say they want to see in our economy and that it is very important!

In the FOX News network, conservative voters have a network promoting the party and policies they believe in! The conservative voter is fed a line from FOX News which they generally agree with! I believe what the viewing public sees on FOX News should be correct information first, coupled with a correct perspective!

Since conservative people represent a high percentage of voters and viewers they certainly deserve to have correct information being reported to them! We all want conservative voters to be voting with knowledge based on true facts.

I am a somewhat conservative person myself! As you know I believe conservative values work well in our personal lives but I have found they do not work so well in the general economy!

It is my opinion FOX News has an agenda to promote the Republican Party above other parties. They are well aware of what they are doing and what happens to our economy when Republicans win election!

FOX News is an important part of the pro-corporate movement. They know without a doubt those policies will not help the nation become strong. They know when elected Republicans will bring those pro corporate policies into the government under the guise of good conservativism. FOX News knows they are selling a con job to viewers!

This is what they are doing. They are selling conservatism as good policy in national economics even though they know in the end it brings contraction at best. As I said Conservatism is good in our personal lives, but is bad when brought to national economic policy because by nature it reduces consumption!

FOX's agenda is also about reducing regulation for the corporations via the Republican Party. FOX News is at the heart of that strategy! They know exactly what they are doing. In fact FOX News IMO is a tool of the corporations and the wealthy to bring about policies seen as favorable to the corporations!

FOX News knows they are promoting blatant pro corporate policies and hindering middleclass Americans and our economy by raising taxes on the middleclass! They know what happens when you do that.

Though I believe FOX News thinks they can sell anything to the public! Given their position in the community I feel FOX News occupies a position of trust and responsibility. People who do not think will follow them.

FOX News works to achieve their goal by bringing about those harmful changes to society by getting conservative Republicans candidates elected to public office! So in my opinion that essentially is their mission statement. Popularize the Republican Party to the public even though they know it will be detrimental to the economy.

I believe the role FOX News has taken on is to be the voice for the Republican movement. They wish to be the number one news organization pushing conservatism to the nation!

FOX News is an intelligent organization and they have allowed themselves to be bought. I am sure they are well aware of what the record of job creation is and has been over the last 96 years.

When observing politics FOX News has seen policies that work and they have seen policies which do not work! They know well what is going on. They understand how the economy responds to both parties economic policies! Yet they continually promote Republicans as being better for the nation and for the economy than are the Democrats.

With Consumer Focused Economics we have always had great economies. With Supply Side Economics, or conservative economic policies we have never have had lasting growing economies. But in spite of the record, FOX News constantly promotes the incorrect Republican policies to the nation. FOX News therefor knows the policies they are pushing will harm the country!

I believe FOX is doing a great disservice to the country. If you promote bad policies once or twice that might be a mistake as it takes time to learn that a given policy does not work correctly. However when conservatism clearly never brings good economies they knowingly are promoting a party with incorrect policy over and over again. Essentially they are performing a malicious act just to elect Republicans!

How much time does a network or do analysts reasonably need to learn that promoting the wellbeing of the middleclass will strengthen the economy more? After you see it a few times that should be learned.

I have seen where Ann Coulter, who is or was employed by FOX, has actually called President Ronald Regan the great savior of the American economy! But really I think he is the only Republican who has ever created a job. He has not done anything Special!

But every time we have used Supply Side Theory, or you could say conservative economic policy it has not delivered us a healthy economy in the end! Are you going to believe the honest facts or are you going to believe the rhetoric of someone like Ann Coulter and the entire FOX News organization?

Those periods when we have had stronger job creation are shown in the federal job creation statistics collected and compiled by the government going back to 1920. The statistics themselves are backing up what I have been saying to you about the economy!

Supply Side Economics came in Ronald Regan's second term. We got the short term pop in the economy which always comes when it is brought into an economy which has just a little strength!

I believe most people know when you reduce corporate taxes and you still have consumers consuming, you are going to see a momentarily improve in the economic picture because you have reduced corporate taxes and it is too early for employment to be negatively affected! It is too early in the process for higher tax burdens on the middleclass to be felt.

The economy collapsed for George H. W. Bush, because the Supply Side Model did not support the consumer! It collapsed again for George W. Bush when he tried it!

Conservatism collapsed the economies for Nixon/Ford and even President Eisenhower! Un-sophisticated economic policies led to the great Depression! But Republicans, FOX News and commentators like Ann Coulter will tell you how wonderful Conservatism is!

Do not be taken for a fool! FOX News is popularizing blatant pro corporate tax cutting and restrictive government spending as proper policy! FOX is a tool of Republicans which is putting this nation in the hole!

In addition even when thousands of people are getting health-care under the Affordable Care Act FOX News will give plenty of time to those who wish to get rid of the Act! I do not see this as constructive for the nation!

FOX News and Republicans will try to paint President Clinton as a bad President. Yet he shrank the massive deficits he inherited from Republicans and actually began policies which gave us four years of surpluses! He created more jobs than any other President in history! But YOU REPUBLICANS are so sure he was the worst President ever.

President George W. Bush brought Supply Side Economics back big time. He destroyed the economy!

My gal actually said to me Bush's economic problems started under President Clinton! OK if that is the case how come Republicans did not recognize the mess and take actions to straighten that mess out? They were in power for 7 years before the crash came! Republicans had plenty of time but did absolutely nothing. So does this somehow say to you Republicans are better than Democrats?

But FOX News, Ann Coulter, Republicans and others will try to tell you it is Democrats who are the bad ones! Well we certainly did not see good economic policy coming from the Republicans when they had control for seven years to change things. They did nothing!

I don't think it can be denied Republicans gave us the Great Depression and the George W. Bush gave us the Great Recession. But Democrats are the bad ones! FOX News works hard to twist the news into negative ways against Democrats and positive ways for Republicans whenever they can!

So if FOX News reports the good things and strong economies Democrats have given us as bad, is that supposed to be OK? I guess because it is all part of the FOX News mission statement of promoting Republicans regardless of whether they are constructive to the economy or not, FOX is just carrying the conservative Republican flag forward!

Even when FOX News knows Republican policy is flawed, one must ask are they performing a reasonable service for the nation. If FOX News is working to promote policies they know are flawed aren't they hurting all of us?

Of course we understand not all news is political in nature. When that happens, it will get reported in a normal fashion, even on the FOX News network! But you can be sure if the news can be twisted in a way where it can be made to appear as an embarrassment to Democrats or any sitting Democrat President, FOX News will be sure to put there wording on the piece to make the news look as bad as possible for Democrats.

For example when American forces apprehended Abu Anas al-Libi in Lybia, which was good, FOX News will make sure to report how it took 2 years to get him. Implying Democrats are slow to bring justice for America. Democrats are incompetent or whatever! That is just an example of a subtle FOX News twist.

But how long did it take for George W. Bush to get Osama Bin Laden? At least President Obama has been able to get both of those animals along with tens and hundreds of others.

FOX News will try to give the impression Democrats are mishandling foreign affairs! When in reality, President Obama has been nailing more bad guys than anyone else has. This is the kind of skewed and slanted reporting I am talking about at FOX.

FOX News will not make a big deal out of how President Obama is keeping us out of the Ukraine conflict or how he is keeping our ground forces out of Libya. But he is striking identified targets in Iraq and Syria with our air force!

It is possible we may have greater involvement with the fight against ISAL or ISIS. FOX News will not report much on how we are seeing the economy coming back with President Obama! Or how it was ruined big time under President George W. Bush!

FOX News just like most Republicans will only see red when viewing Democrats. It is a constant drum beat of negative comments! Even when Democrats give us good policies and good economies, FOX News will report it with a negative twist!

We know Republicans always are on the opposite of Democrats regardless of what the issue is or what the Democrat stance is. I guess they do this to set themselves apart from Democrats. FOX News just backs them up on it all of the way!

For FOX News and Republicans, Democrats will never do anything right. Even though Democrats are the ones who are creating jobs and giving us strong economies *every single time* they come to power. Republicans never give us any lasting job creation!

FOX News reporters, never have anything constructive to add to the discourse. Listening to Ann Coulter, Megan Kelly, Shaun Hannity and the others has got to disturb anyone capable of thinking the news out to its logical conclusion.

I believe FOX News is un-American. Their reporting is harmful to the nation!

If I was a religious person and I am not, I would probably characterize them as doing the devils work! They are working people up needlessly. They are creating negative views about everything which is actually good for America.

Don't you think Democrats occasionally do things which are good for the nation? Are you going to say to me Social Security has not been good for America? Democrats recovered the nation from the Great Recession and the Great Depression!

Democrats brought us basic regulations for a safe economic environment to exist. They have given us the Affordable Care Act! Democrats gave us OSHA laws during the Nixon years, and the G.I. Bill? Civil rights, Women's rights, the 19th Amendment and so on. All were very constructive laws and came because of Democrats!

But because FOX News is in such vocal opposition, they whip people up into believing something is bad when there is nothing to be concerned about at all. A good example is opposition to the Affordable Care Act. I believe the core beliefs of the FOX News network are fundamentally misguided!

Diehard Republicans and FOX News portray the Republican Party as being better for the country, and our economy. But it is all a part of the Republican illusion which is promoted by FOX News? Virtually every time Republicans come to power they give us contracting economies. But FOX News still supports them regardless of how bad they are.

What impartial information does FOX News have that shows Republicans are better? Does the federal job creation statistics back up Republicans or FOX News beliefs?

With all of the analysts FOX News has, why do they constantly get their own analysis of the Republican Party so wrong? Surely FOX News would not support a contracting economic model, because they are supposed to be a good constructive news network!

I believe we have seen how the culture of the Murdoch Empire has gotten in to trouble in other nations for secretly recording cell phone conversations for example. Why would a so called honest, high quality news organization such as FOX News gather private cell phone conversations?

I am not sure of the correct terminology there but you get the idea. It certainly is wrong to listen in on private conversations under any circumstance in my opinion!

So I am trying to make a simple point about FOX News. They are trying to popularize opposition to the one party that has a history of actually creating jobs for our nation. I do not see that as constructive opposition. I would not think their license permits the shading of the news as normal reporting.

Actually here is how a typical broadcast for FOX News works. FOX News will mix some truth into their piece along with the incorrect or skewed information. Because there is a small amount of truth to the piece, viewers tend to assume everything in the report must be accurate!

I understand conservatives have felt they needed a network loyal to conservative values. Or they need a network biased toward understanding conservative thinking. Reporting the news would be one thing, but purposely twisting the news I believe performs a disservice!

I cannot in good faith make arguments to you about politicians or even FOX News. You must be smart and learn to support what is right all on your own. But I believe history is a great tool to use.

What gets me most about FOX News is they will make pretty extreme statements, and no one expects them to back those statements up with any proof. You the viewer are often left to just believe what has been said, simply because a conservative politician or commentator presented it on a conservative network!

We Americans make the assumption that when we tune in to news, it will be given with a certain level of honesty. We assume the things FOX News reports on have got to be more or less the truth, correct and honest. Much of the public just assumes honesty is a part of what we see on the news.

Now by contrast over at MSNBC, when they tell you a certain politician made this comment or that one, they will almost always show you the video or the recording of the politician actually making the preposterous comment. FOX News will not do that as much as MSNBC.

What I do like about MSNBC is that they put effort into catching the FOX News Network, or Republican politicians with their comments. I could use word lies, but that might seem a little harsh. MSNBC does a good job of catching politicians and/or FOX News with their incorrect reporting!

I believe FOX News is the actual voice of the Republican Party on television. What else should we expect to hear from them? When you are watching FOX News, you have essentially tuned into a Republican propaganda news network which does deliver some news. At least that is how I view them.

Imagine if President Obama did to the economy what George W. Bush actually did do to it! There would be no shutting FOX News reporters, commentators, Republicans and critics up. They would be pointing to out how awful those Democrats are. They would say that those Democrats are so irresponsible they should be voted out of office and never returned!

But FOX News will barely report on things like the bridge gate scandal of Governor Chris Christie in New Jersey. Or mention how that the Affordable Care Act is working. FOX News will not point to all the obstruction Republicans are doing and how that harms the recovery efforts!

That is the way FOX News operates. For FOX News, Republicans are only good and constructive in government! Democrats are only bad.

I understand that if you are a Republican you do not want to think negatively about your own party, FOX News or Republican Politicians. You do not like to see the truth and I do understand that completely. But that does not make you or FOX News think in the right way!

In my opinion, President George W. Bush was a total disaster for the country. I am sorry if I hurt someone's feelings and I apologize to President Bush for saying that. However you will rarely hear anything critical on FOX News about Republicans!

FOX News is a very large and powerful news organization. Let there be no mistake, they have the analysts and the wherewithal to understand how economic policies will work in our country. They are not fools and they know what the record of job creation has been with Republicans.

Why would FOX News support a party which clearly is much worse at job creation? That is a question for you to ponder! Why would a good network lend support to a party with economically destructive policies?

As you know I have focused a lot on the federal job creation statistics. When corporations are not creating jobs this means commerce activity is down and that is not a good business environment. Things are much better today than they were 7 years ago.

When commerce is down, corporate profits are down and demand is weak. Our economy is slow and thus less revenue flows through to the government. Government programs can't be properly funded as costs rise and the revenues are decreasing. Which then only causes larger deficits and the economy only weakens further.

I believe FOX News plays a key role in this Republican economic model and deception. It deserves critical commentary! In my opinion the nation would be better off if FOX News did not exist. I believe someone ought to take them down!

What you are seeing on FOX News is only their version of what Republicans can do for the nation. I ask you to just look at the facts. I cannot see how any levelheaded person could possibly align their thinking with the FOX News network or with Republicans!

I know what I have said here contains some pretty strong stuff, so I say to you this entire chapter is just in my humble and personal opinion. I admit I am no expert but my comments are based on my 65 plus years of observations. I have seen what I have seen and I for one do not like it!

WHAT REPUBLICANS
<u>CONSIDER SMALL BUSINESSES?</u>

Have you ever heard Republicans say they do not want to tax the job creators? Then they will say they want to help small business. To me it sounds like they are trying to help the little guy. It sounds like a good, kind and generous thing to be doing!

Of course we all want small businesses to grow and become successful big businesses! But have you ever wondered what Republicans consider a small business to be?

This is another example of what I call "Republican Speak" and the Republican illusion of helping society. A few years back when I learned what a small business was for Republicans, I was in total shock

For Republicans, a small business is not small in terms of the physical size of the company. It is not small in the number of employees they have, or small in the amount of commerce they conduct. None of that is the case with Republican and their small businesses.

I will give you the definition which Republicans use for what a small business is. For Republicans a small business is any company or business with fewer than 100 owners! I am talking owners, not employees!

Now stop and think about that for a moment. Most privately held companies are going to fall within that requirement. The vast majority of privately held companies do have fewer than 100 owners. They are not publicly owned companies and they are privately held. Often we are talking about family run companies.

So basically when it comes to Republicans you could just about say, most privately held companies are small businesses. Regardless of how big they actually are.

It is not unusual for Republican small businesses to have hundreds, and sometimes even thousands of employees. But we only hear Republicans saying how small companies should be helped! Well listen I believe in helping everyone big or small, I do not care.

But again this is pretty typical of the kind of "Republican Speak" I have been telling you all about. Republicans will say something, and it sounds like one thing, but in reality it is something totally unexpected and different. Republicans are not talking about mom and pop-sized businesses here.

When I think of a small company, I think in terms of a few employees say up to 50 employees or something like that. For Republicans their small companies can have thousands of employees doing millions or even billions of dollars of business each year.

So under the Republican definition, I fully agree with Republicans that what they call small companies do create a lot of the jobs. Those size companies are the job creators. For me that is not the issue. But do not think for a minute that Republicans are looking out for the little guy.

Republicans constantly work to help what most people would call large companies but they will just call them small companies to fool some. I guess they do this to have you believe they really are on the average person's side. But never forget Republicans are always on the side of big, big business!

I am here to tell you, it all comes down to Republicans supporting their three interest groups. Big companies, corporations and the wealthy!

It seems like many Republican voters like you have not exactly figured this out. I am not against helping large privately held companies at all. That is an important thing to be doing. But like anything we do need to use proper language when talking about companies!

Republicans know that talking about helping the large corporations or big businesses with tax cuts would be a losing conversation with the vast majority of middleclass Americans. I think middleclass Americans generally feel big businesses and corporations are doing just fine!

IN THE HONEST LIGHT,
THE FINAL CHAPTER

OK in this chapter I will try to quickly summarize why you should not support those Republicans. I am really trying to get through to you here. I am giving you my last arguments!

I understand Republicans totally believe in what they are doing. I want you to understand why I believe Republicans are taking us in the wrong direction!

Keep in mind with Supply Side Economics you have no effective tools to regulate the economy. You cannot do this or that, to heat the economy up. You also have no way to slow the economy if that is needed! You are not dealing with the demand side of our economy!

I think we would all agree if the Republican model were good, the economy should be doing anything but collapsing! It should be doing the opposite, it should be expanding and growing.

I ask you to just remember what happened for George W. Bush with a complete Republican government. For him the economy crashed. That happens not once in a while but literally *"Every Single Time"* Republicans have power they bring about a collapse.

The statistics have shown one failed Republican economy after another failed Republican economy! Reread the statistics if you want starting on page 51.

Wouldn't you think if a certain policy works well in the general economy, both parties should be using more or less the same policy! It would not be the end of the world. We would be experiencing growing economic times. That would be good for both Parties!

Second since Republicans give us contracting economies, it pretty much explains why Republicans are voted out of office doesn't it? Usually after just 2 terms! Voters see the collapse happening by the second term and then feel they need to try the other party at election time.

I do not understand why Republicans are upset if the middle-class is doing well! Sometimes I think that Republicans do not like it when the middleclass is thriving. This basic mindset which Republicans have is also so very wrong!

Additionally we should not be upset to see government being funded properly either. We do want for government, businesses and individuals to be successful, growing and thriving! We want the government to be flourishing just like businesses and individuals. Every time Democrats are in control of government the economy expands. Certainly this is important to you!

Now for me that is enough reason right there to not support Republicans. I myself do not need anything more than that. But there are many more reasons why I cannot support Republicans. Let' skim over just some of the things Republicans and Democrats have already given to you!

Seems to me it has been Democrats who have been practicing what we consider to be proper human and Christian values. I am talking about the things which make life reasonable and acceptable for all. Too often we take Democrat policy for granted.

I realize throughout this chapter we will be talking about many of the same things already discussed. But we are reviewing, now I am putting it all together in one chapter and summing it up. For repeating things I apologize. This is my last chance to make you realize there really are problems with Republicans!

Democrats believe in things like having full and equal rights for women and giving them the right to vote and to hold office. Democrats believe women should have complete control of their own bodies and their lives. What can be a more basic right than that? Are you people thinking things were better in the old days, when we suppressed women?

Women's reproductive rights are being defended by Democrats. Republicans try to defend companies who have owners who do not wish to fund all of the normal medical benefits which the system covers. Since when do we allow companies to pick and choose what they will cover? This is a slippery slope.

Republicans today are clearly pledging they want to do away with Planned Parenthood because a part of what they do involves abortion services! Women want and do use these services!

There is nothing about the Affordable Care Act promoting the use of birth control. It is an individual choice for each woman! But the Act protects women to make their own personal choice.

Electing Republican Presidents will just get you more conservative justices appointed on the Supreme Court. There is nothing in our constitution that says the court must have a conservative lean to it. It is vitally important to have proper justices on the Supreme Court. Do we really want more of these restrictive rulings coming to America?

I cannot believe in this day and age any woman would think that way. We can thank President Woodrow Wilson for taking steps to bringing the country into the twentieth century!

Isn't it also correct to have rights protecting all people from discrimination? Isn't it correct for the handicapped to have equal access to public buildings and transportation? The American's with Disabilities Act was signed during the George H. W. Bush Presidency because of Democrat majorities!

Seems to me the Americans with Disabilities Act pretty much embraces your basic Christian values! I am pretty sure we all feel that has been correct. Those laws were passed because of Democrats in the government!

OSHA laws were passed during the Nixon years. OSHA laws make sure work places and equipment is safe to use. The law was passed but again because there was an over whelming majority of Democrats in congress at the time it passed into law!

Democrats would have been able to pass the law over President Nixon's veto if he chose to veto the Bill. He also knew he would just look bad to the public if he did not sign off on that Bill!

Important child labor laws came to us because of Democrats. That was an important mark for any sophisticated society to reach. Again I say thank you to Woodrow Wilson and Democrats.

The 8 hr. work day and 40 hr. work week is here because of Democrats. It did not just happen! It was Democrats who realized that was the reasonable way to structure our society.

Democrats brought in legislation which has maintained clean air for us to breath, and clean water for us to drink. Clean air and water are your basic human rights aren't they?

Just because you are a big corporation, that does not give you the right to endanger the health of others. You do not have that right! Again those things should be considered as very important to all of us!

All of these laws are in tune with our American values. In return Americans should support American corporations when they are doing the correct thing of protecting the environment. We should reward good companies with our business.

Just look how much longer people are living today verses years gone by. Individually we are enjoying longer and healthier lives because of the protections which these environmental laws have brought to us and to the environment! It is through good laws that we give ourselves a safer better world.

Aren't these the kind of values any sensible family would cherish? Don't families appreciate that Mom and Dad are coming home healthy, safe, whole and at a reasonable hour.

For me the Democratic Party is pretty much the definition of Christian law making. It is the Democrats who are maintaining our quality of life. They are maintaining our health and preserving the safety and freedom of the individual! Those changes to our laws have come to us because of Democrats!

How incredibly important is it that we will not be exposing our spouses, our children and ourselves to known carcinogens? Important environmental laws were passed during the Nixon administration because of Democrats in the government. Again more good proper values have come about because of Democrats.

Looking at the big picture, these changes were not supported by Republicans because it would cost corporations a little money. But it really is better for the overall system when families are saving billions of dollars in medical expenses and living healthier, longer, productive lives which then makes it possible to continue purchasing the products and services of the corporations.

On the other side of these arguments, most of the pro-gun legislation in this nation has come to you because of Republicans in Congress. Since the voting margin's between Republicans and Democrats is so tight Republicans need every single vote they can get! That is why they suck up to the gun lobby!

Democrats on occasion try to bring sensible gun control laws in, but usually they are opposed and beaten back by the Republicans. Are we really a nation which is so paranoid about gun freedom that we cannot have a little common sense surrounding gun ownership?

Some Republicans are proud of opposing Democrats. You just love being against Democrats because you have talked yourself into believing everything about Democrats is bad. What ever happened to the days when co-operation can be constructive for the nation too?

Do you remember the Gabby Gifford shooting, Columbine, or how about Newtown shooter Adam Lanza and many others? Really are short waiting periods that big of a deal if it stops carnage and loss of life? I believe most Americans do support back ground checks. It is not unreasonable and does not prohibit gun ownership. But voters are not holding Republicans accountable!

I must be honest with you and say sometimes I am embarrassed of my countries laws and of our culture. Other nations are not gun crazy and people there are happy. America is at times is a very backward nation. It is like we have little sophistication!

Europeans love their orderly societies and appreciate being sophisticated. Europeans do not think about weapons at all. Weapons are not on their minds.

For a typical European having a good meal, perhaps sharing a little wine and having good conversation with friends are more important daily activities than shooting and/or packing weapons. Europeans understand the value of being educated and embracing peaceful behavior.

They are more concerned about being educated, their relationships and having good employment than in anything else! They wish to live constructive lives.

Democrats brought you the Social Security system. They brought us Medicare and Medicaid. Those are huge and essential programs to the middleclass! And of course we have the Affordable Care Act!

The policy of keeping a strong separation between church and state has been maintained more so because of Democrats than because of Republicans. Republicans seem to want more religion in America not less.

This is another very important area. Government must not support any one faith over any other faith to have excessive influence upon our people. Religion and government must be kept separate from each other. To me Republicans are bringing religious values into society.

Still many of you will turn your backs on the Democratic Party. Where is your appreciation for those laws and our general freedom? You have been brain washed by Republicans into thinking that Republicans are somehow the moral party, or that they have correct policies.

Allowing corporations to decide what forms of medical insurance they will provide is a slippery slope. The Affordable Care Act clearly directs what must be provided. It is both fair and equal for all people. You may do with your life what you want!

Today you can't be refused a medical plan because of a pre-existing condition. People can stay on their parents plans until age 26.

Allowing corporations to choose these things may allow other forms of discrimination based supposedly on religious values to start up. It was sad to see that the Supreme Court rule in this way.

If Republicans were making the decisions today, in my opinion we would have fewer freedoms not more. I thought Republicans were supposed to be standing up for our personal freedoms.

Another good example might be those providing wedding services to the public. Democrats are making sure businesses cannot discriminate in providing their services. It is the American way.

If for example a gay couple wishes to purchase a wedding cake that business owner cannot discriminate against them because he does not approve that it is a guy wedding. So what, it is someone else's life not yours!

Gay marriage has become legal in most states. It is now becoming an accepted part of our society. Don't you think we should all get used to it? Do not expect every individual on earth to conform to your personal values. It really is not that big of a deal.

Republicans have fought tooth and nail to stop the Affordable Care Act from becoming law. Now they are trying to weaken the act further by removing revenues from the medical device providers. Plus they are saying that if you do not work 40 Hrs. per week you are not considered full time and hence you are not entitled to healthcare. Republicans are doing everything they can to undermine the Act!

Today Corporations are giving people fewer hours of work to get around healthcare expenses. This is another good reason to go to a single payer system! Why would you support a system designed around not giving healthcare to the people? Under single payer people will get out of the system more or less what they have qualified for.

Well Republicans just believe the public should not buy anything unless it is done through a corporation? Why would that be thought of as correct thinking? Why can't government provide some services better? Certainly we organize ourselves to provide schools, healthcare, police and fire protection, just like we provide highways and water systems and a whole host of services. We organize our society, it is good!

The Republican approach just makes it possible for employers to stop providing health insurance. That then throws more expense over onto our government and furthers the failure of the system. But the health insurance companies are making more money today than ever before.

I had one of those catastrophic health plans it was not good coverage at all. But because of the Affordable Care Act I now have good coverage. I assure you I did not like my old plan or the old system.

Republicans will try to tell you that because I had the plan, I must have liked it; not so. Under the old system I had my medical insurance for over 23 years and I only saw my doctor one time. That was in the very first year.

In the final years of that plan I was paying $326 every month for that bad and unused catastrophic insurance. I never went to the Doctor because with that plan preventative care was not covered. I assure you I did not like my insurance coverage at all and it cost me a lot of money!

Since the Affordable Care Act has come in, I have already seen the doctor several times I have had two biopsies and a colonoscopy. Millions of good people are being helped with their medical situations because of this law.

Republicans are doing everything they can to undermine the Act! Republicans should get off their rear ends and make the system the people want into a better system!

Today Corporations are giving people part time work to get around healthcare expenses. This is another good reason to go to a single payer system! Why would you support a system designed around not giving healthcare to the people?

I think it should be supported. It is good for all of us and it sure has been good for me. I am thankful for the Affordable Care Act.

With Democrats bettering the quality of life for the average middleclass American that is how to achieve lasting strong profits at the corporations. That is a sound business practice. Everybody will be living better in a growing economy including the corporations.

So many Republicans have given us contracting economies. Democrats always give us vital growing economies. You must not stop thinking about this. I truly hate all of the damage Republicans have done to our economy!

Don't forget Republicans gave us Joseph McCarthy and the Red Scare! Remember how he ruined people who were not guilty of anything at all. How can you people support this from your chosen party?

Republicans have tried to bring us Pat Robertson, Mike Huckabee, Governor Rick Perry, Rick Santorum and other religious minded leaders. If you want to see Joseph McCarty return just vote for Ted Cruz!

Republicans keep pushing for less government regulation. Today Republicans want you to personally guarantee those risky Wall Street complex derivative loans, threw the FDIC! The entire world economy nearly collapsed because of those swaps as they are sometimes called and Republicans want us to do that again, really?

Why would you as an average person be against the Dodd/Frank reforms? Dodd/Frank is protecting all of our investments. Have you honestly been hassled in some way by those regulations? It is keeping the banks and brokerage houses honest as well as keeping us away from these risky investment schemes!

Our economy went through a huge collapse after President George W. Bush. We also saw another huge collapse with President Reagan and the Savings and Loan scandal.

It all came about because of too little regulation. We know the Great Depression was clearly the result of unsafe banking, speculation and investing practices.

I do understand that was a less sophisticated time and we had no regulation at all. But we must learn from both of those experiences. Regulation is in fact needed, it is good!

I want to tell you every Republican President has delivered a weak economy for their Democrat successor. Every Democrat President on the other hand, after first restoring the weak economy they have inherited from Republicans has delivered to them a healthy growing and strong economy!

What I have said is backed up backed up in the federal job creation statistics. The federal government is as impartial as you can get.

Republicans are just trying to pull something over on you when they say that President Obama has been ineffective. President Obama has already done many good things that are beneficial to us.

A national healthcare system has been talked about since Teddy Roosevelt was in office. President Obama made it happen. Certainly the Affordable Care Act has been a huge accomplishment for him.

He is doing a pretty good job of rebuilding the economy in spite of Republican obstructionism. Just last month February of 2016 240,000 plus new jobs were created again! The economy clearly has been heating up.

At this point we have not been looking at the Great Depression or any of the F.D.R. recovery years. If one does include those numbers, you will get to where Democrats have created jobs six times faster than Republicans.

Six times faster! Those are huge differences. In my opinion Republicans are not worthy of being in control of anything at all! *Every single time* they make a disaster of our economy!

Democrats have given us the Social Security System. This has allowed our parents, our aunts and uncles, grandparents, friends and one day our-selves to live with a basic income in retirement.

Many of us do not have retirement plans! Where would we be without Social Security!

Democrats gave our service men and women the G.I. Bill. Truman integrated the services. Democrats created numerous Farm Aid Bills. Democrats stopped home foreclosures during the Great Depression.

Democrats created the FDIC ensuring bank stability and protecting the little guy. These are all vital in today's system. What are you people seeing wrong with Democrat legislation?

Republicans gave us the Great Depression. They also gave us the George W. Bush Great Recession. Republicans gave us numerous slow economies along the way! Just look at the record given in this book.

Republicans are opposing Democrats at every opportunity. Wouldn't it make sense to co-operate with each other a little? How many times have we seen Republicans try to shut the economy down because they did not like the deficit spending? How many times have they opposed raising the debt ceiling?

Democrats literally have saved the American automotive industry multiple times! Republicans and Mitt Romney would have let Chrysler and General Motors go through bankruptcy. American autoworkers today owe their jobs to Democrats. How huge is that?

Democrats have largely made the right moves concerning our foreign policies. We have seen the Arab spring. We got Osama Bin Laden. We are not embroiled in the Ukraine problems. We are trying to steadily rid the world of terrorists.

We did our part to help to get rid of Muammar Gaddafi. We are mostly staying out of the Syrian conflict. Yes in hindsight I think we should have helped Libya more after the downfall off Gaddafi.

We are accomplishing many good things in the world while following President Obama. He has been a good President! Why many people think President Obama has not been good does not make much sense to me. It is mostly just nutty hateful anti Democrat thinking.

Democrats have been correcting the problems we had! Banks, insurance companies, brokerage houses, the finance and housing industries, and auto manufacturers were all failing in a big way under Republicans. Are you going to try and say everything was fine under President George W. Bush?

Another reason to not vote for Republicans is this. Since WWII, Democrats have created 58 million jobs while being in office, for only 28 years. That is not counting any of Barack Obama's time in office. That is an average job creation in excess of two million jobs per year with Democrats. Republicans on the other hand have created only 34 million jobs in 36 years. That is less than one million jobs per year.

After WWII if you remove the one Republican who did create a few jobs (which was Ronald Reagan) you get to where the average Democrat created jobs 4 times faster than the average Republican! Honestly, do you approve of such slow job creation coming from Republicans?

For the better part of 5 years Barack Obama has been creating jobs at around 2.5 million jobs per year! He is not that bad considering where we were and Republicans are not co-operating with him at all!

I believe 36 years of Republican Presidents is plenty of time for them to show us they have good economic policies, if they exist! The fact is Republicans are not good for the economy. I say just hold your nose and vote for the most conservative Democrat you can find.

Ask yourself, why are Republicans voted out of power? Why do people turn away from them? There are usually economic reasons for that.

We know Republicans will never raise the minimum wage because they never do! Even though it is good for the economy Republicans are not on the side of building our economy up. The economy ends up being weak for all business people during Republican administrations!

Recently President Obama stated he wanted tax breaks for the middleclass. The Republican response was they will cut taxes for the middleclass when Democrats give tax cuts to the wealthy! This is returning to the same old incorrect Republican policies of trying to aid the economy with tax cuts for people at the top of the economy!

When President Obama is trying to move our relationship with Cuba forward Republicans have a problem with that! Can you believe that? The best way to move any country away from Communism is to expose them to free Democracies!

This will create the basic desire on the part of the citizens of those nations to experience those freedoms for themselves. One day the Cubans will demand freedom and Democracy!

Can you believe in this modern day and age some Republicans believe in the teaching of only creation in our public schools. Yet this theory is not backed up by any common sense science that I am aware of. It only exists in the minds of believers. It's a nice idea and a nice story, but that does not make it true.

President Obama, then Attorney Generals Eric Holder and now Loretta Lynch have not been pushing racial issues upon the people. You would never know they are black men and women based on their actions as government officials.

Ronald Reagan tripled our national debt and left us 5.4 trillion dollars in debt. President Clinton got us back to surpluses. President George W. Bush then doubled our debt again to over 11 trillion. Then he handed a mess and broken economy over to President Obama! That is your responsible Republican government?

Today President Obama is steadily moving us in the direction of a balanced budget. He is shrinking the deficit spending. He is getting the economy moving forward again.

It is going to take more time than he will have but we are moving in the right direction. We should stick with whoever the next Democratic nominee for President will be and support them in strengthening the economy!

Remember all of the people Republicans have given us. Herbert Hoover, Joseph McCarty, Richard Nixon, Spiro Agnew, George H. W. Bush, George W. Bush, Dick Cheney and even Dwight Eisenhower! All turned out to be bad for the economy or the country. All of these people were disasters to one degree or another. Even Ronald Reagan was not that great. He left the first President Bush a bad economic model.

Republicans have tried to give us Herman Cain, Rand Paul, Rick Santorum, Rick Perry, Michele Bachmann, Pat Robertson, Mike Huckabee, Mitt Romney and Sarah Palin. Next they are going to try and bring us Ted Cruz. They even gave Darrell Issa a voice?

Are you completely kidding me! How about the Marco Rubio or Ben Carson? Are those people Presidential material? All of those people are totally unprepared for the Presidency! They are all nice people but unprepared in my opinion to do that job!

Who knows how many far right-wing religious or ultra-conservative people they will try to get elected? Most of these people have demonstrated they are total nuts!

Do you realize President Eisenhower over threw a Democratically elected government in Iran and gave us the hated Shaw of Iran. That then gave us the Iranian government we are dealing with today!

Cuba went to the communists during his administration. We lost the race into space with him! He invaded Central American nations to save American Corporations there. Central Americans often dislike Americans because of this. He also had terrible job creation!

Nixon did the whole Watergate affair and cover up. He expanded the war into Cambodia. He himself avoided paying income taxes! He was impeached and had to resign his Presidency.

His vice President had to resign also! Nixon had price controls on the economy and left the nation with out of control inflation. He too had no job creation!

Ronald Reagan did the whole Iran/Contra affair. He fired 13,000 air traffic controllers. He popularized Supply Side Economics and taxed the middleclass too heavily! He tripled our national debt and his economic model did not give George H. W. Bush any lasting job creation. It brought us a severe contraction of the economy.

George W. Bush literally ran the economy off of a cliff with an all Republican government helping him every step of the way! Every aspect of the economy was ruined. Republicans had total control of the economy and they killed it worse than anyone else. I will not list all of the things here but there just is not enough room!

Almost all of the humane laws and values we cherish as Americans have come to us because of Democrats. Republicans have opposed pretty much every one of them!

Another reason to not vote for Republicans is they will misrepresent themselves and Democrats to the public! As was the case when Newt Gingrich said if you want a food stamp society, elect Democrats. That is so false!

I believe you can find your way through the rhetoric and chaff if you learn "Republican Speak". Republicans constantly say what sounds like one thing, but really it means something totally unexpected.

I caution you to just be aware of what is going on. Republicans use double meanings in their speech's all of the time! With their "Republican Speak" their tax cuts are for the wealthy and for the corporations. Maybe a crumb comes to the middleclass but the wealthy will get the lions share and become even wealthier!

Republicans never raise the minimum wage.

Republicans always lower taxes and regulation for the wealthy and the corporations.

Democrats create jobs 2 to 6 times faster than Republicans depending on the time frame you are talking about.

With Republican Supply Side Economics you have no tools to regulate the economy. You can't easily heat it up or slow it down as needed. You are without tools.

Republican policies are not focused on giving the nation commerce. Their policies are focused on giving out corporate tax cuts and reducing regulation!

Republicans repeatedly give the nation massive deficit spending.

Republicans believe having a flat tax, which will only remove consumption by the massive middle class, is a wise move.

Republicans will not tax businesses but they will tax the consumer!

Republicans have repeatedly blocked the raising of the debt ceiling!

Republicans do not believe America should be making progress or working together with one another.

Republicans rarely give us balanced budgets.

Republicans repeatedly tell untruths!

Republicans work to make it as difficult as possible for voter to have access to polls and freedoms surrounding voting.

FOX News is popularizing conservative politics in spite of the fact they know conservatism does not work when brought to national economic policy. They have all of the analysts in the world to understand the economy and how it works.

Conservatism does work in our personal lives, but works no place else. By nature with conservatism nobody wants to spend money. You want to hold on to it.

Republicans will bring overly conservative justices to the Supreme Court. Now they are blocking President Obama from appointing a replacement for Justice Scalia.

Republicans are still trying to bring us the Keystone oil pipeline even though it is becoming an un-profitable source for current oil production. Do you think Republicans are going to build it anyway?

Republicans are not working to improve the healthcare system. They are working to make it fail!

Democrats rebuild the sick economies Republicans leave them.

George W. Bush started the totally unnecessary Iraq War, which has cost 4,400 American lives. It led to the Abu Ghraib prison scandal there by creating a great motivational tool for the recruitment of thousands of Muslim fighters. By taking out Saddam he has totally destabilized the Middle East. That country is worse today because we went in there!

Corporations have trillions of dollars sitting in their bank accounts. According to Republicans I always thought the only thing corporations needed to create jobs in American was money. They have had money just sitting in these accounts for years now, and under President Bush we never had job creation!

Don't tell me Republicans know anything about correct economic policy.

I have shown you the kind of tax cuts George W. Bush actually has given to the wealthy and to the corporations. He gave tax cuts to corporations after harming consumption by raising them on the middleclass which killed our economy.

Republicans are never straight forward with us on taxation. They use "Republican Speak" to cover up the true meaning of what they really want to do. Republicans will say they want a tax cut but they say that only to get your vote.

The tax cuts are for corporations and not the middleclass. They have little intention of helping the average American. The reality is they are not thinking of you at all!

Republicans will say, "We must not tax the job creators" for a strong economy. On the surface that sounds right, but how many times have we heard that line? How long are you going to buy it? How long are you going to wait for that to work? That policy surly did not work For George W, Bush! We have never seen job creation when Republicans are in control.

Some corporations and the wealthy keep throwing their money at Republicans, because they believe better times are right around the corner. But Republicans are not thinking about the long term future. They are not thinking correctly!

The only thing Republicans care about is this: they desperately want your vote! Without voter support they are lost. Once they have won your vote away from you, they will act in ways to protect the corporations. They will not think about you for another 4 years.

How can a Christian in good conscience vote for Republicans? Aren't you Christians supposed to be peace-loving people who believe in helping others? Good Christians should not want rampant gun ownership for America. True Christians should want proper healthcare for the country!

Since Republicans have the gun lover votes and the Christian vote they only have to win a small number of people over to their side. So Republicans will throughout a few other lines to win over the balance.

They will say we need less regulation and less taxation and there are those people who love to hear it! You love to hear it even though you yourself are not being harmed or hassled much by too much government regulation.

I cannot think when the federal government has been a problem for me. Republicans say we need to cut corporate tax rates so our companies will be more competitive with foreign companies. Too many middleclass voters seem to buy those arguments because it just sounds too right!

This is why we all need to keep ourselves educated on actual facts. You should not be an uneducated voter. You do not need to become a strong Democrat. You just need to be an intelligent voter. You need to care about the economy and the country! You only need to love America.

Yes I admit I do consider myself to be a strong Democrat. But I am not a Democrat because of love for Democrats. I am a Democrat because I pretty much dislike everything Republicans are doing. They are clearly on the wrong track all of the time!

I love America, I want for our nation to be among the greatest places on earth for us to live and prosper in. I want America to stay strong for the coming generations!

I also am a conservative person just like many Republicans. The thing is I have seen that the nation does prosper much better under Democrat policy than it does under Republicans. This has come down to economic policies more than anything else for me!

We Americans should be thinking of the long run, rather than just eyeing the short term benefits which will not last. We always want stable long lasting growth for the country.

Having said all that, I know I am also a progressive person. I do believe that every society should be making progress and moving forward. As a society we should not be stuck with old-fashioned values when there are better ways. Society should not be stagnant. Societies need to get organized with rules and regulations to help them function in an orderly fashion!

I do not see merely wanting to progress as a society as signifying that I must be a liberal. I will not abandon common sense values. We should not be stuck with old ideas just because our parents used them. I saw problems with their approached. I saw how they often got things wrong!

I am always looking for the most cost effective approach to any given problem. I am my own person. But I believe at times other approaches work better. Sometimes it might be the liberal approach, or the Teddy Roosevelt progressive approach and sometimes the conservative approach works best! I for one can adapt to new things. I am not set in my ways. I want that which works!

You must realize Teddy Roosevelt was a progressive President? He knew over 100 years ago, the wisdom of keeping powerful corporations or trusts in check. He had a pretty good understanding of the problems connected with excessive free-wheeling business. He was a great President in my opinion.

Republicans for years now have abandoned Teddy Roosevelt's principles. America is a weaker country when you overly empower the corporations and ignore the importance of consumption and a strong middleclass!

It goes without saying that Americans enjoy better lives within thriving economies. Strong economies come to us all when our government uses policies which support consumption. That is our holy grail. So why bypass the middleclass with corporate tax cuts when pursuing corporate profits?

In short when it comes to corporate profits, a vibrant economy with lots of people working far outweighs corporate tax cuts. Corporations will be more profitable in a strong economy than they are in a weak economy with low taxes.

I love America. I have spent several years writing and rewriting this book, all in hopes of making people understand the nation will be better off when Consumer Focused Economic values are being practiced. We have seen that repeatedly from Democrats!

Republicans could also use those economic policies if they wanted to. No one should be against that.

Democrats do have a very strong record of providing good times for all. Currently we need to support more Democrats in government. The problem is, so many people are locked into their belief that Republicans are somehow on the right track. Those Republican voters cannot see what is right there in front of them!

Teddy Roosevelt would never support any of the recent Republicans. Teddy Roosevelt correctly understood corporations do not care two hoots about the middleclass. Currently Republicans believe corporations are the key to a stronger America so that is why they support them!

I cannot emphasize this enough, absolutely *"Every Single Time"* Republicans come to power they give us contracting or collapsing economies! That is backed up by the federal job creation statistics. All we have to look at is the mess created by George W. Bush. When Republicans are elected they give us massive deficit spending, few jobs and no lasting corporate profits!

"Every Single Time" Republicans come to power they bring in religious values, more weapons or policies the general public does not embrace. Republicans do dishonest things, or break our laws on a regular basis. Who in their right mind would vote for more of these things? Where is your personal character as an American?

We just saw the economy totally collapse with President George W. Bush. Do not kid yourself and think that he really did a good job, or that it only happens to Republican Presidents once in a while!

If you believe he was a good President you clearly are in total denial of reality. How long are you going to watch this happen?

With such a long list of negative things about Republicans, and with so many very good programs, economies and policies coming to us from Democrats how can you ever support Republicans?

Whatever negative things you might sight about Democrats, I believe there have been many more negatives from Republicans. I believe Democrats are much better for the country, so please be wise!

I cannot think of any other argument to try and convince you Republicans are bad for America. They simply are openly on the side of the corporations. They believe that is correct policy to get to prosperity! It is not!

The prosperity path runs through strong commerce. That is the way to create a strong economy. In addition I would like to remind you we have never had bad economies coming from Democrats!

We may not like voting for Democrats, but as long as Republicans are not bringing us strong economies we must vote for those Democrats to save our financial lives. Mark my words with Republicans bad economies will come to us again. I do not see them changing.

Thank you so much for supporting the Wounded Warrior Project. It is a very worthy cause. I hope you feel this book has helped you understand politics just a little better. At least you might have a different perspective!

I fully agree with you politics is a complicated subject. I do understand people have strong loyalties. I know it is very hard for people to leave their party, or change their thinking.

My intentions in writing the book are for the good of nation. For me there are just too many negative aspects in voting Republican. I cannot support them!

I love being an American. I want you to enjoy a happy and prosperous life. I want all of your desires to be met. I am absolutely sure healthier economies come to us with Democrats. That is just a fact. I am not saying Democrats are perfect, only that they do not exhibit the problems Republicans clearly have!

Few things are more important to our country than a healthy economy. It enables us to fund the important areas of our society. Everything from roads, parks and schools up to our military, and Affordable Healthcare for Americans come to us because of the strong economies which Democrats bring!

We have more of the things we want when the economy is strong. America is better nation with Democrats in control of the government. I believe progressive values mixed with a conservative approach generally deliver a better society!

We only have one chance at life! So I say to you above all else, live your life constructively; love your family, and your pets. Your life and your time on this earth is far too short, to have problems in relationships or with family members. Live your life with a positive nature, you will be happier!

Always be considerate and thoughtful to others. Make kindness a part of your daily life and life will be good to you! You must be a wise person and educated voter *every single time*!

Thank You Very Very Much!

Gene Enree

www.ingramcontent.com/pod-product-compliance
Lightning Source LLC
Chambersburg PA
CBHW022341290526
45786CB00014B/2042